The Oyston Files

Andrew Rosthorn

Published by

Red Sea Books Publishing House

Ivy Cottages Tockholes Darwen
Lancashire BB3 ONA
United Kingdom

Cover image by Mark Chapman

SBN: 978-1-9160963-4-9

In memory of:

Liliane Tierney, Joan Moyles, Sharon Moyles
and Kirstie Moyles

Acknowledgements

I thank my father, Dick Rosthorn, a local government officer who showed me how well clean government suits double-entry bookkeeping. He once took me to Sansepolcro, the birthplace of that pioneer of double-entry bookkeeping, Leonardo's mathematical collaborator Fra Luca Bartolomeo de Pacioli.

I thank Eric Leaver, the chief feature writer of the *Lancashire Evening Telegraph,* who posted me his own copy of the first and most shocking message from the conspirators.

Four reporters who helped me are now much-missed; James Stansfield, Graham Nown, Ray Fitzwalter and John Burke-Davies.

Among my surviving colleagues and helpers from the last days of hot metal, I thank Chris Blackhurst, Francis Wheen, Robin Ramsay, Harold Heys, Jon Whittaker, Jon Harris, Robert Satchwell, Bill Amos, Jan Needle, Alan Hart, Andrew Chapman, Andrea Muldoon, Adrian Darbyshire and Martin Tomkinson

I found many collaborators, in the best sense of that word, among the dozens of politicians, police officers, private detectives, solicitors and barristers professionally engaged in these disturbing events. Despite their help, I dare only thank Dale Campbell-Savours, the assiduous Labour MP for Workington, Mrs Lily Henderson MBE, still the Conservative councillor for the Highfield Ward of Blackpool Borough, and Harold Elletson, Conservative MP for Blackpool North from 1992 to 1997.

I could not have written the book without access to the files of three of the combatants. I therefore thank Owen Oyston, Frank McGrath, and Michael Murrin, but not equally.

Mrs Olivia Frank, a former secret service combatant from a harsher world, helped me to publish this book. She noted how well *wilderness of mirrors*, borrowed from T.S. Eliot by James Angleton of the CIA, suited the confusing *para-politics* of Lancashire in the days of Margaret Thatcher. But no matter how many of those mirrors were blinding me at the time, all mistakes remain mine, and mine alone.

Contents

Foreword

Three tonnes of documents and tape recordings discovered in an old manor house revealed the depths of corruption and political decay reached in Lancashire towards the end of the twentieth century.

Opening the archives at Claughton Hall in the Lune valley outside Lancaster reminded me of the French historian Emmanuel Leroy Ladurie discovering the truth about the real lives of peasants in the middle ages by finding the Fournier inquisition register in the Vatican Library.

Bishop Fournier, tracking heresy in the Pyrenees, interrogated shepherds and peasants in the small village of Montaillou. The record of his intimate conversations with ordinary men and women survived only because he became Pope Benedict XII. Six hundred years later, in 1975, Leroy de Ladurie's wonderful book *Montaillou, Cathars and Catholics in a French Village: 1294 to 1424* [1] changed all our ideas about real life in the fourteenth century.

The twentieth century archive at sixteenth century Claughton Hall covered only the fifteen years in which a group of well-connected political conspirators set out to ruin and imprison an opponent of the government of Margaret Thatcher.

---

[1] Montaillou: Cathars and Catholics in a French Village 1294-1324, Scolar Press, Aldershot, 1978

In our time, which has been the era of the telephone, the trail of political villainy can be very faint. Hitler left no written order for the Final Solution, allocated no financial budget for death camps.

Politics pursued in unrecorded telephone calls leaves historians unable to resolve discrepancies between the unreliable memoirs of unreliable politicians. Lee Harvey Oswald's journey to Russia, the murder of President Kennedy and the decision to start the Vietnam War remain unsolved mysteries of the telephone age.

The documents and tape recordings had accumulated at Claughton Hall by an accident of history, during a prison sentence being served by the 64th richest man in Britain. The country's richest prisoner had been stalked for years by enemies whose stated aim had been to see him jailed.

Owen Oyston, an estate agent and media tycoon, was the opposition Labour Party's principal private financial contributor during the long premiership of Margaret Thatcher between 1979 and 1990. His defence lawyers had gathered many thousands of police documents at Claughton Hall. Hundreds were secured under a law, later changed, that required Crown prosecutors to reveal evidence 'unused' by the prosecution. The tape recordings revealed how Oyston's friends in the Labour Party had been targeted with corruption allegations for nearly ten years.

Amid thousands of Home Office computer printouts lay boxes of tape cassettes. These were recordings of conversations between the men who had wanted Oyston in jail, a group that included at least two Conservative government ministers.

The conspirators had stolen the income tax records of their political opponents, a crime never previously recorded in the two hundred year history of income tax in Britain.

Some of those targeted and questioned under caution by the Lancashire police in an abortive £20 million police investigation named Operation Angel were eventually elected as members of parliament in prime minister Tony Blair's New Labour landslide victory of 1997.

The total cost of the conspiracy was a quarter of a billion pounds, largely paid by the British Exchequer and by Owen Oyston personally.

When Oyston was jailed for six years for the rape and indecent assault of a young woman, a conspirator who had been pressing the Greater Manchester police to arrest him for four years, released his own files and declared, 'I'm the man who put him where he is today'.

A skilful investigation by a senior policeman who had once hunted German war criminals led to the sacking of the Chief Constable of Lancashire, dismissed after interfering with police procedure to cover up for the daughter of a millionaire after her car left the road and killed two young mothers.

Reporters from the *Sunday Times* had shown how her father corruptly acquired and rented public land to caravanners in Blackpool. The documents at Claughton Hall showed how he had hired a private detective to steal the bank overdraft balances of local politicians. Prime minister Margaret Thatcher stayed overnight at his Lancashire home several times during the long campaign of dirty tricks. In London he lunched at the House of Commons with the man who had led her party leadership campaign.

Robert Atkins, the MP who ran the election campaign of Margaret Thatcher's successor, was revealed as one of the informants in Operation Angel. The police had tried to obliterate the names of high-level conspirators in computer printouts, hiding their identity in the documents that survived.

One of the plotters was Mrs Thatcher's former home secretary, Lord Waddington. He tried to persuade the Director of Public Prosecutions to start a corruption case against some Lancashire politicians. The DPP, Sir Allan Green, found no evidence and refused the request, but was then forced to resign after being observed talking to a street prostitute.

Police activity resumed after Sir Allan's resignation and urged on by the conspirators, fraud squad officers raided Preston town hall, effectively ending the political careers of the town's Labour leader and his deputy. They were ruined politically and financially.

Some of the victims were rich, some were very poor, some were very foolish, some were non-political, some were famous, many were young and fragile. In 2018, one of the four children orphaned in the death crash that led to years of hatred, committed suicide. Her body was found hanging from a tree in a wood on Wolf Fell, barely ten miles from Claughton Hall.

The lives of the victims were ruined because they were all caught up in the careless exercise of the enormous power exerted by central government in the United Kingdom of Great Britain and Northern Ireland.

The story of how it happened, and who was to blame, lay in the Oyston Files.

Andrew Rosthorn

CHAPTER 1

'Night Out Mums Die in Crash'

Those of us who can remember the beginning of the story agree that the years of hatred and political corruption began in an instant.

At 3:20 a.m. on Sunday, August 10, 1975, two young mothers walking home after a night out in Blackpool were killed by a Ford Escort driven by the daughter of a millionaire. The Escort overtook a taxi on the A583 a few seconds before the crash. The taxi driver and his three passengers saw headlights flash across the footpath and glimpsed two bodies being thrown high in the air. In laconic police terms the car

> mounted a footpath, crossed a junction, mounted the footpath again and continued something like 120 yards before coming to rest. During the early part of its journey on the footpath it knocked down two women, killing them outright.

This terrible road accident made the front page of the papers on Monday afternoon. Four young children would never see their mothers again and no-one would ever know how Liliane Tierney, 24, and Sharon Moyles, 26, came to be walking home on the footpath of the Kirkham Bypass. Had they been to Blackpool? Were they short of their taxi fare home?

Lancashire police were appealing for witnesses. They could not have guessed that their investigation of this road accident was going to cost their chief constable his job. David Graham, the reporter who covered the death crash story for Monday's *Lancashire Evening Post,* could not have imagined that twenty years later he would be reporting its political aftermath for national newspapers and television.

There was a cover-up. It led to a poisonous feud that ruined dozens of lives, forced the resignation of a minister in John Major's Conservative government and landed Lancashire's richest man in jail. Two years after the accident, the chief constable was sacked for misuse of police transport and manpower and 37 charges of intervening in motoring cases involving wealthy or influential people in Blackpool.

The most notable complaint against the chief was that his actions ensured that Janette Harrison, 20, the driver of the car that killed the young mothers on the A583, would not be prosecuted for causing death by dangerous driving, under Section 1 of the Road Traffic Act 1972.

When the millionaire's daughter eventually came to court, she faced only a charge of careless driving under the lesser Section 3 of the Act. In the magistrates' court Miss Harrison was most unusually defended by a Queen's Counsel, a top barrister making a surprising appearance in a lower court. Her QC argued that when the police had decided not to recommend proceedings against Janette Harrison for causing death by dangerous driving under Section 1 of the Road Traffic Act 1972, they had demonstrated a basic weakness in their evidence. That weakness also applied under the lesser Section 3 charge of careless driving. The QC argued that the Section 3 charge had been 'a face-saver' and he persuaded the magistrates to acquit the young driver, even though a later inquiry would one day find that 'there could not have been a more flagrant example of dangerous driving.'

The 'stitch-up' had been achieved without public outcry. Someone saw to it that the newspapers were kept in the dark - and no reporter was in court. The driver of the taxi, overtaken by the Escort before the crash, was not called to give evidence. Only the relatives of the dead mothers were left to ask questions about what had been happening to judicial process in this part of the County Palatine of Lancashire.

The cover-up was so complete that the mother of Sharon Moyles wondered whether newspapermen were part of the conspiracy to hide what had happened to her daughter. In 2002, she said:

> I couldn't understand what was happening. There was absolutely nothing about it in the newspapers. When I telephoned the *Evening Post* office, two days after the magistrates' court hearing, I was just told they knew nothing about it. When I told the paper about it, they said it was too late by law for them to report it. I called the TV. It was the same. Too late. [2]

Mrs Moyles, then 54, decided to adopt her orphaned grandchildren. Kirstie was five and Liam was eleven months. In 2002, at the age of 80, she could still recall how her anger intensified as she watched people in authority imposing a news blanket. An inquest into the two deaths, had opened a week before the magistrates' court hearing but there had been no newspaper coverage. A routine telephone call to alert local reporters was never made. This early conspiracy to make sure that reporters stayed away from court hearings breached a famous legal maxim expressed in 1923 in a dangerous driving case by Lord Hewart, a lord chief justice who had been born and educated in Lancashire:

> a long line of cases shows that it is not merely of some importance, but is of fundamental importance, that justice should not only be done, but should manifestly and undoubtedly be seen to be done. [3]

The inquest that had been convened in the small town of Kirkham, in an unheated room without reporters, was as disturbing as the acquittal of Janette Harrison. When a traffic policeman rose from his seat to offer some extra information to the coroner, the grieving relatives sitting behind him saw how quickly he had been silenced. A senior officer was seen tugging the

---

2 Interview Andrew Rosthorn

3 https://en.wikipedia.org/wiki/R_v_Sussex_Justices,_ex_parte_McCarthy

traffic officer's tunic to pull him back into his seat. This was noticed by the wife of the taxi driver involved in the crash. She whispered support to Pat Carter, the sister of Sharon Moyles.

> I'm a policewoman in Southport. Don't worry. There's no way they can cover this up.

Pat Carter remembered in 2002:

> The taxi driver was never called to give evidence. Four men in the taxi said the Escort overtook them. They saw headlights on the pavement and the lights picked out the figures of the girls being thrown in the air. No one can know just how Sharon and Liliane came to be on the footpath that night.
>
> I was baby-sitting for Sharon that night. I was the one who had persuaded her to have a good night out in Blackpool, instead of just going into Preston. They had some money on them when they were killed, but I think they hadn't quite enough for a taxi all the way home. After the hearing, one of the PCs came up to us to say: "After what's happened here, I feel like packing the job in." He made his feelings very clear to us.

Mercifully, for the reputation of the Lancashire Constabulary, the cover-up of the Kirkham double fatal was eventually exposed after one of their own officers complained about 'dissatisfaction' felt by officers in Blackpool over the failure to prosecute Janette Harrison for causing death by dangerous driving.

In a 1980 judgment, Lord Denning, Master of the Rolls, summed up the situation:

> In 1976 rumours were rife in Blackpool. Gossip abounded. About the goings on of the Chief Constable of Lancashire. He lived in the town. Not only about the Chief Constable himself. But other police officers too. And well-known citizens. These were sort of ruinous. It was said that in motoring cases some offenders were not prosecuted when they ought to have been; that firearm certificates were issued to friends and acquaintances when they ought not to have been; that police cars were used for private purposes; and that there

> were close associations with undesirable characters. There was at any rate one courageous member of the police force. He was a sergeant. He reported these goings on to Her Majesty's Inspector of Constabulary and to the local Member of Parliament. They took it up with the Home Office who regarded it as so serious that they asked the Police Authority to carry out an investigation.'[4]

Det Sgt Harry Roby of Blackpool CID had sent a list of complaints about Chief Constable Stanley Parr to Her Majesty's Inspector of Constabulary and to the Labour MP for Ormskirk, Robert Kilroy-Silk. In August 1976 the Chief Constable of Hampshire, Sir Douglas Osmond, arrived to question senior officers in the Lancashire force and to report in secret to the Lancashire County Council police committee. [5]

Sir Douglas had previously investigated Nazis in the German Gestapo as deputy assistant inspector general for the Allied Control Commission for Germany in 1945. Obstructive senior police officers in Lancashire were no match for him. He found hard evidence for most of the complaints listed by the whistle-blower and declared that some senior officers in the chain of command had told him lies.

He also put the indomitable Sgt Roby, 50, through a long interrogation that concluded with this glacial compliment from Sir Douglas:

> Did not impress as a man with a grievance, stood up well to two days of questioning.

[4] https://api.parliament.uk/historic-hansard/lords/1978/mar/08/osmond-report

[5] https://api.parliament.uk/historic-hansard/lords/1978/mar/08/osmond-report

Sir Douglas told how a driving charge was changed

›se two men lied to me'

Cover-up claim over mystery death smash

A DRIVER had a case for careless driving dismissed at a magistrates' court.

But, says Sir Douglas Osmond, this is "the case which causes me more concern than all the other cases of alleged intervention."

Sir Douglas states that he is forced to the conclusion that Lancashire's Chief Constable was subject to pressure to reduce the charge against the driver from causing death by dangerous driving to the eventual careless driving charge heard in court.

He also claims an elaborate cover-up attempt during

...Douglas then asked for all papers on the accident to be sent to him by Assistant Chief Constable Mr Ronald Rowbottom.

First Mr Rowbottom said there were no papers at Hutton but two days later he told Sir Douglas they had been found.

The papers included the ... of a ... sent by Mr Sephton to Hutton in which he recommended going ahead on the Section One offence.

It was returned to Sephton marked with the Chief Constable's initials and saying: "No evidence of dangerous driving, but let the court decide." Sir Douglas mentions vague marks on the memo near the Parr initials.

In view of the "total falsity" of Chief Supt Sephton's first statement Sir

The 37 complaints against Chief Constable Parr comprised improper interference in traffic cases, misuse of police transport and manpower and improper associations with people in Blackpool. Sir Douglas heard how a 17-year old youth, under caution for dangerous or careless driving in Garstang, had said to police:

> My father is on holiday in Tenerife with Stanley Parr and I will see Mr Parr when he returns.

Two days later, Stanley Parr contacted the reporting police officer and instructed him to come and interview the youth at the young man's home, in the presence of Stan Parr and his father, described by Osmond as '*surely a most unorthodox action*'.

There was 'Miss U', the daughter of a prosperous caterer known to Mr Parr, given a caution after speeding through a radar trap at 60 per cent over the limit when others were prosecuted for driving through the trap at lower speeds.

A member of the police committee had not been prosecuted after brake defects were found in his lorries. Osmond concluded that:

> I was left in no doubt that the officers in Blackpool had for some time regarded the lorries of S. Ltd. as having some sort of special protection. Once

again, Sgt Roby's criticism can be supported by evidence and in this case there is also evidence of an early intervention by the Chief Constable.

Sir Douglas looked into the Kirkham double fatal:

For reasons which will appear, this matter was more difficult to investigate and causes me more concern than all the other cases of alleged intervention. There could not be a more flagrant example of dangerous driving.

He noted that Janette Harrison, had not been *properly interviewed* by the police on the day of the accident. After giving a negative breath test at the roadside she had been taken away by her father for a hospital check. The police had questioned her the following day in the presence of her father, Fylde Coast property developer Bill Harrison, a man known locally as *Mr Kirkham*. The Harrison family solicitor had been present at the interview.

Sir Douglas noted that Janette Harrison

overtook a taxi and then turned normally across it to return to the nearside; instead of straightening up, however, her car mounted the footpath. When interviewed, she was unable to give any reason for her driving but claimed that something had obstructed her view.

On the very day Janette Harrison was being questioned by the police, another policeman was warning, in the privacy of a mortuary, of her father's baleful influence in Kirkham. In this grim location PC Woods from Kirkham police station put some hard facts to John Carter, a farmer married to Sharon Moyles's sister, who had identified the bodies of the dead women.

John Carter remembered that PC Woods used a 1971 phrase from lawless days in Northern Ireland to describe Bill Harrison's malign influence in Kirkham:

While I was talking to Police Constable Woods of Kirkham, when we were alone at the mortuary, he gave me very clearly to understand that the Harrisons were very influential in that district and nothing was ever likely to be done if they were reported for speeding or parking offences. They were a sort of *no-go area*. They had to be left alone.

The warning proved timely. Not until 1977, when a copy of Sir Douglas Osmond's secret report fell into the hands of journalists on the *Lancashire Evening Post,* did anyone outside the police service see how quickly Bill Harrison had moved to protect his daughter.

Two young mothers of four children were killed.

William Harrison

CHAPTER 2

'If I can be of help to you, you know this is what I am for.'

Although the Osmond report was an ultra-secret, the deputy chairman of the Lancashire Police Authority decided to strike his own blow against corruption in Blackpool. Jack Ashton, a Conservative former council alderman from Preston, deplored the way that two men from Blackpool were dominating the amalgamated Lancashire police force, under the command of a former chief constable of Blackpool and chairmanship by the Tory leader of Blackpool.

Jack Ashton arranged to meet reporter Bob Satchwell of the *Lancashire Evening Post* on board a yacht in the Isle of Man. Satchwell took a camera down into the saloon to find that Ashton's personal copy of the Osmond report lay by the washbasin in the 'heads' of the yacht. He flew home with a snapshot of every page.

With David Graham and the crusading editor, Barry Askew, the men from the *LEP* examined every word of Sir Douglas Osmond's careful description of how Bill Harrison had forced the pliant Tory leader Len Broughton to bend Chief Constable Stanley Parr to his will. Bill Harrison would later admit to a BBC *Tonight* TV reporter that he had telephoned the Tory leader Len Broughton after the accident. He said it was because Broughton had told him:

> If I can be of help to you, you know this is what I am for.

Former alderman Jack Ashton left his copy of the Osmond Report ready to be photographed by a reporter in the heads of a yacht berthed in the Isle of Man.

Harrison told the BBC that he had asked for a senior policeman to be put in charge of the case for a forensic examination of the taxi that had been overtaken by his daughter before the crash. Len Broughton told the BBC that Bill Harrison called at his home to persuade him to contact the chief constable.

Osmond reported:

I was later informed that Councillor Z [Broughton] of the Lancashire County Council wished to see me regarding the part he had played in this matter. I interviewed him on 10th October, 1976, when he made a statement to the effect that Mr Y [Harrison] was reasonably friendly with him as a result of the development of a caravan site in Blackpool. Mr Y [Harrison] had approached him to the effect that he had not been altogether satisfied with the way in which the police were handling the accident enquiry and he was concerned that the truth was not being obtained.

He was suggesting that the taxi and its driver were more involved than appeared and that it was most likely that the two deceased women had been in some way connected with two male passengers being carried in the taxi at the time. He was attaching a great deal of importance to this, wishing it to be proved, since it might explain the reason for his daughter's accident if the women had alighted from the taxi on the offside. Mr Y [Harrison] also wished the taxi to be forensically examined and for the result to be considered by his own advisers. Councillor Z [Broughton] told Mr Y [Harrison] he would take the matter up with the Chief Constable; he would have been wiser to have told Mr Y [Harrison] to take the matter up with the Chief Constable himself.

The following day Councillor Z [Broughton] telephoned Mr Parr, who said he would look into the case.

Councillor Z [Broughton] states that some days later the Chief Constable told him he was satisfied this matter was being fully investigated but there were certain aspects he wished to look into further. He did not say at that time, however, that the police were satisfied that the taxi played no part in the cause of the accident and had not been involved except that its occupants were to some extent witnesses. Councillor Z [Broughton] also says that at some stage, either on one of the two occasions described or another, the Chief Constable had told him that there would be some proceedings taken in this matter but he had not said what these would be for.

Councillor Z [Broughton] told Mr Y [Harrison] of this outcome but Mr Y [Harrison], he states, was still adamant, about the involvement of the taxi. Councillor Z [Broughton] told him that he had done all he could on his behalf. Thereafter Councillor Z [Broughton] had seen the Chief Constable perhaps on two occasions at meetings when the only comment was by the Chief Constable who indicated that inquiries were still going on and that nothing had been decided as to future action.

It would appear therefore that Councillor Z's [Broughton's] involvement was complete before the change of decision was made, over the period from the 5th to the 10th September, and it is possible that some other factor influenced the Chief Constable to call for the papers over that weekend.

This tedious account of the details of the investigation is regrettably necessary in order to demonstrate the mystery which still surrounds the case and the obstructions which were put in my way.

The timetable of events is now apparently established and appears to be as follows: -

10th August, 1975

Accident occurs. Two persons killed. *Prima facie* case of causing death by dangerous driving against Miss Y.

12th/13th August

Mr Y sees Councillor Z.

13th/14th August

Councillor Z telephones Chief Constable. Some mention of case between them in subsequent weeks.

27th August

C/Supt. Day speaks to C/Insp. Gradwell (twice) regarding the file. |

28th August

Incomplete file taken to Headquarters. Memorandum attached by C/Supt. Sephton recommending Section 1 proceedings (copy only available).

4th September

File returned to C/Supt. Sephton marked by Chief Constable "S.1. No evidence of dangerous driving but let Court decide". C/Supt. Sephton writes Coroner asking for inquest to be adjourned.

5th September

File called for by Chief Constable to be delivered to his house in Blackpool. (Scrap of paper, now disappeared, was then attached in Chief Constable's handwriting changing the decision to Section 3).

10th September

C/Supt. Sephton writes to Coroner telling him of change of decision. Alters Section l decision on accident card to read Section 3.

30th September

Inquest held. Verdict "accidental death".

8th December

Miss Y prosecuted Section 3 - case dismissed.

10th March, 1976

File sent to County Hall - notification by C/Supt. Day of interest of Councillor Z. Scrap of paper bearing change of decision by the Chief Constable was then on the file.

At the inquest into the deaths of the young mothers, held on September 30, 1975, Janette Harrison said she could remember nothing of the accident.

Pat Carter, Sharon's sister, said later:

Until then, although very emotionally involved, I had felt very sorry for Miss Harrison, the young driver. I knew she had never intended to kill my sister.

> But when the coroner seemed so much concerned with comforting her, and being upset that she had some scratches on her face from the shattered windscreen, and so little concerned with probing the causes of the accident which killed two women, the mothers of four children, I became so upset I had to leave the courtroom. Miss Harrison seemed to show no real remorse and was so composed and apparently indifferent that I lost all sympathy for her. Only by repeatedly ringing PC Woods at Kirkham did we find the day of the magistrates' hearing. I was astonished that there was no Press and no public in the court and I could hardly believe it when the magistrates dismissed the charge of careless driving. I was so upset that I rang our solicitor, but he told me there was nothing we could do about it. I told my mother and she got in touch with the *Lancashire Evening Post.* [6]

John Carter, the man who had been warned about the Harrison family in the mortuary, said:

> I came away feeling that it had been a pantomime. The coroner seemed to so sympathetic towards Miss Harrison. He was not really pressing for the facts in an accident which had killed the mothers of four children. Police Constable Bailey, who had taken details at the scene, attended the inquest with a lot of papers setting out exactly what had happened. But he was asked only one or two questions. Once, when other evidence was being given, PC Bailey half rose, as if he was going to intervene with some of his information, but he was restrained by a senior officer sitting behind him. Afterwards, PC Bailey said to me, "I feel like packing the job in."

Liliane Tierney's mother shouted out '*Rubbish!*' during the proceedings. When the coroner warned that he might hold her in contempt of court, she marched out of the inquest into her daughter's death. In 2002, Pat Carter remembered her own despair when Gordon Mellalieu, an inexperienced solicitor from Kirkham, representing Sharon's family, chose to put only one question to Janette Harrison:

> We had been warned not to use a solicitor from Harrison's hometown. But Gordon Mellalieu had once acted for us in a land matter. He did very little for

---

[6] Interview with author

> us in this case. I was aghast when he said to me later: "I think you are over-involved emotionally." A few years later I heard that his own child had died in a road accident. He's dead too now, but I often wonder whether he ever reconsidered what he said to me that day and how he let us down.

Bill Harrison's initial fix was so alarmingly successful that by the time his daughter was acquitted at Lytham magistrates court on December 8, he was beginning to achieve overkill. His successful interference with police procedure had left two courts looking stacked against the grieving families. Someone had seen to it that the Press was absent from both the public hearings. The Press were not so much squared as left in ignorance.

The cover-up was so complete that it eventually provoked an injured reaction from Mrs Joan Moyles, the grandmother of the orphaned children. She had seen the Lytham magistrates acquit Janette Harrison of careless driving. She had tried and failed to get the media to report the case.

She was still angry about the cover-up, when a Labour Party canvasser happened to knock on her door. Joan Moyles told the canvasser about her frustration with the police force and triggered a series of events that would catapult Bill Harrison into what he later described as 'twenty years of hell'. Somewhere in the Lancashire rain forest a butterfly had beaten its wings.

The Labour Party canvasser related Mrs Moyles's story to the Labour leader of Preston. Councillor Harold Parker was a remarkable man of the people who had been born to a single mother living in poverty. He had passed the entrance examination to the grammar school but the cost of the school uniform had been beyond his mother's savings. At secondary school:

> He was so bright that his teacher spotted his ability with figures and recommended him to work in the office of a local mill, which was quite a

thing. When he was 15, he was running the wages department for Horrockses Mill.[7]

Harold Parker passed on Mrs Moyles's complaint to Ron Atkins, the Labour MP for Chorley. He also alerted the editor of the *Lancashire Evening Post*, an intervention that ultimately wrecked Parker's long and outstanding political career.

Joan Moyles remembered:

One evening Harold Parker came to call on us. He took us to see the editor of the *Lancashire Evening Post*, at night when no other work was going on. They gave us whiskies and asked us to tell them all that had happened. At last someone wanted to listen to us!

The newspapermen discovered that Sir Douglas Osmond was already investigating other complaints about Chief Constable Parr. Mrs Moyles then persuaded Ron Atkins MP to organise a petition to the police authority that called for the Kirkham cover-up to be added to the existing complaints against Stanley Parr. She gathered three thousand signatures. Bill Harrison, who had sowed the wind, was about to reap a whirlwind. Thanks to the intervention by Mrs Moyles he was doomed to feature in Osmond's devastating report, which reached the police authority in January 1977.

In December that year, after an eight-day tribunal, the 40-year career of Stanley Parr ended in dismissal. He had been the first man in the history of the Lancashire force to rise from police constable to chief constable. He had served in the Royal Navy in wartime. He had tried to resign from his post but the police authority had insisted on sacking him. After being sacked he managed to alert the *Sunday Times* about the corrupt relationship between Bill Harrison and Broughton, but he died soon afterwards.

Mrs Moyles said 25 years later:

[7] Daughter Deborah Robinson quoted in Lancashire Evening Post, August 6, 2009.

> I still pray every night for Stanley Parr; that he shall have eternal rest. I don't hold him to blame for all that happened. Others were worse. Every night for 25 years I have prayed to God that it would all come out one day.

People began to wonder what power Bill Harrison held over the county council leader. How could he have persuaded Broughton to intervene in the case of Janette Harrison? How could he have persuaded Broughton to make the telephone call that ruined the chief constable?

The *Daily Mail* crime reporter Jim Stansfield heard that Len Broughton was now so worried about his own future that by night his neighbours could see him pacing the floor of his bedroom endlessly.

Bill Harrison quite accurately blamed the *Lancashire Evening Post* for turning his daughter's tragic case into a *cause célèbre*. But he seemed unaware that it was the outraged Mrs Moyles who had galvanised the *LEP* editor into action, by showing the newsmen that they had been well and truly duped into missing the shabby cover-up after the death of Sharon Moyles.

When the balloon went up, as the Osmond Report started leaking and when people began to ask awkward questions, Bill Harrison came to a seriously wrong conclusion. Harrison disastrously decided that it had been one of his business rivals, the ambitious Blackpool estate agent Owen Oyston, who had pushed the *LEP* editor Barry Askew into running the newspaper investigation that ruined Stanley Parr.

That was not true. Oyston had been friendly with Stanley Parr for many years. They both lived and socialised in Blackpool. Oyston took no part in the destruction of Parr and had even tried to defend him when he was in trouble. Writing in *Esquire* magazine in 1992, Chris Blackhurst described what came over the wounded Harrison after the newspapers leaked the Osmond Report

The Oyston Tapes

A seamy saga of smears, death and vendetta...

Or how two Tory MPs,

Sir Peter Blaker MP; Robert Atkins MP

a fish and chip shop

Michael Murrin

owner, and a Blackpool wheeler dealer with a secret grudge

Bill Harrison

tried to ruin a socialist millionaire

Owen Oyston

An investigation by Chris Blackhurst

THE POLICE ACCOUNT IS matter of fact. The car "mounted a footpath, crossed a junction, mounted the footpath again and continued for something like 120 yards before coming to rest." The report goes on: "During the early part of its journey on the footpath it knocked over two women killing them outright."

The time was 3.20am, the date: August 10, 1975, the place: on the Kirkham by-pass between Blackpool and Preston in Lancashire. The dead women, Lilian Tierney, 24, and Sharon Moyles, 26, were from Preston. Close friends, they had been on a "girls' night out" to Blackpool. When they ran out of money for a taxi, they decided to walk. As a result, four young children never saw their mothers again.

Janet Harrison, 20, the driver of the car, was also on her way back from Blackpool but was more fortunate. After passing a breathalyzer test, she was treated for shock at Blackpool's Victoria Hospital and allowed to return to her home in Kirkham.

On December 8, 1975, she appeared before Lytham magistrates' court on a charge of driving without due care and attention. She was represented by a QC, while the police were advised by a local solicitor with little experience of criminal prosecutions. At the hearing her counsel made great play on the police not finding enough evidence to bring a more serious charge of death by reckless driving and claimed they were only proceeding at all in order to save face. Janet Harrison was acquitted.

The court case appeared to mark the end of a sad, painful story. In fact, it was only the beginning of a longer and much seamier saga. For the case against young Janet Harrison, though seemingly dead, refused to lie down.

60 Esquire MAY 1992

> The more Harrison thought about the Post's campaign the more he detected the hand of Oyston, his former business associate. Oyston was a major advertiser in the paper and was a friend of Askew. He came to believe that Oyston had encouraged Askew to vilify Parr and also his daughter. Even today he is convinced that it was Oyston's doing.

Harrison told a *Sunday Express* reporter:

> It is very possible that Owen Oyston, as a principal advertiser with the Lancashire Evening Post, had considerable influence on the paper's coverage of my daughter's case.[8]

In great secrecy, Harrison started an expensive dirty tricks campaign against Oyston. The feud ran for ten years before Harrison's involvement was discovered and a further nine years after it had become public. In 1999, when Harrison died at 77, of an unexpected heart attack in hospital, Oyston and Harrison were still locked in expensive legal disputes.

On the eve of a 1996 High Court hearing in a conspiracy to defame case brought by Oyston against Harrison, Harrison told Adrian Darbyshire of the *Blackpool Evening Gazette*:

> I've had twenty years of hell with Oyston, starting with the road accident involving my daughter in 1975.

The hell that hit Harrison was not orchestrated by Oyston but conjured by Barry Askew, editor of the *Lancashire Evening Post.* Askew was not one to worry about being accused of muckraking. He had won awards for exposing corruption and cruelty in mental hospitals and often presented *What The Papers Say* for Granada Television. His buccaneering reputation would eventually persuade Rupert Murdoch to make him editor of the *News of the World.*

---

[8] Telephone conversation between William Harrison and Andrew Rosthorn, for Sunday Express.

Askew admitted having doubts about leaking the Osmond Report. He went first to secure the backing of Lord Barnetson, his proprietor at the United Newspapers group. Then, just as he was preparing to publish, he was confronted by a remarkable policeman. This was a man who had once been described by *Paris Match* as

> the greatest detective of the twentieth century.

Det Chief Superintendent Joe Mounsey, head of Lancashire CID, called on Barry Askew and pleaded with him to hold back on publishing the Osmond Report,

> for the sake of the public and their faith in the police force.

Joe Mounsey

Mounsey was the man who broke the Moors Murders case. As a dogged and intelligent head of CID at Ashton-under-Lyne he had promised the mother of a missing boy that he would find her son's body. Two years later, working from a grainy photograph of Myra Hindley posing on a nondescript stretch of moorland, Mounsey led 60 policemen into the wildest terrain in England and by digging, against the advice of two chief constables, his men found the body of John Kilbride and cracked the crime of the century.

Under Mounsey, between 1969 and 1974, Lancashire CID reached a *satisfactory conclusion* in 180 of the 181 murders on their books. When a big story was running, crime reporters would seek him out on a Saturday morning at Brucciani's coffee bar, in Fishergate, Preston, where he used to wait for Mrs Mounsey to finish her shopping. You could rely on Mounsey for an honest answer. He was a plain dealer. Now it was Mounsey coming to ask for help. Askew said later:

> Joe pleaded with me. Not for himself, but for the force. He feared the consequences. But I had to turn him down. [9]

Askew didn't leak the Osmond Report. He detonated it. It cried out for publication, being superbly written by a man who had once pursued German war criminals. There was a gripping account of how Osmond had tackled the secrecy around the Kirkham double fatal and

> the mystery which still surrounds the case and the obstructions which were put in my way.

Mounsey would have recognised the intelligence and authority of the Osmond Report before deciding he must go to beg with Askew for its suppression. For Bill Harrison, the publication proved devastating. Many in

[9] Interview with author.

Blackpool and Kirkham could guess which *mystery death smash* had caused *County Councillor Z* to contact the chief constable on behalf of a relative of the driver.

Five days after publication, Robert Kilroy-Silk MP raised in parliament

> the conduct of the Chief Constable of Lancashire as outlined in the report of the Chief Constable of Hampshire.
> The matter is urgent because there are fears that the issue will be covered up and swept under the carpet. Two members of the police authority are named in the report. Too many local people are involved in this for it to be dealt with by the Lancashire Police Authority.

There was no escape for Harrison. There had been a slim possibility that an independent tribunal appointed by the police authority might not concern itself with the chief constable's actions in the Kirkham crash cover-up. But Ronald Atkins, a Labour MP, raised it in the House of Commons on March 31, 1977, asking Home Secretary Merlyn Rees:

> Is my right honourable friend aware that the Lancashire police tribunal is not considering the more serious cases, including what has been described as the most disturbing, involving the deaths of my former constituents Mrs Tierney and Mrs Moyles, in which there was intervention by County Councillor Leonard Broughton, the Chairman of Lancashire County Council? What action will the Home Secretary take on this?

None was possible, for procedural reasons, said Rees. But by 1978, Lord Harris of Greenwich was able to tell the House of Lords that the chief constable had been sacked. It had been 'a sad and dismal business' which had led to a further investigation into public life in Blackpool 'being carried out by Mr Imbert, the deputy chief constable of Surrey.'

Lord Harris said the dismissal had caused

great distress in the Lancashire police force and to many people living in that county.

Bill Harrison was still on the warpath and threatened to sue United Newspapers as owners of the *Lancashire Evening Post* and the *Blackpool Evening Gazette*. When it was suggested that the two editors might be well advised to call on Harrison and eat some humble pie at his lovely home, Askew refused to go. That came as no surprise to the journalists. Later in his career he would decline an invitation to lunch with the Queen of England – on the grounds that he was too busy.

Fortunately for Askew, the editor of the *Blackpool Evening Gazette*, the patient and diplomatic Brian Hargreaves, was prepared to tackle the painful duty of taking tea with Bill Harrison, admiring the porcelain collection and hearing how Harrison had become friendly with Airey Neave, a former Colditz prisoner of war, escaper and MI9 agent, who was murdered by the Irish National Liberation Army at the House of Commons in 1979 just after Margaret Thatcher's election as leader of the Conservative Party.

Exactly how a former grocer and caravan site operator from Blackpool came to be friendly with the MI9 man who had engineered Mrs Thatcher's election and personally served the Nuremberg indictments on Hitler's deputy Rudolf Hess, was not explained. It is now believed that one of Harrison's solicitors had been a prisoner of war in Germany, and therefore in clandestine contact with Airey Neave at MI9 in London.

Brian Hargreaves managed to earn a reprieve for both papers from libel actions threatened by Harrison. But both papers had to pay damages to Chief Supt Ronnie Day, head of the traffic section of the Lancashire Constabulary, for unjustified allegations in their unprivileged stories about the Osmond Report.

Osmond had mentioned Ronnie Day in his examination of the Kirkham case. He described how Day had attempted to answer a very tough question about how the Chief Constable had come to be involved in the Janette Harrison case

> Chief Superintendent Day says that in the (confirmed) absence of the Assistant Chief Constable it was his practice to take Section 1 cases to the Chief Constable for decision. This is not confirmed by other members of the Headquarters' staff who say that Chief Superintendent Day used to act for the Chief Constable and it was most unusual for the Chief Constable to become involved. The likely explanation is that the Chief Constable called for the papers after the early intervention of Councillor Z [Broughton].
>
> Was the Chief Constable's original decision to proceed under Section l (after Councillor Z's approach) the right one?
>
> In my view it was. There could not be a more flagrant example of dangerous driving (in spite of the Chief Constable's comment that there was no evidence), and Miss Y gave no acceptable explanation; two people were killed and it was surely right for the circumstances to be fully investigated under the umbrella of Section 1.
>
> To do otherwise is carrying the exercise of police discretion to an absurdity. Chief Superintendent Day, who admits that he always had the view that the case was one for Section 3 rather gloatingly justifies this view by pointing out that even the Section 3 case was dismissed. This argument is unacceptable; to proceed under Section 3 was an admission of weakness, a point of which defending counsel was not slow to take advantage.

Sir Douglas described the file as *incomplete* because it no longer contained a report by the police traffic inspector for Blackpool, the man who had supervised the investigation of the death crash. This was Inspector Ted Flasby, who had been called from home to reach the crash scene at 04:00. Flasby's report, with a recommendation that Janette Harrison should be prosecuted under Section 1, had been left out of the accident file that went down the line at police headquarters.

The file was handled by senior officers who unusually sent it from headquarters to the chief constable's home in Holly Road, Blackpool, where it stayed for four days. At the Duchy of Lancaster office, an official in charge of prosecutions told Sir Douglas Osmond that the file was *a frightful mess*, that *the whole case stinks*. This official had also received an interfering telephone call from County Councillor Len Broughton.

When Osmond showed the file to Insp Flasby, its originator, the file was seen to bear signs of having been quite crudely altered, with a figure 3 obliterating a figure 1. It was marked in a way that would have confused a lesser investigator than Sir Douglas. Insp Flasby told Sir Douglas Osmond:

> During the week or ten days following the accident, I took part in the general supervision of PC Bailey, the officer dealing with the accident. I spoke to him on several occasions, read statements which he had taken and made suggestions.
>
> From my visit to the scene and from the part I took in the subsequent enquiries, I formed the opinion that this was a case where the driver of the car involved should be prosecuted for an offence of causing death by dangerous driving, contrary to Section 1 of the Road Traffic Act. My opinion is based on my sixteen years as a traffic officer.
>
> The file in respect of this matter was not submitted in the normal way for my recommendations or the recommendations of the traffic sergeant who attended the scene. Had the file been submitted to me, I would most definitely have recommended that Section 1 proceedings be taken.
>
> From the file, it can be seen that it was finally submitted by PC Bailey for proceedings against the driver under Section 3 of the Road Traffic Act, on 16th September, 1975, and that I checked it and signed it on 17th September, 1975, prior to submitting it back to Fleetwood [traffic headquarters].
>
> On seeing the file on this occasion, or it may have been a few days earlier, when the file was returned to P.C. Bailey after the decision to prosecute for Section 3 had been made, I recall seeing on the file a recommendation in the Chief Constable's handwriting for Section 1 proceedings. This took the form of 'S.1.' `with the Chief Constable's initials plus a hand-written comment which included the words 'No evidence of dangerous driving'.

My recollection is that this recommendation was on a plain sheet of paper which also bore some handwriting of Mr Sephton. However, I have been shown a photocopy of a memorandum dated 28th August, 1975, regarding the accident and it could well be that the original of this document is what I saw because the comments on this document are virtually as I recollect them. Also on the file at this time was the final decision to go for Section 3 but I cannot recall what form this decision took except that I can remember that the file bore the instructions of Mr Sephton to proceed for Section 3 and that the figure '3' had been written over what appeared to be a figure '1'. It can be seen that the accident card on the file bears such instructions.

Sir Douglas questioned Len Broughton about his friendship with Harrison and their involvement in a caravan site deal. He discovered that in 1975 and in 1976, Bill Harrison's name had appeared on a list of possible financial subscribers for the Lancashire Constabulary's important Peel Night dinner. In 1976, the year after the death crash and the year before the chief constable was sacked, it had been Len Broughton who had entered Bill Harrison's name on the seating plan for a Peel Night dinner with the chief constable.

In 1978, the dismissal of Chief Constable Parr brought Fleet Street reporters into town and Bill Harrison began to reap the whirlwind he had sown after the accident. The *Sunday Times* managed to persuade the sacked chief constable to give them an interview. He intrigued them by suggesting that after the Kirkham case

two councillors should clarify their role in the events.

The fact that the former chief constable revealed Bill Harrison's questionable business deals with Len Broughton was revealed in some detail in the *Sunday Times* a week later. A Liberal councillor rose in the Blackpool council chamber, a forum formerly dominated by Len Broughton, and declared that for ten years the behaviour of Blackpool Council had been *morally appalling*.

On April 16, 1978, *Sunday Times* reporters Will Ellsworth-Jones, Jon Connell and Chris Ryder detailed *three golden deals* in which Councillor Broughton was dubiously involved with various bingo hall operators, slot machine owners, bookmakers - and Bill Harrison.

CHAPTER 3

Three Golden Deals

Blackpool had seen this kind of thing before.

The world's first working-class holiday resort had always been corrupt, making a living on easy pickings from the pockets and purses of Lancashire mill workers, probably the most disciplined hands in the industrial history of the world, and quite possibly the most honest. Their long hours and exacting work called for regular Sunday breaks and when trade was good, they could afford to stop work and take a holiday without pay in the summer. The higher real wages earned by men, women, and children in the 1870s allowed them to pay for a holiday out of their own savings, often invested in 'going-off-clubs'. [10]

At first, they took weekend trips to Blackpool, often for religious rallies on the beaches. A few textile and engineering workers could afford to stay over in Blackpool for a few extra days after the weekend. These increasingly predictable absences forced the mill owners to accept the new summer holiday idea as a *fait accompli* and to get on with the annual overhaul of boilers and machinery in slack days after the holiday weekends.

So began the Blackpool summer season, starting with Burnley Fair in early July and ending with Oldham Wakes in September. Thousands of holiday makers from one industrial town after another would arrive week

[10] *The British Seaside: holidays and resorts in the twentieth century*. John K. Walton, Manchester University Press, 2000.

after week in strict rotation at one of Blackpool's three railway stations; 1,300,000 arrivals in 1883; three million in 1903.

The industrial towns that lie fifty miles around Manchester still form the biggest conurbation in Western Europe. Money blown in Blackpool was seldom ever seen again in Bolton, Bury, Burnley, Bradford or Birkenhead. It piled up in Blackpool like windblown sand, vanishing into the pockets of boarding house operators and the aprons of the hucksters on the Golden Mile.

After the railway reached the coast in 1846, hundreds of day trippers gambled their careers by staying on in Blackpool at the end of the season, in the hope of finding a job and an easier life than the one waiting for them back in the worktowns of Lancashire and Yorkshire. The other Fylde Coast resorts, St Annes, Lytham and Fleetwood, actively discouraged these working-class trippers.

L&Y wartime excursion train arrives at Blackpool in 1917.
The young men are away at the war.

Merchants and millowners were also taking money away from the mill towns, but they were spending it on building grand houses of Accrington brick and Haslingden stone behind the sand dunes of St Annes and Lytham. The crack train out of the Fylde every weekday morning was the express that rushed the merchants from their homes in St Annes and Lytham to the Manchester Cotton Exchange.

Coupled in the rake of Lancashire & Yorkshire Railway coaches would be the L&Y club car. Each man going *on 'change* would have his own regular armchair. The textile men often gambled in the club car, sometimes even on variations in the numbers of cattle in the fields alongside the line.

Unlike the other resorts, Blackpool went hell for leather after the working classes, catering for people arriving with their own food in their own hampers, lugging most of their own bedding and usually demanding little more than a roof over their heads and 'use of cruet' at dinner time. In 1879, Blackpool became the only British holiday resort allowed by law to charge ratepayers two old pennies on the rate to pay for advertising its attractions to the masses.

The historian John K. Walton described what happened when land was sold off to small speculators in the 1840s, with minimal building control.

> Houses were packed on to small plots of land, with unpretentious brick and stucco frontages and the minimum of space at the back. Any individual who attempted to go significantly up-market was vulnerable to his neighbours, who might sabotage his efforts by putting slums or pigsties next door. The Cliftons of Lytham, recognising the situation, gave up their original plan to build semi-detached villas with planned gardens on their perfectly-sited Blackpool estate between what is now North Station and the sea, and joined the scramble to build poky little terraces of the standard type. This set the pattern for the rest of the Victorian years.

Walton also described the 'light touch' that voters in council elections demanded from their local government:

> The Corporation was more concerned with keeping property taxes low and pacifying the legions of small business people who were made uneasy by high levels of municipal spending. Thus no public park was provided: the beach was thought to be sufficient for visitors, and all offers of land from private donors came with strings attached. Sewage treatment was kept to the minimum necessary to avoid visible pollution of the beach. No public baths were provided for the locals, although they were often promised at election time. A public library was established early in 1880, when it was thought likely to be an attraction for 'better-class" visitors; but priorities changed, this proved not to be the case, and the library was neglected. Outside the realm of the holiday industry, Blackpool was as parsimonious as any authority whose voters were drawn mainly from small businessmen and owners of house property.

The loose building controls were so slackly enforced that by the turn of the century, thousands of builders had broken the regulations, and more and more rooms had been let to cram people into small houses, so that even in the late twentieth century, the place struck strangers as incorrigibly scruffy. The American Bill Bryson reported that Blackpool had 'more public toilets than anywhere else in the world – elsewhere they call them doorways.' Publication of the English Indices of Deprivation in 2019, revealed that after the notorious coastal hamlet of Jaywick in Essex, the next eight most-deprived areas in England were found in Blackpool, ranking along with Middlesbrough 'as the most deprived districts regarding income deprivation among children.' [11]

With so many residents on the make, Blackpool politics had long ago descended into villainy. The Town Clerk committed suicide in 1956, which was the year that the parents of Janette Harrison, Bill and Glen, arrived from Hull to set up their grocery shop - Jubilee Stores - at Dowbridge in Kirkham.

---

[11] https://www.gov.uk/government/publications/english-indices-of-deprivation-2019-research-report

Two years later, the Chief Constable of the Blackpool Borough police force was forced to resign and in 1973, the *Daily Mail* photographed a senior Blackpool council official collecting a bribe in his dressing-gown on a Sunday morning, caught red-handed on his own front doorstep. In 1977, a Liberal politician committed suicide, leaving a note for the police that revealed his utter despair about the dirty politics of Blackpool. In 1978, the *Sunday Times* arrived in Blackpool, prompted by remarks made by the dismissed chief constable Stanley Parr who had urged them to investigate '*three golden deals*' arranged by the leader of the Blackpool Conservatives, Councillor Len Broughton.

The three deals might have shocked readers of the *Sunday Times* but were pretty familiar to many of the *sandgrown 'uns* who are the minority of Blackpool residents actually born in 'the greatest seaside resort on earth'. The first of Broughton's '*golden deals*' was the sale of a lease to run bingo games and slot machines in the old Central station, once the very heart of Blackpool and the former fount of its wealth, disgracefully closed by British Railways with the connivance of national and local politicians.[12]

The *Sunday Times* showed that Councillor Broughton's wife had been in business with two bingo operators, Billy Greenwood and Sid Driscoll. Greenwood and Driscoll had been negotiating with council officials, instructed by Len Broughton to purchase the Central station gaming site for £460,000, without competitive tender, for their firm Formisdeal Ltd. A year later, Formisdeal was sold to the bookmakers Joe Coral for £2.3 million.

[12] 'It's here that the picture becomes extremely murky. Simply let it be said that representations in high places – and they must have been very high, at BR Board or even government level – led to the astonishing announcement in summer 1964 that Central Station was to be closed and North Station retained. Skilful clandestine politicking had won the day, with the council successfully pressing BR to sacrifice Central for North. The closure was approved by Transport Minister Ernest Marples.' The Central Question by Barry McLoughlin, The Progressive Press, Preston 2014.

The *Sunday Times* reported:

> In 1972 British Rail offered another site, North Station, for sale or long lease. The Council's conditions for development were that the site should not be used "as a major shopping unit".
> A record of discussions with the council on the site says "one or two shops would be acceptable, but certainly no intensive shopping use."
> In the light of this stricture a London property firm which had been interested in the site decided to cry off. But Formisdeal took a gamble and bought the site for about £435,000. It then applied for planning permission for a scheme which included a 27,028 sq ft supermarket and five double-storey shop units as well as office accommodation and other developments. In other words, a major shopping development.
> A town hall planning technician, reporting to his superior on the application emphasised "the council's repeated decision not to consider intensive shopping development on this site." He wrote: " It would be morally inexcusable for the council to change this policy now and would he a political embarrassment to the council after such a policy has been widely publicised, to turn full circle."
> Nevertheless, this is exactly what the council did. In early summer 1973, the borough surveyor recommended refusal to the planning committee, one of whose members was Broughton. The surveyor's views were echoed by a Labour member who argued that British Rail was being sold short. He then remembers vividly a bitter argument between himself and Broughton, who supported the application. Broughton says now that he cannot remember committee decisions on this particular site but that he would have simply judged the application on its merits.
> So Formisdeal, on the basis of the planning committee vote, was able to sell to Coral a site whose value had been transformed. [13]

The *Sunday Times* team started looking into the activities of Bill Harrison after Len Broughton claimed to have met Bill Harrison for the first time in 1970, when Harrison came to the council with a controversial proposal to run an overnight park for touring caravans on council-owned marshland at Marton Mere.

[13] Sunday Times: April 16, 1978

This seemed unlikely, since both Harrison and Len Broughton had grown up in Kingston-upon-Hull and made their fortunes after arriving in Blackpool. Broughton, one of 12 children, had been a clerk in the Hull council housing department. He claimed he only met Harrison 'three or four times' after the 1970 meeting and that one of these meetings was the one prompted by the Kirkham double fatal road accident.

CHAPTER 4

A Xerox Rep v. the man With More Front Than Blackpool

Robert Atkins, a former copier salesman for Xerox, once described himself as

> a seat of the pants operator who has never lost any campaign that I have organised or been involved in.

He won the highly marginal Preston North seat for the Tories in Margaret Thatcher's 1979 election victory, later planned her successor John

Major's campaign for the Tory leadership and eventually became the deputy leader of the British Conservative Party in the European Parliament. As a prospective parliamentary candidate for Preston North, supported by Bill Harrison, he had blundered into the white-hot row that followed the leaking of the Osmond Report on Stanley Parr.

Personal lives of crash mothers attacked by Tory

A PROSPECTIVE Tory MP today launched a scathing attack on the personal lives and characters of two young Preston mothers killed on the Kirkham by-pass.

Candidate for Preston North Mr Robert Atkins made his allegations in a statement on the background to the Parr Affair, in which he also bitterly criticises Sir Douglas Osmond's team, whose investigation led to the sacking of Lancashire's Chief Constable.

He said today he had conducted a personal investigation into the Osmond report. "I have information about the two women which suggests certain things about them to me. I don't know whether it is true."

Mr Atkins says he has centred his investigation on a double-fatality road accident case — one of alleged intervention by Mr Parr in the process leading to a court appearance by the daughter of a Fylde Lancashire builder.

She had driven the car which hit the two Preston women and police charges against her were changed from causing death by dangerous driving to driving without due care and attention. She was acquitted by a Magistrates Court.

DISTURBING

Sir Douglas Osmond said

Sir Douglas Osmond

"Let Mr Atkins and the 'Lancashire Evening Post' be very careful! The basis of their dubious campaign to lower police morale in Lancashire is founded on a report whose substance on quite a number of matters is quite wrong," he added.

Mr Atkins said he has information from the men who defended and prosecuted the double fatality case at court and from the clerk of the court used.

"A number of members of the police committee are sick and tired of not being able to say anything about all this," said Mr Atkins.

"There will not be a new inquiry," he stated. "If there was then the Osmond

David Graham of the *Lancashire Evening Post* had taken the notorious telephone call from Robert Atkins and reported to his editor that Atkins was saying the young mothers killed by Janette Harrison's car were just a pair of prostitutes on a night out in Blackpool. This shocking intervention backfired on Bill Harrison, provoking public attacks from both the editor of the *Lancashire Evening Post* and from the Labour Party leader on Preston Council, Councillor Harold Parker, whose daughter later married the editor of the *Lancashire Evening Post*. On March 3, 1978, the *LEP* had reported

> A prospective Tory MP today launched a scathing attack on the personal lives and characters of two young Preston mothers killed on the Kirkham by-pass.
>
> He said today he had conducted a personal investigation into the Osmond report. "I have information about the two women which suggests certain things about them to me. I don't know whether it is true."
>
> Speaking at last night's annual meeting of the Preston North Conservative Association, he said: "I am frankly nauseated by the apparent witch-hunt which is being provoked by Mr Ron Atkins [Preston North Labour MP] and his comrade Mr George Rodgers, MP for Chorley. I say witch-hunt because Ron Atkins is deliberately using the cloak of parliamentary privilege to talk about matters, some of which are at best unsubstantiated allegations and at worst malicious. Let Mr Atkins and the *Lancashire Evening Post* be very careful! The basis of their dubious campaign to lower police morale is founded on a report whose substance on quite a number of matters is quite wrong."

The newspaper's hostility horrified Bill Harrison. He convinced himself that behind the nasty newspaper campaign was a business rival. The man he had in mind was known to be a drinking pal of Barry Askew and known to be the part-time employer of Harold Parker. This was the Lancashire estate agent, Owen Oyston, a mercurial character, a former actor, once described as 'a man with more front than Blackpool'.

Oyston had previously crossed Bill Harrison in a land deal in which three developers had ganged up to force the house builder Derek Barnes, controller of Britain's biggest land bank, into paying top dollar for a patch of land. Harrison got cold feet, felt isolated, pulled out of the deal and eventually missed the payoff. Bill Harrison was also mortified by the knowledge that late one night in Blackpool he had boasted to Owen Oyston and his wife, Vicki Oyston, that running the caravan park on council land in Blackpool meant that every week he had been obliged to deliver cash in a suitcase to the council leader Len Broughton. [14]

Harrison developed the idea that it must have been Oyston, 'the principal advertiser with the *Lancashire Evening Post'* who had encouraged Askew to pursue Stanley Parr. In fact, Oyston was friendly with Parr, took no part in the newspaper campaign and frequently socialised with the chief constable. Oyston was known as the 'socialist' son of Selsby Oyston, an energetic Durham miner and part-time bookmaker who had made a new life for himself as a boarding house owner in Blackpool in the 1930s.

Owen John Oyston had been born in County Durham in 1934 and was two years old when his father bought the boarding house and moved to Blackpool. The boy went down with meningitis at the age of five and missed almost three years of school. He was sharp enough to help with running the boarding house and carrying bags for the Geordie coal miners, who were their patrons, but at St. Joseph's Roman Catholic College, where the future barrister George Carman QC was head boy, the Christian Brothers, who handled the teaching, complained that Oyston was 'shy'. Oyston said, 'The only thing I passed was lamp posts' and years later he bought the abandoned Roman Catholic school buildings 'just for the pleasure of knocking them down.'

He left school at 16, found no work as an actor in London and for a while survived on one pint of milk every two days. He sometimes appeared on

[14] Interview with Andrew Rosthorn

Granada TV in Manchester as a continuity announcer and once acted as a barrister in Granada's afternoon TV series *Crown Court*, but he made no further theatrical headway and threw in the towel to start work as a commission-only sewing machine salesman in London. When the sewing machine firm collapsed, he started his own sales firm but a sudden government credit squeeze forced him out of business.

In 1960 he left London with seven pounds in cash and four gallons of petrol in his Jaguar. Back in Blackpool, his parents were about to sell their house. Young Owen struck up a friendship with Fred Ritchie, their estate agent, and started selling property for the agent on a 'commission only' basis. When he asked for a partnership to marry Vicki Burns, a tall Blackpool school teacher, herself the daughter of a bookmaker from an industrial town in Lancashire, Fred Ritchie turned him down:

> Somewhat distressed by this rejection, in view of my dedication to him, I then placed my first advertisement under the name 'Oyston', trying to sell four houses. This was in 1962. As a consequence, Fred Ritchie called me into his office, expressed his objection, paid me off and dismissed me. [15]

Father and son then opened the Oyston Estate Agency, run from Oyston's house. Owen had ten shares. Selsby had two hundred. Owen's brothers, Ian and Robert, joined later and the business began to flourish in a hard and competitive world. They broke the rules, pioneered *no sale - no pay* deals, bought a computer and made no charge for placing ads in newspapers. Branches stayed open seven days a week and in the evenings. Everything was heavily advertised on TV at 'off-peak' rates. After 20 years, they claimed they were the 'largest family-owned estate agents in Britain.'

Ian died in 1976, when Owen moved his family into an old manor house once owned by Samuel Morse. Claughton Hall had been dismantled and rebuilt by millionaire linoleum manufacturers as a bijou castle on a hilltop outside Lancaster. Oyston's employees called it *hassle castle*. While running 97 agency offices in North West England, the former actor went on television, starring in his own commercials by falling unforgettably backwards into a swimming pool in amazement at the deals his company was offering.

He cast a wide net, gaining a reputation in the City of London for being an early bird, early into commercial radio, early into free newspapers, early into cable TV. In 1982, assembling a consortium to bid for the licence for commercial radio in Lancashire, he brought in Russell Harty from BBC

---

[15] Interview with Andrew Rosthorn

television, the peerless West Indian cricketer Clive Lloyd and two England rugby captains, Billy Beaumont and Richard Greenwood, winning the franchise for Red Rose Radio.

The ambitious Labour leaders of Preston, Councillor Harold Parker and Councillor Frank McGrath, backed and eventually joined the Red Rose team. In 1987 at the height of the stock market boom, Owen and Robert pulled off an astounding deal, to sell 35.9 per cent of their business to the Royal Insurance Group for about 33 million pounds. It was the height of the Thatcher boom. Oyston was cash-rich, courted by city financiers and Labour politicians, but woefully unaware that he had now acquired a secret and implacable enemy.

CHAPTER 5

Enter the man from Allied Crowbar

Michael Murrin was an unforgettable political wild card, a member of no party who damaged the careers of a dozen serious politicians in both the big parties.

Lady Dulcie Atkins, wife of the Tory government minister Sir Robert Atkins, once told a Preston newsagent,

> Watch your back. Murrin is a very dangerous man. He ruined my husband's political career. [16]

Louise Ellman, Labour MP for Liverpool Riverside from 1997 to 2019 and former leader of Lancashire County Council, told Dale Campbell-Savours MP,

> Before I saw what that man could do to good people in public life, I had no idea how vicious English politics could be. [17]

Michael Hugh Murrin had grown up in the South of England and claimed to have been introduced to political cynicism by meeting a friend of his father. His father's friend was the British spy Greville Wynne who had been captured by the KGB in Budapest after the Russians had outwitted a British attempt to rescue the doomed master spy Oleg Penkovsky.

Wynne had been very lucky to get back to Britain in a spy exchange for a very important Russian agent, Konon Molody [Gordon Lonsdale].

Mike Murrin was a completely self-tutored political agitator, living in a semi-detached house in Goodwood Avenue, in the Fulwood suburb of Preston with his wife Judith, a schoolteacher, and their daughters. He sold

---

[16] Mrs Doreen Cook, 1996

[17] Interview with Andrew Rosthorn and Dale Campbell Savours MP

life assurance for the lightly regulated and aggressive Allied Dunbar firm, known in the trade as *Allied Crowbar*.

Michael Murrin

He first took a hand in Lancashire politics in the second year of the long premiership of Margaret Thatcher, just before the Falklands War, when her personal popularity had fallen to a record low of 25 per cent. The Conservative Party had become even more unpopular than Thatcher, so that the unexpected result of the county council elections of 1981 was that control of Lancashire County Council went to the Labour Party, with Mrs Louise Ellman unexpectedly becoming Labour leader of Lancashire.

Ellman's new policy of self-help, investing council funds into 'job creation' projects, was bound to annoy a central government then ideologically reducing state intervention according to the principles of Friedrich Hayek.

Murrin recounted his headfirst dive into local politics in a 1991 letter to Dale Campbell-Savours MP:

> Lancashire County Council imposed a supplementary rate. At that time I was a life assurance salesman and found that many of my clients were suffering severe financial hardship as a result of the recession. I formed the Preston & District Ratepayers Association to fight on their behalf.

Someone working at Preston Town Hall told Murrin to 'watch the docks' and watch how the Labour team running Preston Borough Council would be diverting the proceeds of the derelict land grant under which the town would be financially rewarded by the government for closing down their municipal dock.

The consequences of this irresponsible remark were huge. Telling Mike Murrin that corruption was in the offing was as deadly as giving Béla Lugosi a full moon.

Funded by cash from ratepayers' coffee mornings, this unorthodox agitator, an English *Poujadiste* if ever there was one, set about a 'dirty tricks' plan:

> In 1983 I began an investigation into local government in Preston and Lancashire.
>
> I paid Christopher More, a private detective trading as CILS, to obtain the bank account details of the Labour leader of Preston, Harold Parker. Parker was being paid by a company owned by the estate agent Owen Oyston. I made statements to police alleging corruption involving Oyston and local councillors.
>
> On July 27, 1983, I wrote to David Waddington MP asking him to persuade the Minister to call in a redevelopment scheme for Preston Dock or 'otherwise investigate the project'. On August 6th, 1983, David Waddington MP wrote to me agreeing to raise the Preston Dock plans with the Secretary of State for the Environment.
>
> On December 8, 1983, I wrote to Councillor Harold Parker, leader of Preston Borough Council and a friend of Owen Oyston, asking him to resign as

> chairman of the Preston port sub-committee because he was working for Oyston as a self-employed consultant. [18]

Murrin forced his first resignation, on December 22, 1983, when Owen Oyston, a friend and political ally of Louise Ellman, resigned as an unpaid director of Lancashire County Council's controversial regeneration firm Lancashire Enterprises Ltd. Oyston was now Murrin's key target code-named 'T1' in correspondence.

> On January 4, 1984, Christopher More, of CIL Services, reported to me the National Westminster Bank balance on the previous day of Harold Parker. He also noted the outstanding mortgage balance of Parker's account at the Bradford & Bingley Building Society, Parker's NatWest business account balance and, obtained from Oystons by deception, the exact amount paid monthly by Oyston to Parker.

On January 24, 1984, Murrin noted:

> I am now involved in further in-depth of questioning of quality sources and expect to have further information within seven days. The source of information is of the highest quality but very sensitive.

Years later, he described some of his tactics:

> I gathered allegations by other people of corrupt behaviour by the Deputy Labour leader of Preston, Councillor Frank McGrath. I met Tom Cato, a Tory businessman from Fleetwood who had been a client of Christopher More's agency. Tom Cato made allegations against Owen Oyston.
>
> At this time, I wrote to the Chief Constable of Lancashire and was invited to visit the headquarters, to meet Assistant Chief Constable Mander. I made a statement to Mander but I was disturbed when Mr More of Commercial, Insurance and Legal Services told me he was certain that the contents of my statement were being passed back to Oyston.
>
> I was eventually told by Mr Mander that the police could find no evidence to substantiate my information and that, as far as the police were concerned, the matter was closed.
> On February 4, 1984, Christopher More reported to me that Oyston Greenwood estate agency in Maghull, Liverpool had paid standing orders since February 1983 to the NatWest and Co-operative Bank accounts of Harold Parker and his firm Activus, totalling £550 per month.

---

[18] Letter to author

> More noted that the figures matched those obtained earlier by him from the National Westminster Bank. He also told me the names of Harold Parker's loan guarantors and the fact that his mortgage had not been paid in February 1983.
>
> On March 27, 1984, a BBC TV Sixty Minutes *Watchdog* programme, based somewhat on my own work, was screened. The programme claimed that Owen Oyston's consultancy work with Parker was improper. The programme forced a Preston Council debate on the Dock.
>
> At a public meeting afterwards, I revealed I had been behind the *Watchdog* programme and I invited Councillors Parker and McGrath to sue me.
>
> On April 28, 1984, the Preston Tory councillor Audrey Scott introduced me to Robert Atkins MP at her home in Preston.
>
> On May 11, 1984, Robert Atkins MP invited me to meet him at his home and gave me an introduction to the Fylde developer, William Harrison.

In May 1984 Murrin began to tape record the telephone calls in and out of 21, Goodwood Avenue.

Robert Atkins was 'absolutely appalled beyond belief' when the tapes were discovered in 1992 by Chris Blackhurst of *Esquire* magazine. [19]

> It is unbelievable behaviour. Conversations you have with people are not always articulate and don't always make sense.

But it made sense to Murrin, whose main target 'T1' was now Owen Oyston. Chris Blackhurst described the Murrin approach:

> The overall message of the tapes is simply, 'Get Oyston', and the spirit of the enterprise was best accomplished by Murrin passionately breathing into his own recording device: 'I'm going to have him. One way or the other. I am going to have him'.

The writer Graham Nown, who lived in Southport, stumbled on transcripts of Murrin's tapes after they fell into the hands of libel lawyers. Nown had just published a biography of the Leeds-born American gangster Owney Madden, a man who was once released from Sing Sing prison on

[19] *Esquire*, May 1992: *The Oyston Tapes*

parole after paying a million dollar bribe to Franklin D Roosevelt's Democratic Party. [20]

Intrigued by the Murrin tapes, Nown assembled slices of the telephone traffic recorded in 21, Goodwood Avenue and revealed how Mike Murrin had orchestrated the illegal activities of a shadowy team of conspirators.

Soho, mid 1970s, Martin Tomkinson between Jeffrey Bernard and *Private Eye* editor Richard Ingrams. © ERIC HANDS / NATIONAL PORTRAIT GALLERY, LONDON

TACTICS

Michael Murrin talks to Martin Tomkinson of the *Digger* magazine.

Tomkinson: Apparently your great friend likes dressing up in funny regalia.

Murrin: Are we talking about Hitler uniforms?

Tomkinson: We are indeed.

---

[20] *The English Godfather,* Graham Nown, Ward Lock, 1987.

Murrin: What I heard was that he had a party for a group of businessmen who were mostly Jewish, and that he marched out in a SS uniform.

Tomkinson: Right. Well you see that matches everything I heard, except it was a Christmas party, I heard, and it was 1985. Now what's just been pointed out to me it's apparently old information, but I just wondered whether he made a habit of doing this.

DRUGS

In the search for an elusive drugs connection Murrin talked to Geoff Scott, husband of the Preston Tory Councillor Audrey Scott.

Murrin: I mean, personally, if it had just been a case of bribery, I would have given up this years ago. I mean it's just not worth the bloody effort.

Scott: No, no.

Murrin: But it's not a question of that. What I'm interested in is the association of these people with drug dealers.

Scott: Yes, yes.

Murrin: I mean lets be quite clear about why I'm in it. I'm in it because I see a situation where politicians are coming into the control of the drugs dealers.

Scott: Yes, yes.

SMEARS WERE SPREAD

Following a rumour: Murrin talks to a Norman Dearden

Murrin: Child pornography?

Dearden: Yes.

Murrin: You heard that story, did you?

Dearden: From somewhere, but where I can't remember at all.

Murrin: What was the ... what was the gist of it? That Oyston had an interest in pornography?

Dearden: Er, there's a bit going on up at his place, North of Lancaster.

Murrin: Can I draw the distinction and see which way you interpreted it? Were they using children up there for pornography, or were they just indulging in looking at films?

Dearden: Er, From the way I understood they had children up there.

Murrin: You're kidding me. Really?

Dearden: From what I understood, yes.

Murrin: Is there anyway of tracing that?

Dearden: I can't think where it came from now. I just can't think at all. It's probably some months back now. You know, it's just gone.

It spreads to Martin Tomkinson at the *Digger*...

Murrin: As I understood it, he was looking at videos and that sort of thing.

Tomkinson: Yes.

Murrin: But I've just been in touch with a person who was talking to me. And, as he understood it, they actually had children up there.

Tomkinson: Oh really? Yes, well, right OK. If, well, you know, you get any sort of solid evidence, that's fine.

Murrin: Well, what I'm really saying to you is –

Tomkinson: Yes…

Murrin: If that is the case then, um, all it means is that I want the bastard sooner than later.

To the *Lancashire Evening Post* municipal correspondent Peter Dugdale

Murrin: Child pornography. Did I mention that to you?

Dugdale: Oh really?

Murrin: Right, well, what I heard was that, er, that he had an interest in child pornography. Well, what I'm hearing now is that the interest was not in the form of magazines or films, but he's actually had children up at his castle.

Dugdale: Um. And have we any way of getting to prove that?

Murrin: Well, let's put it this way. Every piece of information I have on him I run through a system. So, I take it from one source, I take from another... If it comes from a third source, then I think there's something in it. And then I put it out to independent verification.

Dugdale: Ah.

Murrin: Now, every time I have done that the independent verification has proved the information to be accurate.

Later:

Murrin: I mean, if your Editor is so spineless that he can't pursue, or even allocate, a bit of time to something of the gravity that we're talking about, then it's pointless me dealing with the paper.

Later still:

Murrin: I've got tape recordings. The source of information just told me that it was actually children up there. I've got that on tape. I also have on tape that he dressed up as an SS officer and pranced, paraded around a party of businessmen who happened to be all Jewish. And that has been verified I've also got on tape that he had compromising photographs of one of his colleagues which he'd used to blackmail him. And also got a model agency in Manchester which I've been told is, er, supplying him with prostitutes.

Dugdale: Um. Um.

The rumour travels back to paymaster Bill Harrison.

Murrin: Those reports concerning child pornography -

Harrison: Yes?

Murrin: They refer to actually having children on the premises.

Harrison: Yes, but have they proof?

Murrin: Um.

Harrison: Do they have proof?

Murrin: Well, that's what we're working on.

Harrison: Mm. Can't understand people. But, of course, these people they're different, aren't they? They're more of the animal type.

Murrin: Mmm.

Harrison: Well... animals don't maltreat their children like that, do they?

Murrin: No. Heh, heh.

And then Murrin talks to Sir Peter Blaker, Tory MP for Blackpool South.

Murrin: There is a note in the post. You probably haven't opened it. The child pornography didn't refer to films and papers, magazines. It referred to sexual abuse of children on the premises.

Blaker: Oh, that's what the note says does it?

Murrin: That's what the note says.

Blaker: I see. From a reliable source?

Murrin: Ex-policeman.

Blaker: Well, really. Well, things are shaping up then.

Murrin tells Blaker about Oyston's deal with a pension fund controlled by the Derbyshire Labour leader, Councillor David Bookbinder.

Murrin: I've sent a letter to Edwina Currie.

Blaker: Yes. I saw that. You sent me a copy. I wouldn't bother with her. Ha Ha Ha. She's too busy making a name for herself and she won't have time to pursue this. Oppenheim's your man. [*Tory MP for Amber Valley*] Er… Oppenheim's taking this seriously, I talked to him yesterday.

Murrin: Is he taking it seriously?

Blaker: Oh yes. What? The Oyston Question?

Murrin: Yes.

Blaker: Very much. He's got a research assistant.

Murrin: Yes. I spoke to the... I saw the research assistant Wednesday of last week.

Blaker: The research assistant I haven't met. But Phillip, who I haven't previously talked to very much, but I had a talk with yesterday over a cup of tea, he's taking it very seriously. Er he's much interested in getting Bookbinder into the soup, which he believes Bookbinder deserves to be in. He's, Bookbinder's a real so-and-so and he's much interested in the Derbyshire County Council pension fund affair. Umm, I've put him in the picture a little more widely about the nature of Oyston, which he seemed to know something about already.

Murrin: Yes.

Blaker: I think perhaps you will send him some documents. Will you?

OYSTON BLAMED FOR RUINING THE CHIEF CONSTABLE

An ex-policeman called Brown calls Murrin...

Brown: It's Mr Brown.

Murrin: Mmm.

Brown: Ten years ago, Mr Imbert, Assistant Chief Constable...

Murrin: Mmm.

Brown: of Thames Valley, came to the Fylde to investigate various aspects of police... Parr... perpetrated by Oyston. Mr Imbert is now the Chief Commissioner for the Metropolitan Police. I reckon he'd like a copy of that.

Murrin: How do mean, perpetrated by Oyston?

Brown: Well he set all that stuff up did Oyston.

Murrin: What? He set up the investigation?

Brown: No. No.

Murrin: He set up the thing with Parr?

Brown: Ah yes. Everything.

Murrin: Did Imbert go into Oyston?

Brown: Don't know. Got called off the case.

Murrin: Did he?

Brown: Well Imbert was called back. Change of government, you see, and change of policy. You sent that to them. I think you should send a copy somewhere else.

Murrin: What is he now?

Brown: He's the chief of the Metropolitan, the whole works.

ANOTHER SMEAR SURFACES.

Murrin talks to Paul Halloran of *Private Eye.*

Murrin: Spoke to a fellow today who is a senior employee with Oyston, left some time ago. He has said that Oyston said at one time that he had compromising photographs of 'C'

Halloran: Uh huh.

Murrin: Which he used to exert pressure. That's the implication. Now that's the first direct thing I've got of blackmail being used. But he's saying quite adamantly that Oyston was saying that he had photographs showing 'C' in compromising situations.

Andrew Hogg of the *Sunday Times* calls Murrin who had responded to a story about a Manx-based drug-money launderer Patrick Diamond and his mysterious offshore company called Oyston Ltd.

Hogg: You wrote to the Editor last week regarding Patrick Diamond.

Murrin: Yes.

Hogg: I wondered. I know a little bit about our interest in this Mr Diamond.

Murrin: Yes.

Hogg: I was curious about what prompted you to send the letter, whether you're a journalist or…

Murrin: No, I'm just a wayward northern eccentric.

Hogg: Yes.

Murrin: Ha, ha, ha. I've had a long running enquiry going on into a gentleman called Mr Oyston.

Hogg: Mm.

Murrin: Do you know about Mr Oyston?

Hogg: I don't, but I would suggest there's probably someone here who might know about him. Barry Penrose. He wrote the other two articles about Diamond.

Later:

Murrin: You're on the 'Inside *(sic)* Team?

Hogg: Yes.

Murrin: Right. There was one of your fellows who came up here with a chap from the BBC called Andrew Jennings.

Hogg: Yes.

Murrin: And Jennings did an article, er, a TV *Watchdog* programme some years ago concerning Mr Oyston paying local councillors and the Preston Dock redevelopment. I'm trying to fish for the guy's name but I... it eludes me.

Hogg: Yes.

Murrin: But, the bottom line of that was that I got involved at that time in some enquiries concerning Mr Oyston. Constantly, from the beginning, there were rumours, or information was being passed around concerning drugs; that there was an element of drugs trafficking involved.

Hogg: Yes.

Murrin: This is going back six years now

Hogg: Really, why?

Murrin: Blackmail and bribery.

Murrin tries drugs on *The Independent*

Murrin: From then, I made statements to the local police and I employed an enquiry agent who provided me with information. I was told by this enquiry agent that the information I was putting in the statements was being fed back to Oyston and his associates.

Reporter: Hmm. Hmm.

Murrin: Information I was told was coming out of police headquarters. At the time I was not issued with a writ, but an approach was made. The investigator told me that an approach was made to him to try and buy him off - to stop him working for me. A female friend of mine and a friend of my wife's was approached and asked about her sex life, and had I ever made a pass at her. I have always been told from Day One, and there have always been rumours, and I can't put it more strongly than that, of Mr Oyston being involved in criminal connections and drugs.

Reporter: Hmm.

Murrin: Now I came across a company search when I was at Companies House in London. On that company search, the company was called Oyston Ltd. It was formed in the Isle of Man under nominees, with nominee shareholders in Hong Kong. On that company search were nominee directors, formation agents, under the name of Patrick Diamond. Patrick Diamond is well known for his drugs connections and money laundering activities. He served a prison sentence for the same.

Paul Halloran of *Private Eye* asks Murrin for money

Halloran: I had a chance to effectively report back, since we spoke. And my people don't like your operation at all.

Murrin: Why?

Halloran: Because the primary problem that we had, has not been overcome. We don't know who we're dealing with.

Murrin: Well, we can overcome that problem. I think.

Halloran: Now, they, they won't, under any circumstances, entertain any arrangement unless there's cash up front.

Murrin: Well, as I said, I think we can overcome those problems.

Michael Murrin tells Sir Peter Blaker that Andrew Rosthorn knows about how he taped the *Private Eye* reporter Paul Halloran asking for money.

Murrin: I told him about the *Private Eye* incident and he asked me whether he could have a copy of the tape recording of the conversation with Halloran. He's sent it down to Hislop, the editor. I have been put in the position where I was basically being asked for a bribe for the stuff to appear in the magazine.

Blaker: By one of his staff.

Blaker: The problem with someone like Hallrahan, or whatever is name is, is that he isn't a beaver. He's an idle drunken so-and-so who wants to make some money. That's no good. We want someone who wants to make his name as a journalist.

Allegations linking Oyston to Patrick Diamond reach Westminster and Rosthorn calls Murrin.

Rosthorn: Right now, the guy I went to see is, er... Dale Campbell Savours, who is a member of the Parliamentary Accounts Committee.

Murrin: Right.

Rosthorn: Now he was very, very appalled at the behaviour of the Labour leaders in Preston.

Murrin: Yeah.

Rosthorn: Shocked by it, and very depressed. Now, strangely, he knows Paul Halloran quite well. He was completely pole-axed by that tape. He, like Hislop, said he personally hopes there is some kind of reasonable explanation behind it. Now, the next stage is that he is definitely ready to table a question at Parliament.

Murrin: Right.

Rosthorn: And we've actually penned out a parliamentary note - this House notes certain things - now what these are is Oyston Limited, the Hong Kong thing. It asks Oyston to confirm to the

House... actually to say whether he has, at any time, had any links with the Isle of Man person.

Murrin: Who, with Patrick Diamond?

Rosthorn: Right.

Murrin and Sir Peter Blaker discuss the chances of jailing Oyston.

Murrin: It is not beyond the possibility that he tries to do a runner.

Blaker: A runner?

Murrin: Yeah…

Blaker: Rio?

Murrin: Somewhere.

Blaker: Yes, well that will be a victory of sorts, but not such a good one as the one we want. Not the one we want.

Murrin: No, we want him here. We don't want him to do a Biggs.

Blaker: Behind bars, that's right absolutely.

Murrin: He's sticking two fingers up and is laughing at us.

Blaker: Yes.

MONEY, MONEY, MONEY

Murrin talks to Sir Peter Blaker about money

Blaker: There are funds still available.

Murrin: Oh yes?

Blaker: I don't know whether Robert talked to you about the quantity of the funds talked about.

Murrin: No, he didn't.

Blaker: Well, we've got up to ten thousand.

Private detective Chris Guest More has tracked the cash from Bill Harrison and seen it landing in Murrin's bank account.

Murrin: How are you?

More: I'm all right, and you?

Murrin: A bit peeved.

More: Why?

Murrin: You calling me a liar. Ha, ha, ha. Sunday.

More: I didn't call you a liar.

Murrin: You did.

More: When?

Murrin: Well, you said I haven't got the financial backing.

More: *(Indistinct)*

Murrin: Ha, ha, ha. Me being ultra-sensitive? Do you want a copy of the bank statement?

More: No, I've got it thanks.

Murrin: Five grand went into that account. And I've got another five thousand on account to call on.

More: OK, sir.

Murrin and a caller named Ivan...

Murrin: No, the fellow I'm after is called Oyston.

Ivan: Oyston?

Murrin: O.Y.S.T.O.N... that's who I'm after... It's one of those maverick operations of mine that sort of got out of hand, to be honest with you. If I pull it off and it does break open, it will be a major thing. It will be bigger than Poulson ever was. And I would hope to try and capitalise on my years of effort. But, of course, if I don't pull it off and I can't break it open in the Press, then it will all be down the tubes. Although I have actually cost the man something like five and a half million quid in hard readies.

Ivan: I'm sure he's grateful to you.

Murrin: Yes, he'd have been better off paying me, wouldn't he? This is one of the ironies, you see, because I said to Judith, if he'd approached me in 1982 and said, 'Look, Murrin, here's ten grand - now sod off and buy yourself a house on the south coast', I would have gone.

Paymaster Bill Harrison complains about a private detective

Harrison: I don't want to see my £20,000 just go into the sea.

Murrin: Well, I don't think you'll see that.

Harrison: Well, I've not seen anything for it yet, have I? So what I had in mind…

Murrin: Yeah.

Harrison: We've got to flush things out somehow.

Later:

Harrison: Well if we'd got that you see... that would, I thought, be a good start. Chris More said, well, 'I have the Inland Revenue special investigation branch, they could look at something.' But I never hear anything. It's like dealing with the dead. You know what I mean?

Murrin: Yeah.

Harrison: You know how I feel?

Murrin: Oh, yes, I know –

Harrison: I feel as though... I've taken a suitcase with twenty odd thousand in and thrown it off the bloody North Pier...

Later still:

Harrison: At least I could have said, well, I was a stupid fool.

Murrin: Yeah.

Harrison: For a half hour.

Murrin: Yeah, yeah.

Harrison: Now I feel I've been a stupid fool for a year.

Murrin: I don't think you have been. I don't honestly.

MONEY ISN'T EVERYTHING

Murrin and Sir Peter Blaker

Blaker: His problems do not involve money. He's got lots of money.

Murrin: Yeah.

Blaker: And if... *(indistinct)* it will not be nearly as much as he's got.

Murrin: But what if he was on charges?

Blaker: Well, that would be a different matter. That doesn't involve money. That involves being sent to jail.

Murrin: But then, he must not think he's going to be in that position.

Blaker: Why?

Murrin: Well, surely, he wouldn't get involved in something like this if he thought he was going to be facing criminal charges, would he?

Blaker: I don't see why not. I think he might bluster it out, or bluff it out. He probably doesn't know he's going to face criminal charges.

Murrin and Paul Halloran of *Private Eye* discuss *News on Sunday*

Halloran: Because, what's happening, they've run out of money, you see.

Murrin: Yes.

Halloran: And Owen wants to help.

Murrin: Does he?

Halloran: So he could be the owner of a national Sunday newspaper before much longer. Which makes it even more tasty.

Murrin: Well, what do you make... how do you, er… see all that fitting in with the other stuff?

Halloran: Well, it makes him vulnerable, doesn't it?

Murrin: I don't know.

Halloran: Yes, I think so. But we are in good shape.

HIGH PLACES

Sir Peter Blaker talks to Murrin about Robert Atkins

Blaker: You know that Robert's in the government now?

Murrin: Yes, I did. Yes.

Blaker: Which is good for him. Mind, he deserves to be. Done a great job. Well, I'll wait to see what your letter says. But, er, I think we should keep Robert in on this, by the way.

Murrin: Oh everything that you've got, he has got

Blaker: Yes but I think we should keep him ...What I'm saying is that you and I should keep him involved, in spite of the fact that he's going to be much busier.

Later:

Blaker: I think it would be a good idea to meet when you're next in London.

Murrin: Right.

Blaker: I'll try and get Robert along.

Murrin: Yes.

Blaker: In spite of his ministerial jobs, he's still interested in the subject.

After hearing about Inland Revenue action against Oyston, Blaker tells of meeting Bill Harrison in the House of Commons

Blaker: There are two points you are making. One is the... is that there's something happening with the Revenue which looks favourable to us, and secondly coming back to drugs, yeah?

Murrin: Yes.

Blaker: Well, keep up the good work. I saw our friend who went for a cruise. I saw him today and shook his hand. He happened to be down here for luncheon, not luncheon given by me. And I was walking along the corridor and there he was. So I shook him by the hand heartily and said, 'We're keeping up the good work.'

Murrin: Is he a happy man?

Blaker: He looked very happy. Yes. He gave me the thumbs up sign so... We didn't have chance to talk because he was in the middle of a crowd all going into a dining room and I was going into the dining room next door. So it was just a pure fluke. But anyway, I told him... I had the opportunity of saying, 'Things are moving on.'

Murrin: Now what about police involvement?

Blaker: Well. have we got to the point where we can...

Murrin: Not yet. The steps I've taken today... is that I've gone back to my sources at the Revenue today. I've told them what I've heard and I've also phoned the...

Blaker: What you've heard, you mean, about the drugs?

Murrin: Yes, and the, again, reaffirming what I've heard about the offshore involvements.

Blaker: Offshore involvement?

Murrin: Bank accounts.

Blaker: Oh, that's come up again has it?

Murrin: Yeah. Channel Islands I'm being directed to, which fitted in with their theory. Channel Islands has been mentioned before.[21]

Murrin and Harrison discuss strangling Oyston's advertising revenue

Harrison: People are beginning to believe in you?

Murrin: Well, I mean, one chap who advertised in the *Lancashire Life* magazines, as soon as Oyston took over, he cancelled his advertising.

Harrison: So did my son-in-law.

Murrin: Right, well this guy –

Harrison: That's Livocks Furniture, they were the biggest advertiser.

Murrin: Of which furniture?

---

[21] Murrin tape 21 transcript.

Harrison: Livocks.

Murrin: In Blackpool?

Harrison: My son-in-law.

Murrin: Your son-in-law owns that?

Harrison: Yes. It's thirty five thousand a year they spent.

Murrin: Why did he cancel?

Harrison: Because he doesn't like his politics. He's always voted Conservative, and he likes a Conservative attitude.

Sir Peter Appears Pleased

Murrin: He has put up additional money, [*for the News on Sunday newspaper]* but of course, what we really want is for him to take it over.

Blaker: Yes, we want him to be the Maxwell of that outfit.

Murrin: That's right.

Harrison: With the highest possible profile.

Later:

Halloran: Uh huh.

Blaker: Yes. Well that's - that's good news.

Murrin: Good news, good news.

Later:

Blaker: We haven't got to the point yet, have we? Where Robert and I can go to the cash people.

Murrin: Not yet, no. But at some stage, you know, if it starts to break in the Eye. But from that stage, it is going to become known to the people who matter, where the information has come from.

Blaker: Well Robert and I will be ready to, we'll be ready to go into action at that point.

POURING IN THE POISON

Murrin tells Harrison about his plans.

Murrin: Now, the key question is what are they putting up the finance for? Blackpool Football Ground seems to be the major contender at the moment.... So what I'm doing at the moment is I've arranged for somebody to contact these people. No connection between us. He will provide them with the information that I've got anyway. So, in other words, he'll pour some poison in.

Later:

Murrin: Now if we can isolate the client, we might be able to screw up the deal, mightn't we?

Harrison: I would think so, yes. But that's not really what we want is it? What we want –

Murrin: Well, it depends. What do we want?

Harrison: We want to get the person stopped, don't we?

Murrin: Well, if we can block the finance that he's proposing to set up for whatever deal it is, I mean we've got to, we must find out which deal it is that he's looking at, because it might be something we don't know about. But if it's the Blackpool thing then we really need to find out who is involved and see if we can cut off his line of credit.

ANOTHER OPPORTUNITY

Murrin talks to McDougall, a businessman in cable television...

Murrin: I've been involved in stalking this fellow now for about four years and I mean what we're talking about is we're talking about reports of… are you there?

McDougall: Yes, I just shifted to my other ear so I had a bit of pad in front of me.

Murrin: We're talking about tax evasion. Inter-company fraud. Drug abuse. Prostitution. The very faint possibility of blackmail and there are unsubstantiated and unconfirmed murmurings, I can't put any more than that. But there are persistent rumblings of a connection with the drugs business. What I'm looking at is I'm looking at a spread of something in excess of 40 companies.

Murrin tells Peter Hounam, *Sunday Times* chief reporter, that Owen Oyston has been in touch

Hounam: From what Vicki [*Oyston*] was saying to you then, they're in dire trouble?

Murrin: No, no, no. That is not true. No, that's not right. No, she was only saying that it had hurt them very badly in an emotional sense and it had affected the family. Now, you've got to remember what I've done to him Peter. He walks into a bloody merchant bank in London and the first question they ask him is: 'Before we do talk business Mr Oyston, have you been involved in running drugs from Hong Kong?' I mean, Jesus Christ, you know I hurt the guy, didn't I? Not that I was the one who put the information into the merchant bank but, I mean, it was a pretty successful campaign wasn't it?

Hounam: That's right. I mean I can't answer these questions for you, can I? It's up to you, you know.

Murrin: Well, I mean, let me say to you one thing straight away, right? If I was going to do a deal and turn to being a crook or taking bribes, I wouldn't be asking you would I? You're the last person I would talk to.

Hounam: I see. I think if you are trying to set him up, you've got to try and get him to... you don't want to disabuse him of your importance, you want to sort of blow it up out of all proportion. Likewise, you should go for a fairly substantial sum.

Murrin: Yes, but I mean, if we are going to do that, then we've got to organise it haven't we?

Hounam: Yes.

Murrin: I'm quite prepared to... put my head in that noose.

Hounam: Right.

Murrin: I'm quite prepared to do that. But really, I mean you know... what I'm doing, I mean, it's suicide.

Hounam: You must be mad to take this risk.

Murrin: Well, either mad or desperate.

Later:

Murrin: I've spent eight years on this bleeding thing. Let's spend another 12 weeks or 12 months and if I can set the guy up to bribe me, then let's have it done that way. What I don't want to happen is for me to do that and then find I'm being prosecuted for something or other and put across the papers as being a bloody blackmailer or something.

And still later:

Murrin: Well, you see what I'm saying to you, Peter, really the bottom line is that...I am exceedingly vulnerable.

Hounam: Yes.

Murrin: I have made that totally clear to Oyston. I have also made it totally clear to him that as far as I'm concerned, I've been dumped by the other side. Because nobody is going to lift a finger to help me.

NO REGRETS

Murrin interviewed by radio reporter Judith Burns

Burns: Now, you were using a private investigator and people have said that you were conducting a witch hunt against various individuals on the Preston Council. Are those accusations justified?

Murrin: Well, we certainly used a private investigator. But all that those investigators have ever done is to check information which was already in my hands.

Burns: Do you think it was fair to go delving into people's bank accounts?

Murrin: Well, I don't think life's very fair. If you can't stand the heat, you get out of the kitchen, and if you enter public life, you should be accountable to the public. If I were in that position, I would feel that I'm accountable to the people who put me into office.

Burns: So you'd do the same thing again?

Murrin: Oh, I would do the same thing again tomorrow morning if I had the opportunity, yes.[22]

---

[22] Murrin tape 26 transcript, August 1985.

CHAPTER 6

Blow by Blow

In February 1982, Mike Murrin opened a new offensive by sending a rude letter to a new target, Mrs Louise Ellman. The county council leader was openly involved with Owen Oyston in a kind of industrial self-help scheme involving millions of pounds of taxpayers' money. On February 15, Mrs Ellman sent a stroppy letter to Murrin

> It is clear from the tone and contents of your letter that you have little knowledge of, or sympathy with, the needs of the Preston and district area.

On the same day Owen Oyston and his soon to be divorced wife Vicki appeared in the newspapers together, posing on the sunny terrace of Claughton Hall as Oyston backed the county council scheme:

> I applaud what the politicians have done here. For the first time this idea will break new ground, a marriage between the county politicians and business expertise. We are hoping to have several millions of pounds from the county council and institutional sources.

In March, Mrs Ellman unveiled the county council's job-creation project, a commercial trading firm to be called Lancashire Enterprises Limited, based in the old dock offices at Preston and funded by the county council with up to two million pounds of public money 'limited by guarantee'. LEL was to be chaired by her friend, Jim Mason of the Co-operative Wholesale Society, with Owen Oyston serving as an unpaid director.

Brian Hill, chief executive of Lancashire county council explained in a letter to the Chorley Tory MP Den Dover that LEL would work 'independently from the county council and may invest in ventures and business opportunities on a commercial basis as part of its objective to help alleviate unemployment and to assist in the regeneration of the economy of Lancashire.'

Murrin's reaction was to send a copy of Louise Ellman's frosty letter to the prime-minister, asking Mrs Thatcher to comment 'in detail'. He had already warned Robert Atkins MP about ambitious and risky LEL investment plans after hearing that Owen Oyston had been to Iceland to persuade Nordic trawler owners to start landing fresh fish at the dying port of Fleetwood.

Murrin discovered that Louise Ellman, Jim Mason and Harold Parker, the Labour leader of Preston, had recently resigned from a number of small loss-making businesses. He felt that a trading firm run on public money, investing in small businesses in ravaged towns like Skelmersdale and Rossendale would be sure to alarm the ideologues who were running Britain in the long high summer of Thatcherism.

Murrin was no Thatcherite. He was not even a Tory. But he went into overdrive when the Tory leader in Preston, Councillor Joe Hood, tipped him off that the Labour politicians were getting involved in the big money re-developments at Preston Dock, where the council would be spending a £12 million government derelict land grant.

The Labour leader Harold Parker and his deputy, Councillor Frank McGrath, had decided to reject the advice of the professional consultants Debenham, Tewson & Chinnocks and turn down a redevelopment scheme for the dock proposed by Mowlem plc.

They wanted Preston to bring in a new development consortium assembled by Mrs Ellman's LEL firm, to include Jim Cookson's project developers, North of England Development Association, the civil engineers Balfour Beatty, a subsidiary of BICC, and the bankers NM Rothschild & Sons Ltd.

The council's previous consultants had resigned when Parker and McGrath insisted on getting their own way over the project. In a letter to the *Lancashire Evening Post* in July 1983, Murrin asked:

> How much longer have the poor bemused ratepayers of Lancashire to suffer the iniquities of Lancashire Enterprises Ltd without any voice in their activities?
> Can anything be more scandalous than the intrigues concerning Preston Dock Development and the involvement of LEL?

To Murrin's fury, and to the astonishment of the Tory councillors in Preston, the Labour-controlled port sub-committee awarded the £55 million Preston Dock Riversway project to Balfour Beatty, at the eleventh hour against the combined advice of property consultants and council officials.

There was bad blood afterwards. Michael Day, former managing director of Mowlem Property Developments, later complained to police and trade journalists that during negotiations with the Preston councillors he was called to a bedroom at the Hilton Hotel in Park Lane, London, to meet Owen Oyston.

Day stated to the police:

> Mr Oyston suggested that Mowlem would make substantial profits out of this building work and if we cared to give some of this to him and his associates, he would make sure that the project would be given to Mowlem and any further negotiation would cease.

Robert Atkins MP agreed to meet Murrin for a discussion about LEL and the dock project. Murrin wrote on July 27 to David Waddington, the Ribble Valley Tory MP, asking him to persuade the environment minister to call in the Preston dock scheme or 'otherwise investigate the project'.

Things got dirtier when Murrin used £1,200 from ratepayers' coffee mornings to hire a Preston firm called Commercial, Insurance and Legal Services to investigate Councillor Harold Parker, the Labour leader of Preston. Parker was known to have a part-time consultancy with the Oyston estate agency, but the estate agency was not involved in projects in Preston and Councillor McGrath had recently publicly threatened to take Oyston Estates to court for non-payment of business rates.

Sure enough, CILS reported that Parker was being paid by Oystons. Murrin then reported Parker to the police and called on him to resign from the port sub-committee. Two weeks later, on December 22, Owen Oyston resigned from his own unpaid directorship at LEL.

> I only agreed to become involved on the basis that the company and my own involvement was supported by councillors of both the two major parties in the county, Councillor Len Broughton, Conservative, and Councillor Louise Ellman, Labour, were on the board. Both were friends of mine and both approved my appointment. The company was successful with this cross-party political consensus. I worked hard for the company setting up deals and giving it a solid property base without any payment. Unfortunately, the Labour-controlled county council and the company were attacked by the media.

On January 4, 1984, Chris More of CILS gave Michael Murrin the previous day's NatWest bank balance on Harold Parker's personal bank account. He also noted the outstanding mortgage balance of Parker's account at the Bradford & Bingley Building Society, the balance on Parker's NatWest business account and, obtained from Oyston's by deception, the exact amount being paid monthly by Oystons to Parker.

Murrin reported on January 24:

> I am now involved in further in-depth of questioning of quality sources and expect to have further information within seven days. The source of information... is of the highest quality but very sensitive.

He noted allegations of 'corrupt behaviour' on the part of Councillor Frank McGrath and said that Roger Ratcliffe of the *Sunday Times* had told him Oyston was paying off the debts of Harold Parker's struggling publicity and marketing firm.

Murrin talked to Andrew Jennings, an intrepid reporter with the BBC and future nemesis of Sepp Blatter at the Swiss-based International Olympic Committee and Fédération Internationale de Football Association.

Jennings was working on a *Watchdog* television programme about local government and managed to find a firm called Associated Productive Companies Ltd., registered at 68, Topping Street, Blackpool, in premises owned by Oyston Estate Agency Limited, with James Mason and Louise Ellman listed as directors. He pressed ahead for an explanation and on February 20, solicitors for Oyston telexed the BBC to state that Owen Oyston 'has never been a shareholder and resigned as director on February 1, 1984.'

Jennings wrote a draft for a BBC television programme about corruption and sent a copy to Murrin, an act with astonishing consequences for all those named by Jennings.

1. Leading Labour lights Louise Ellman and her colleagues in Lancashire start a training workshop in Skelmersdale in 1979. It's a noble idea and you can't fault it. But they come badly unstuck when Kitchen Queen default on huge debt. Multi-millionaire socialist Owen Oyston bails them out. So no egg on their face. And they owe Owen.

2. They set up another training workshop in Rossendale. OO is now major stakeholder in their company, Associated Training Workshops Ltd and he has inside information that

the MSC will fund it. So he buys a mill and installs ATW and then the MSC pays him, via ATW, £11,000 a year rent. That's very naughty, there are internal rows at the MSC [*Manpower Services Commission]* but OO's back is protected by then regional director of MSC, Dewi Rees. Dewi tells his colleagues: "We won't let him do it again." So Owen is directly paying his property company rent given to his ATW by the MSC. MSC sources tell me that a rigid rule is that no private interest should benefit from these public funds.

3. Having hidden their Skelmersdale failures, Ellman, Mason and the cream of the Lancs Labour movement set up Lancashire Enterprises Ltd, funded by rates to create jobs. Again, you can't fault the idea.... Unless of course you are a Tory. And they bring in OO as a director. That's all in early 1982... They spend some of that cash renting premises from OO in Preston. Again, as in Rossendale, OO is wearing 2 hats and benefiting from public money.

4. Red Rose Radio. It stinks. There is no justification for the Labour leadership of Lancs County Council and Preston Borough Council turning up at the public consultation meeting and backing one out of 5 contenders. [see my chapter 4] The result: OO gets his lucrative, it's already in profit, station and Parker and McGrath get shares they clearly could never afford to buy. We're virtually certain OO has given them owt for nowt.

Murrin gave this legally dangerous document to the Lancashire Constabulary. He wrote a letter to the Chief of Constable of Lancashire that earned him a strange Sunday afternoon interview with Assistant Chief Constable Mander at county police headquarters out in the countryside at Hutton.

> It was fixed for a Sunday afternoon, so I would not be seen by other officers, who might have tipped off Oyston.

> I made a statement to Mander but was disturbed when Mr More of Commercial, Insurance and Legal Services told me he was certain that the contents of my statement were being passed back to Oyston.

> I was eventually told by Mr Mander the police could find no evidence to substantiate my information and that, as far as the police were concerned, the matter was closed. It was not until 1987 that I was told by another informant that they had been told Mrs Louise Ellman had a close personal relationship with a senior police officer based at Hutton.

The police did in fact question Mrs Ellman.

On February 4, Chris More reported to Murrin that the Oyston Greenwood estate agency in Maghull, Liverpool, had since February 1983 paid £550.00 per month in standing orders to the NatWest and the Co-operative Bank accounts of Harold Parker and his firm Activus.

Chris More CAVENDISH PRESS

The private detective noted the figures matched those obtained earlier by stealth from the National Westminster Bank at Liverpool Road,

Penwortham, where he discovered that Owen Oyston had guaranteed Parker's loans and that Parker was behind with his mortgage repayments.

This information went to Andrew Jennings, as evidence for his *Watchdog* programme, screened in the old nationwide *Sixty Minutes* slot as a warning about the dangers of Tory and Labour politicians getting too close to businessmen and suggesting that that Councillor Parker's consultancy post with the Oyston firm looked improper.

Murrin was triumphant in the aftermath of *Watchdog*. The Tories in Preston forced a council debate on the dock redevelopment scheme. At a chaotic public meeting in Preston, Murrin revealed that he was the man behind the *Watchdog* programme and invited Councillor Parker and Councillor McGrath to sue him.

Frank McGrath told the newspapers

> We probably have a case against the BBC and against another group of people. We will be taking action over the programme not because of what it did say, but what it did not say.

Although the *Lancashire Evening Post* reported on April 27, 1984, that the politicians were likely to sue Murrin, it was Owen Oyston who instructed Peter Carter Ruck & Partners to file a writ for libel against the BBC and Andrew Jennings.

A day later, delighted with the recent success of Murrin's buccaneering politics, a Preston Tory councillor, Mrs Audrey Scott, invited Murrin to come to her house in Preston and meet Robert Atkins MP, a fateful moment in the history of Lancashire.

Murrin reported

> Mr Atkins said he would explore the possibility of finding a backer.

In the political shorthand of those days, not long after the Falklands War, it was agreed that Audrey Scott had launched an Exocet. Two days later Murrin told the ratepayers he was sending new information to the police and since his life was now in danger. He had insured it for a hundred thousand pounds. Brian Ellis of the *Lancashire Evening Post* reported:

> Michael Murrin admitted today he was taking 'safety precautions' and would consider asking for police protection. 'I could be very vulnerable,' he said.
> The town's ratepayers' chairman believes he could be sitting on a bombshell sparked by the BBC *Watchdog* programme last month.
> 'New information has come in, which if proved correct, could escalate this whole thing beyond anything that I had originally thought or considered would be possible', he said today.
> Mr Murrin whose association is still looking for financial backing to continue an investigation into the dock project has also insured his wife.
> Sole beneficiary is a firm of private investigators instructed to use the cash to complete the inquiry.
> 'The policies are left in trust in the event of anything happening to either myself or my wife – an accident or anything else.
> 'If both of us die there will be £200,000 going to this company whose brief will be to continue the inquiries into every piece of information we have. They will see the thing through to its end. It will go on – I believe it has to go on.'

On May 11, Robert Atkins invited Murrin to his home, Manor House, Lancaster Road, Garstang, to introduce him to a new 'funding source'. This turned out to be Bill Harrison, the corrupt property developer who had funded Atkins's early political career and the man for whom Atkins had disastrously intervened in the death crash scandal.

A day later, Murrin went to meet Harrison at Greyfriars Hall in Preston and on June 28, as Murrin moved into a secret grouping with Robert Atkins and Bill Harrison, he bade farewell to his Preston & District Ratepayers Association. They had already sacked him as chairman and in the words of their new chairman Bryan Chapman

> He was more or less carrying on a witch hunt.

Little was known about the private life of Bill Harrison and certainly not his friendship with Mrs Thatcher's close colleague Airey Neave, terminated when the MP for Abingdon was killed at the House of Commons in 1979. Harrison's friendship with Airey Neave may have been the reason why, during the 1983 Tory conference at Blackpool, Bill Harrison hosted Margaret Thatcher and her entourage at Greyfriars Hall, a huge Edwardian home two miles north of Preston.

It was the year before the IRA bomb attack on Margaret Thatcher and her cabinet at the Grand Hotel in Brighton. Greyfriars, hidden behind the Ingol golf course in Preston, was seen as a safe place for a prime minister to stay during the party conference week at Blackpool. Mrs Thatcher and other cabinet ministers eventually stayed in Bill Harrison's home on five occasions.

Murrin kept the identity of his new backer secret from all but Robert Atkins and the private detective Chris More. More had already mounted a small investigation into Oyston, using funds from Tom Cato, a Fleetwood Tory annoyed by Oyston's interference in the stricken Fleetwood fishing port.

Early in 1985, someone tipped off Harrison that Oyston had secretly told his estate agency staff he wanted to take the agency to the stock market as a public company. By that time, pushed by Murrin and his BBC *Watchdog* programme, the Lancashire Constabulary had started to investigate the activities of Oyston and the councillors Parker and McGrath. The police acted on a complaint from a Tory councillor, Jack Heatley but four years later, the Director of Public Prosecutions, Sir Allan Green QC, would report to Home Secretary David Waddington that 'no evidence of any criminal activity was revealed.'

Chris More's devastating ability to penetrate banking secrecy, using untraceable 'old pals' contacts with bank security officers had impressed Bill Harrison. Murrin said Harrison was

> a strong-willed and determined man who liked to have things done his own way and always expected to take control.

Harrison demanded a direct investigation deal with Chris More which annoyed Murrin:

> At this point I was pushed out of the picture and the funding source took over.

In the year 1985, Harrison paid more than twenty thousand pounds to CILS. On May 4, Murrin broke secrecy by revealing

> The man who has financed the enquiry is Mr W. Harrison of Greyfriars, Walker Lane, Fulwood, Preston. I was introduced to him by Mr Robert Atkins MP. Mr More of CIL has indicated to me that Mr Harrison's net worth is in excess of five million pounds. He is reported to have had Mrs Margaret Thatcher MP as a guest in excess of five occasions. Harrison has indicated that he has raised the enquiry with Mrs Thatcher. Mr More has told me he was approached by Mr Barry Askew who attempted to buy him off. Mr More has further indicated to me that persistent rumours occur concerning drugs trafficking but the scope of the enquiry is such that he has been unable to pursue every lead.

More went to his former clients at the *News of the World* office in Manchester and managed to get a file of cuttings on the stormy business career of Owen Oyston from their reporter Keith Beabey. These were handed over to Harrison and Murrin. But by August 7, 1985 Harrison was complaining to Murrin that More had been paid '*a lot of money*' for investigating and had '*nothing to show for it.*'

I feel as though I've taken a suitcase with twenty odd thousand in and thrown it off the bloody North Pier.

After Harrison complained to Audrey Scott, the Tory councillor and her husband Geoff joined Murrin in trying to solve the case of the missing detective. On August 2, Murrin telephoned Chris More:

More: Michael.

Murrin: Hello Chris.

More: Yes.

Murrin: I've had Geoff Scott on.

More: Yes.

Murrin: Harrison's jumping around like a bee in a bottle.

More: Yes, I know.

Murrin: Can't get hold of you, thinks you've done a runner on him, all sorts.

More: Right, go on.

Murrin: Well, that's it. He thinks you've buggered off with his money and you're not going to finish the job.

More: Well he owes me money, so let's have it right.

Murrin: Yeah. Well I'm not involved in that, I'm only telling you what I'm being told.

More: OK.

Murrin: And...

More: How can you do a runner when you put your phones on bloody transfer?

Murrin: Chris, he gets a bit hysterical, doesn't he? Isn't he a bit excitable?

More: Sometimes. And very talkative.

Murrin: OK, I'll phone Scott.

More: I've been asked to phone Harrison, what do I do?

Murrin: Well phone him.

More: Phone him?

Murrin: Yeah.

More: OK. What's his phone number?

Murrin: 774771

More: 774771

Murrin: Yeah.

More: OK. I'll try and get through to him today.

Murrin called Harrison on August 5:

Mrs Harrison: Preston 774771

Murrin: Mr Harrison there please?

Mrs Harrison: He's just outside. Just a minute. Who's speaking please?

Murrin: Mr Murrin.

Mrs Harrison: Just a moment please.

Murrin: Thank you. Hello.

Mrs Harrison: Sorry to keep you waiting, he was just speaking to someone.

Murrin: Oh I see.

Mrs Harrison: He's on his way.

Murrin: OK. Right.

Mrs Harrison: Thank you.

Harrison: Hello.

Murrin: Hello?

Harrison: Hello. Mr Murrin?

Murrin: Oh, hello Mr Harrison. I said I'd phone you this evening.

Harrison: Yes, well I haven't heard from our friends.

Murrin: Well he said he was phoning you today.

Harrison: No.

Murrin: Have you - have you been out, has he not been able to contact, or what?

Harrison: Well, my wife's been in solid since one o'clock.

Murrin: Were you out this morning? I know he said he was going out to phone this morning, because I phoned him…

Harrison: Well, he knows I go out every morning, Mr Murrin.

Murrin: All right.

Harrison: He knows that. He knows over the past year.

Murrin: Yeah.

Harrison: I've said I'll telephone you

Murrin: Yeah.

Harrison: After two o'clock. When he's come in, come to see me, it's always been after two thirty. He knows my routine. Friday we were in. Once again, it would be - would be after lunch, you know.

Murrin: Yeah.

Harrison: I go out in the morning...

Murrin: Yeah...

Harrison: But mind you this morning, I did go out early, but my wife was here. And we've staff in the morning, you know. No, he hasn't called today. So I haven't anything to tell you. Have you spoken to him since?

Murrin: Well, I spoke to him this morning.

Harrison: What did he say?

Murrin: He said he was phoning you this morning.

Harrison: Did he tell you anything. Any progress?

Murrin: Not on that particular round, no.

Harrison: No progress.

Murrin: Well I mean he - he hasn't told me anything in detail for a long time, because obviously, I mean if anybody's going to hear anything it should be you. It shouldn't be me.

Harrison: Oh, well, a dead man will have heard more than I've heard from him for the past three months.

Murrin: Have you heard from Geoff Scott?

Harrison: Well, he did make a call the other day, but he spoke to my wife. I wasn't in.

Murrin: Ah.

Harrison: I just... and I think she said I was expecting a call from the man, and so that's it. Status quo. No, this morning I - I was out at half past nine, and - but my wife was in.

Murrin: Yeah.

Harrison: Busy morning for me, Monday. Fridays and Mondays are busy, but you know, this phone is - it's always got somebody here.

Murrin: Yeah, yeah.

Harrison: Almost. Almost always. My... I was right down the garden just now, but my wife took the call, and I'm here, aren't I? So this is what happens, you see, and this is what worries me. You know no news to me, from our - that source - is bad news, isn't it? Really? That's the way I've thought it out. Some people all the time say no news is good news, but from this one, no news is certainly not good news. But he has frequently said he would ring me back, like the day after tomorrow or something like that when he's had more information, or when he's seen so and so, but it's always been me, or virtually always been me, who's done the ringing. So anyway, I'll ring him tomorrow.

Murrin: Right, well I'm due to phone him again on Wednesday.

Harrison: I think we've got to keep on his back. Mmm?

Murrin: Yeah, got to get him moving in the direction you want, haven't we?

Harrison: Well, I've told him, I don't - you know, when he first started, I said I don't want any reports, I want some positive action.

Murrin: Yeah.

Harrison: And at first I gave him a lot of money, you know, regular. Several thousand pounds regularly.

Murrin: Yeah.

Harrison: And haven't given him any for about three months now, two months, two months, probably two or three thousand, I think it was. So he's not done so bad. He's had more than I've had, because I've had nothing from him. Nothing at all. Plenty promises, Mr Murrin, you know, like -

Murrin: Well, they're cheap enough, aren't they?

Harrison: Like certain people are going to run 1000 miles or 100,000 miles and can't hide, and this is it, my life's finished, but their life isn't finished, they're carrying on and feathering the nest, the life of Riley.

Murrin: Well, we'll have to see. You're going to try and phone him tomorrow are you?

Harrison: I will.

Murrin: OK.

Harrison: Well, what do you want me to do, do you want me to phone you back at all, or what?

Harrison: Oh, you can give me a try tomorrow night, eh?

Murrin: OK.

Harrison: I'll let you know what he says. If we've had a success. All Right?

Murrin: OK. I'll give you a ring tomorrow.

Harrison: Fine.

Murrin: Bye.

Harrison: Bye.

Murrin called Councillor Audrey Scott. She knew that Harrison was annoyed by More's failure to ruin the careers of her fellow Preston councillors, Harold Parker and Frank McGrath, leaders of the Labour group.

Audrey Scott: Oh, well the impression I got was that she came in the shop, expressed concern that they hadn't heard anything from Chris More for a while.

Murrin: Yeah.

Audrey Scott: And that things seemed to be ebbing away -

Murrin: Yeah.

Audrey Scott: And was under the impression that Geoff had spoken to Chris More, Chris More had told him that he wasn't surprised because this fellow had cried off –

Murrin: Yeah.

Audrey Scott: Obviously been warned off. Geoff rang Harrison and mentioned to him, with respect, that he thought perhaps he was talking where he shouldn't, and Harrison accepted that and said well, OK, I'll make sure I don't in future. Geoff rang Chris More, and said, you know, I've done this, and Chris

More said, 'Right, well I'll ring Harrison on Monday'. Now, that was what I understood.

Murrin: Well, he hasn't heard from him anyway.

Audrey Scott: And he says that he didn't speak to Geoff?

Murrin: No.

Audrey Scott: Ah, well, he's probably doing what he said he would do, which is, which is, crack on that he hasn't spoken to anybody, probably Geoff's put the frighteners on him, because…

Murrin: Well, he says...

Audrey Scott: If he has frightened this fellow away, then he's a fool, isn't he?

Murrin: Well. Yes.

On August 16, 1985, Murrin tape-recorded Harrison complaining about More's promises to pass stolen information about Oyston to the *Blackpool Evening Gazette*:

Harrison Well if these people don't go ahead this week with what they said they would do - publish something about the Double O Man…

Murrin: I don't know what you're on about there.

Harrison: It's all to do with Oyston, he's behind everything and once you destroy the myth... you see we both agreed that everybody thinks he's so powerful and wealthy...

Murrin: That he's out of reach?

Harrison: Beyond reproach

Harrison demanded 'warrants for arrests or something like that'

Harrison: Well if we'd got that, you see, that would, I thought, be a good start. Chris More said, 'Well. I have the Inland Revenue special investigation branch. They could have a look at something.' But I never hear anything. It's like dealing with the dead. You know what I mean?

Murrin: Yeah.

Harrison: You know what I mean?

Murrin: Oh yes, I know.

Harrison: I feel as though I take... if I take a suitcase with twenty odd thousand in and throw it off the North Pier...

Murrin: You'd have got more out of it.

Harrison: At least I could have said, 'Well I was a stupid fool.'

Harrison was planning to mount a surprise legal raid on More's office using the devastating power of an Anton Piller court order, to search for the fruits of his ordered investigation into Oyston and the Labour politicians.

More was too quick for him. He headed off Harrison's legal action by telephoning Harrison's solicitor at 09:30 on the day planned for the Anton Piller searches. More revealed something to Harrison's solicitor that morning that would have obliged the solicitor to reveal Harrison's unlawful activities to the court.

Harrison withdrew his legal action. In what More later described as 'a tactical rather than a legal approach to the problem' the detective handed over a document to his angry client. It was a five-page report, typed on CILS headed paper under the title **Re: Councillor Frank McGrath**. One day it would be the subject of questions in parliament.

It was an obvious breach of the Official Secrets Acts. It was also the first recorded occasion in the two hundred year history of income tax in Britain in which personal tax records of politicians had been bought and sold. A series of damning phrases introduced five pages of personal tax and employment details:

> Your initial instructions in this matter requested that we obtained information with regard to information which may possibly be held by the Inland Revenue.
>
> Our enquiries with regard to Mr McGrath's current employment with the Institute for the Deaf, St Pauls Road, Preston, established their tax affairs are dealt with Preston 1 District...
>
> Enquiries with the Inland Revenue showed that Mr McGrath commenced employment on this reference...
>
> The Tax authorities were able to advise...
>
> Tax records show earnings from this source as being...
>
> We note the last tax return Mr McGrath submitted to the Revenue...
>
> Investment income was shown with an account at the Halifax Building Society...
>
> There is a file note at the Revenue stating that the balance owing to the Chemical Bank was...
>
> Revenue records show Mrs McGrath's earnings as...
>
> We now await your further instructions, together with revised fee limit.

On August 16, the Tory leader of Preston, Joe Hood, told Murrin that Councillor Jack Heatley had been to county police headquarters to make corruption allegations about Labour councillors, especially Harold Parker.

In September, when Owen Oyston, the journalist Barry Askew and Councillor Frank McGrath were known to be bidding against a firm called Cable TV for a Lancashire cable television franchise, Geoff Scott assured Murrin that Joe Hood and Robert Atkins MP had told him the Oyston group application would fail.

Scott said Cable TV, backed by the Tory MP for Blackpool South, Sir Peter Blaker, would win. He said Joe Hood and Robert Atkins

> have stated that the Chorley-based Cable TV Consortium will get the franchise being offered locally. The Oyston, Askew and McGrath consortiums will be blocked, as they were before, because of their suspected involvement in corruption.

Murrin's activities, backed by a further ten thousand pounds from Bill Harrison, intensified in 1986, but Harrison still wanted more results from Chris More. More duly put the frighteners on Harold Parker.

Harrison: I said, "Look, I've paid you all this money. Tens of thousands, may be getting up to twenty."

Murrin: Yes.

Harrison: And he said... I said, 'Look I've had nothing for it.' I said, 'I was going to get...'. I said, 'When you were going to write it... You were going to write me a report.' And then he said, 'Well, we'll leave it for a day or two, because something is imminent.' And I've got all these things down. Imminent. May be five occasions.

Murrin: And nothing hard.

Harrison: Nothing ever came. When I'm talking about things imminent, from memory, I've got my notes in front of me, but from memory, 'Let the BBC bring a team up.'

Murrin: Yes.

Harrison: A day after tomorrow. It's all arranged.

Murrin: Yes.

Harrison: And this man McGrath... having lunch with somebody and it's all been arranged. And then he approached me another time and said, 'I have a man who is willing to spill everything. He wants ten thousand in the hand.' And then another time, 'Well'. he said, 'I've seen Parker and Parker said, 'Well my best place is ten thousand miles away, isn't it?' But nothing happened, you see.

Harrison called Murrin on February 27, 1986, to tell him he was meeting More and let slip the fact that he was in contact with Mrs Thatcher's trade minister Lord Young of Graffham, Robert Atkins's boss at the DTI. Murrin noted:

> At the beginning of the conversation he mentioned that he had been asked to get involved in this thing, and I quote, 'in the North West by Lord Young'. Now I've not heard that before. That's the first time he's said anything like that, although in the reports and that - that are along with this tape - there was a reference at the beginning of this matter that Harrison had very close connections with Thatcher.

Lord Young's autobiography *The Enterprise Years* tells how Margaret Thatcher asked David Young to organise political attacks on the Labour Party in the provincial towns in the run-up to the 1987 general election. Being more of a businessman than a politician, this former assistant to Sir Isaac Wolfson and former director of P & O acknowledged getting invaluable help in a grubby area from Robert Atkins MP.

There was an echo of this after Harrison died in 1997, when Murrin revealed that Harrison had expected to get a knighthood for his unconventional campaign against the Labour Party in North West England.

Murrin chased the new developers of Preston Dock hard. On March 4, in a Preston wine bar, he met an accountant with a criminal record who had been trying to persuade Preston Council to build three ice rinks at the dock development. Discussing Balfour Beatty, the accountant told Murrin:

> You never catch Balfour Beatty paying a politician. They always put them on the sub-contractors' payroll.

At Murrin's suggestion, Chris More arranged for a reporter from the *Daily Star* newspaper to confront the financially embarrassed Labour leader Harold Parker with documents gathered by illegal penetration of banking and tax secrecy. But there was no evidence that Parker was getting money from Balfour Beatty.

Harrison and Murrin launched an offensive against Oyston's booming family firm by bribing an accountant at the estate agency, using one of Harrison's employees as a go-between. Ms Sheila Catlin was a former employee of Oystons. She met Murrin on March 17, 1986, and three days later at the Carr Wood residential caravan park in Preston she gave Murrin the telephone number of Richard Arnold, a disaffected Oyston accountant with a drink problem.

Catlin knew that Arnold had written memos to Oyston about things like personal income tax, Value Added Tax on racehorses and Pay As You Earn technicalities, to try get himself a payoff from the company. He had pulled the stunt at other firms before. Oyston stonewalled Arnold's threats.

On March 20, Murrin feverishly noted:

> Oyston separating from wife. Divorce papers, eight women named.
> X slept with Oyston. Oyston Hong Kong - two years ago, bought bullion.
> Oyston sleeps with Ellman. David Brown, estate agent Hyde, suing Oyston £1 million.

Murrin first telephoned Arnold and followed up with something that Chris More had suggested. He telephoned the Inland Revenue Special Office in Liverpool on March 20. It was a tactic that Harrison had called for.

Murrin spoke to Stephen Long, an investigator at the Special Office who called at Murrin's home in Preston next day. Three days later Murrin got an assurance from Stephen Long that the Inland Revenue might be interested in further information about Oyston.

On April 8, 1986, Murrin met Richard Arnold in Stockport, but without cash they made no progress. Arnold wanted money for his information and refused even to confirm the existence of the dodgy memos to Owen Oyston about tax irregularities.

Later, at Bill Harrison's office in Progress Park at Kirkham, Murrin saw Harrison hand two thousand pounds in cash to Sheila Catlin, which was used to buy from Arnold lists of the 1984 salaries and expenses of senior employees and directors of Oyston Group.

Catlin came back with copies of Arnold's 1984 warning memos and a mass of sensitive files on the planned stock market flotation of the Oyston Group. Her haul included some of Oyston's personal income tax calculations and letters from City advisors warning Oyston about the danger of talking up the prospects of the flotation in the press. She handed the stolen files to Murrin on December 15.

One of the Richard Arnold's 'private and confidential' memos read:

> It is my opinion that in the eventuality [of an Inland Revenue PAYE audit after the TV exposure of the Harold Parker affair], the Inland Revenue would have a field day in the face of such blatant and naïve tax evasion.

On December 16, Murrin delivered the material to Stephen Long at the Inland Revenue Special Office in Bootle. A few hours later, Sheila Catlin's contact in the Oyston offices at Blackpool, telephoned to tell her that Inland Revenue officers were searching files in the offices. At Oyston's home, Claughton Hall, he was asked to turn out his pockets by Inland Revenue officers. Murrin said later:

> I was told by Mrs Catlin that Mr Arnold had refused to accept any payments for the file and the cash was handed back to Mr Harrison.

Murrin had lit the blue touchpaper. He triggered two Inland Revenue investigations at Oystons, just as the firm was being lined up for the stock market. By now, any journalists, politician or businessmen with a grudge against Owen Oyston knew that Mike Murrin was the man with the answers.

Just a few days after the taxman Stephen Long came calling to inspect Murrin's information, the restless political agitator in Goodwood Avenue came to the attention of another wealthy and influential business rival of Oyston.

This was Sir Peter Blaker, a Tory MP with longstanding connections at the Foreign Office and in British Intelligence, a man who had invested in a consortium that was bidding against Oyston for a government licence to install cable television in the streets of Lancashire.

CHAPTER 7

Enter Sir Peter Blaker

Oyston's enemies and business rivals soon found that the man in Goodwood Avenue had answers for anyone wanting to know more about the astonishing rise and rise of Owen Oyston. Cable television rivals, competing against Oyston for cable franchises in Lancashire and Merseyside came knocking on April 16, 1986, when Mike Murrin tape-recorded a meeting with John Seddon, a franchise bidder who claimed Oyston had once invited him to jump into bed with a woman during late-night negotiations at Claughton Hall in January 1985.

Just one day later, a man called McDougall called at 21, Goodwood Avenue. McDougall came to see Murrin on behalf of Peter Blaker, Conservative MP for Blackpool South, with family business interests in cable television in Hong Kong.

Murrin later explained how he had encountered Sir Peter:

> I met John Seddon a cable TV pioneer who had suffered serious problems with Oyston on Merseyside cable TV projects. Seddon put me on to Peter Blaker who had cable TV interests in Preston. Blaker was at that time trying to get the Preston cable TV franchise. I used the name of Robert Atkins as a reference in my dealing with Blaker. I met Atkins and Blaker together on three occasions. The total amount of money used in the investigation was £25,000. Bill Harrison gave me £5000 and paid other bills direct. It was, in my opinion, very good value for money. [23]

---

[23] Murrin interview with author.

On May 20, 1986, Murrin met Blaker at the Crest Hotel in Preston

I showed him my scrapbooks showing a chronological history of my campaigns. He was impressed by the way in which I had kept a record of my activities. I made it clear to Sir Peter I was acting as an individual and was only interested in investigating the allegations of corruption centring on Oyston.

I made it clear I was in debt and could not fund the investigation from my own pocket and that I was searching for funds.

On May 27, Murrin wrote to Blaker to say he would be seeing Paul Halloran of *Private Eye* about Oyston.

I have formulated and planned, in detail, a strategy which, if followed through, will ensure that our objective is achieved. Our motives are very different, but our objective is the same.

Sir Peter Blaker

The next meeting between the soft-spoken former government minister and the insurance man from Allied Crowbar came on June 9 at Sir Peter's home in Ashley Gardens, London SW1. Cash arrived a month later in the form of a cheque drawn on Sir Peter's solicitors Piper, Smith & Basham for two and half thousand pounds, the first tranche of ten thousand.

Here was Blaker, a privy councillor and a former Foreign Office minister in the Edward Heath government, funding Murrin's political dirty tricks campaign in the knowledge that Mike Murrin, Chris More and Bill Harrison had already looted private bank accounts, purloined income tax records and bribed accountants to steal company records.

Sir Peter was a man with the powerful connections expected from being the son of the chairman of the Hong Kong & Shanghai Banking Corporation and married to the daughter of Sir Pierson Dixon, permanent British Ambassador at the UN. Caught up at the start of the Second World War when travelling with his brother in North America, Blaker had signed up as an officer with the Argyll and Sutherland Highlanders of Canada and fought eastwards from the beaches of Normandy until the day he was severely wounded on the borders of the Netherlands. After the war, he was elected President of the Oxford Union, then called to the Bar before being sent as a Foreign Office diplomat on postings to Cambodia and Canada.

At New College in Oxford Blaker shared a staircase with Anthony Wedgewood Benn. They toured America together as former presidents of the Oxford Union. Benn, the son of Viscount Stansgate, became Blaker's lifelong friend, despite later renouncing his inherited title and living on the other side of the political spectrum. As Tony Benn, the president of the Stop the War Coalition, he contributed a friendly postscript to Sir Peter Blaker's obituary for *The Guardian* in July 2009.

Benn had noticed that from the moment his friend had won Blackpool South for the Conservatives in 1964, Peter Blaker had always spoken for 'the right wing of the security services'. Blaker had called for Britain to support the USA in the Vietnam War, supported the US invasions in Cambodia and Grenada, pressed for Britain to join the US boycott of the 1980 Moscow Olympics and stood on the Khyber Pass in Pakistan to urge support for the mujahedeen resisting the Soviet invasion of Afghanistan. He was knighted at the age of 60 in 1983 and asked to stand down from ministerial office by Margaret Thatcher to chair the backbench Foreign Affairs Committee.

On June 20, after Mike Murrin met Sir Peter in London, he went back north to see Stephen Long, an inspector of taxes at the Inland Revenue Special Office in Liverpool. Long contravened the Official Secrets Act by telling Murrin that the Revenue had already interviewed Oyston. Long asked Murrin if he had any more information for the Revenue and Murrin said:

> I am working on securing the file from Mr Arnold. [24]

In July 1986, Oyston sold 36 per cent of his estate agency to Royal Insurance for a record sum, which prompted Murrin to write to Sir Peter Blaker's solicitors:

> The enquiry agent has been instructed to carry out enquiries into reports of tax evasion and company fraud. His fee has been agreed at £2500 plus VAT.

Murrin reported to Sir Peter that after Oyston's deal with Royal Insurance Murrin would be concentrating on:

> Cable television and the funding of Lancashire Cable. 2. Reports of sex parties and drug abuse. 3. Reports of tax evasion.
> Following my interview with Mr R. Arnold, an accountant who worked for Mr Oyston, I secured further confirmation of previous reports concerning PAYE and National Insurance irregularities. I have good reason to believe these reports to be accurate and I have been asked to provide further

[24] Murrin tape recording, transcribed by author at Oyston Mill, Preston.

information as soon as possible. In view of the power vested in the Inland Revenue and the likely outcome of an in-depth enquiry I am seeking further information concerning reports of tax evasion and possibly company fraud.

Murrin told Sir Peter he was going to meet the *Private Eye* staff reporter Paul Halloran. Murrin had learned of a secret income tax investigation at the Oyston estate agency. It was an inquiry primarily concerned with cash payments to workmen who erected and dismantled 'house for sale' signs. In a letter dated September 22, 1986, Murrin leaked to Sir Peter's solicitors and to Halloran everything he had learned on visits to Inland Revenue tax offices in Preston and Liverpool.

The Revenue have confirmed that they intend moving in for the £250,000 at some stage and that their own investigations are to continue. You know as well as I do that they are extremely thorough. Their enquiries are as a direct result of information provided by me.

Murrin learned that the Inland Revenue had swooped on the Oyston Estate Agency. At a critical time during the sale of estate agency to Royal Insurance when the news would have affected the share price of Royal Insurance, Pay As You Earn tax inspectors had called at Claughton Hall. They asked Oyston to turn out his pockets and hand over the keys of the castle. The Inland Revenue Special Office eventually agreed a tax settlement. On October 1, 1986, Murrin reported to his backers:

Confirmation has been received that the Revenue have enforced a settlement of six figures for the PAYE irregularities identified by my source.
If the information recently received from the same source proves to be as accurate then I am assured that this would result in the special investigations department undertaking an in-depth investigation. I am using my own sources to secure copies of files to support the information received. [25]

Stephen Long, one of two tax inspectors who had called on Murrin at

[25] Murrin personal notes handed to author.

Goodwood Avenue, had unlawfully revealed to Murrin the amount of the financial settlement that had been agreed between Owen Oyston's firm and the Special Office. This was the only known occasion in the two hundred year history of income tax in Britain on which politicians bought and sold the tax records of their opponents.

Oyston had been entitled by law to confidentiality in his personal and business tax affairs, especially when a Peat Marwick tax accountant, Mrs Carol Barrie, had been working on the case at the Oyston office and negotiating with Inland Revenue under strict secrecy required by the stock market situation. Murrin tape-recorded a discussion with Long about two parallel tax inquiries into the personal affairs of Oyston and the estate agency:

Long:	Well it's interesting. There is one individual that does attract my attention, er, simply because it's similar to one I have done in Liverpool and er, this sort of corruption, especially if it's going on for some many thousands of pounds could stand an investigation, I think. It could be worth looking at.
Murrin:	Well it is coming across very similar to the Liverpool set up, all the way through.
Long:	Unless I'm mistaken, which I could be, of course. What we need is evidence.
Murrin:	That's right.
Murrin:	No.
Long:	Certainly the fellow [Oyston] who John Robertson looked at was. And er, there may be one or two other individuals in that sort of league.
Murrin:	Is he only six figures of did he go to seven?
Long:	I think it got towards seven certainly, it was certainly erm, five hundred thousand the last time I heard, but. I never

actually got the final figure I don't think, but I got the latest situation on it and it was er, it was round about half a mil, what they finished up at I don't know. But it was certainly worth looking at obviously for that sort of amount.

Murrin: Well it surprised me, quite honestly it surprised me that it was only that.

Long: Well er, I don't know the facts of the case so I can't comment. Like John Robertson I tend to keep my own cases to myself and I don't tend to discuss things with anybody.

Murrin: I mean for all you know it might still be going on.

Long: Erm, that's a possibility certainly. I understood that it was finished and certainly later developments suggested it was.

Murrin: That it was finished?

Long: Yeah. It certainly suggests that way. But – er - you know the developments that happened after that. Taxation comes *INAUDIBLE* their own and no doubt you'll be looking at more, so, yeah, but we're always interested, especially if the sort of tax at risk is getting towards six figures then I think we have to be interested. Obviously if somebody pocketed a few thousand, we're not interested in that. Although I could feed that to the local Inland Revenue er, it's of no interest to me personally because you know the type of cases we take on, and they have to be big.

Murrin: Well when I get any more information, I'll send it on.

Long: All right Mr Murrin.

Murrin: All right. OK?

At one point in the recorded conversation, transcribed by Michael Murrin, the civil servant Stephen Long speculated about who would pay to discredit Oyston.

Long: The most intriguing question of all is...who the hell is to bait good money to get this fellow? I mean apart from yourself. There certainly is one individual, and I suspect you might have more.

On December 22, 1986, Murrin told Sir Peter about interviewing Bill Nabb, a solicitor and a 'man of undoubted integrity' who had worked for Oyston.

> My contact and Mr McNabb [sic] then went to see Mr Richard Arnold FCA. Papers were secured and the agreement was reached that Mr Arnold should talk to the Revenue.

A two-page report from Michael Murrin to Sir Peter noted:

> Oyston did bring gold back from Hong Kong.
>
> The papers secured show fraudulent claims for expenses, non-payment of PAYE and National Insurance due.

In a letter to Sir Peter, arranging another meeting in London, Murrin wrote:

> Events are now moving at a rapid rate and I will need clearly defined instructions as to the areas I am to cover and the objectives I am to aim for. If I am to pursue the wider objectives then, clearly, there are implications which could be of national, as opposed to local significance. If the deadline is to be met then I will be involved in twelve weeks of solid work and the detailed planning will need to be re-co-ordinated and regular meetings arranged.
>
> The main point is whether or not we aim for the local or national objectives. I assume I will be given clear instructions covering this point when we meet.

Murrin's meeting with Sir Peter improved his position with Bill Harrison, his original 'funding source'. Harrison's solicitors wrote 'formally' to Chris More, telling the private detective who had penetrated the Inland Revenue that he was now off the case.

Early in the general election year of 1987, Murrin wrote to George Gordon, chief reporter of the *Daily Mail,* attempting to link his prime target Owen Oyston with a Merseyside property developer called Ted Spencer who had fled to Spain in March before the collapse of his firm Merseypride plc.

Spencer's flight generated a famous headline 'ET Phone Home' when the *Liverpool Echo* unveiled his picture:

> THIS IS the man who made millions playing Monopoly with Merseyside... he was never out of the headlines as his friendship developed with Liverpool's flamboyant deputy council leader Derek Hatton and powerful Knowsley councillor Tony Beyga.

Murrin set about winding up George Gordon by linking Oyston, through E.T. Spencer, to the *Daily Mail's* target of the hour, the left-wing deputy Labour leader of Liverpool, Councillor Derek Hatton. But when the *Daily Mail* lost interest, Murrin wrote a 'green ink' letter to George Gordon, with copies to editor David English and proprietor Lord Rothermere:

> Whatever else you may lack, you certainly make up for in cheek...
> If it has not yet sunk in, then let me say quite clearly that I do not take kindly to being messed around and I do not dance to anyone's tune....
> I will personally ensure that when this story does break, be it in five weeks, or five years, that it becomes generally known that the *Daily Mail* failed to act due to its parochial attitudes and gutless nature. In the parts of Southern England where I come from, we refer to it as ALL MOUTH AND NO TROUSERS...

In letters written on March 8 to Sir Peter Blaker MP and to Robert Atkins MP, he urged that the destruction of Oyston by prosecution for tax evasion was to be their main aim:

> The more recent objective of crippling the ship has moved ahead and the 'rev' are now involved. I am now seeking ways of pushing them to seize documentation and / or prosecute....
>
> If 'rev' go further then T.1 can be picked off at leisure as he will, in effect, be crippled and unable to fight back effectively. If the hand is played with cunning and skill then we have the advantage of surprise never letting it be known how much or how little is known.

Murrin informed Paul Halloran of *Private Eye* on March 5:

> I have now secured a small amount of further funding to enable me to proceed with my enquiry. If you are interested in the story then perhaps the most constructive move would be for you to decide what area you are particularly interested in and for me to utilize the cash I have in hand to secure bank account details etc.

But in March 1987 Oyston's business affairs were booming. After the runaway financial success of Red Rose Radio, the Labour Councillor Frank McGrath revealed to the *Lancashire Evening Post* that his personal investment in the radio station had made him a millionaire. An alarmed Murrin warned Sir Peter:

> I stress again that he will get away unless action is taken to prosecute. I must have got him in a bit of a sweat but it is now beyond my control and totally in the lap of the authorities.

Murrin talked to Blaker about Oyston's prospects. Sir Peter made it clear that he wanted Oyston in jail.

Murrin: ...It is not beyond the possibility that he tries to do a runner.

Blaker: A runner?

Murrin: Yeah...

Blaker: Rio?

Murrin: Somewhere.

Blaker: Yes, well that will be a victory of sorts, but not such a good one as the one we want. Not the one we want.

Murrin: No, we want him here. We don't want him to do a Biggs.

Blaker: Behind bars, that's right absolutely.

Murrin: He's sticking two fingers up and is laughing at us.

Blaker: Yes.

A month later Murrin stumbled on a valuable nugget. It turned out years later to be 'fool's gold', but that didn't make much difference to Mike Murrin, to the House of Commons, or even to Owen Oyston. It generated enough smoke and fire to generate questions in parliament and eventually an Early Day Motion which named Oyston and hurt him badly on the Stock Exchange.

Using funds from Sir Peter Blaker, Murrin uncovered two mysterious companies that were both called Oyston Limited. On a microfiche reader in the Harris Library at Preston he found a firm called Oyston Investments Limited, registered in the Isle of Man.

It turned out to have Asian directors with Bolivian connections and had been registered with a cheque drawn on the infamous Bank of Credit and Commerce International, known to readers of *Private Eye* as the 'Bank of Crooks, Cocaine and Impostors'. Then, to his amazement, he discovered another firm called Oyston Limited, registered at Companies House and based at Stamford Hill in London.

The agitator from Preston had opened doors on the complicated money laundering activities of a Northern Ireland-born lawyer called Patrick

Diamond, based in the Isle of Man. Murrin's discovery of these companies was a disaster for Owen Oyston, even though Oyston had no connection with the firms carrying his unusual name. John Huber, the US Drug Enforcement Agency's man at the American embassy in London, told Murrin that Oyston Limited in the Isle of Man was a drugs money laundering firm. Huber told Murrin that in 1984 Metropolitan Police investigating a Chinese syndicate importing heroin into London and Blackpool had raided a flat where Diamond was staying overnight on his way to America.

The police had found four thousand dollars in cash and a copy of a Blackpool newspaper in Diamond's possession, with a small amount of cocaine in a drawer. Diamond got a four thousand pound fine and eight months in jail for possessing cocaine. Murrin noted that he could now 'prove' that the man who had set up the mysterious Oyston firms had a Blackpool connection.

Diamond had laundered hot money through 170 companies before his arrest on the Isle of Man by Scotland Yard officers who had been sworn in as Manx special constables. The men from the Yard discovered that a Manx travel agency had sold Diamond air tickets for a number of young women to fly tourist class to Florida before returning home first class, with extra cabin baggage, from New York.

Diamond was also jailed for eighteen months for receiving £100,000 in cash proved to be proceeds from the £26 million Brinks-Mat bullion robbery at Heathrow in 1983. London's most famous 'thief-taker', Det Supt Tony Lundy, travelled to the Isle of Man to give evidence for the defence at Diamond's trial. Lundy told the court in Douglas that Patrick Diamond had helped him:

> in one of the biggest worldwide police operations I have ever been involved in. Due to things he has told us a worldwide operation has taken place involving police agencies from a number of countries.

A month later, the US Drugs Enforcement Agency arrested and convicted Michael I. Levine and ten other Florida businessmen for racketeering, money laundering and smuggling marijuana worth thirty million dollars. The *Sunday Times* reported that Diamond was getting police protection from a certain Scott Errico, an American drug trafficker and self-confessed hit man for a Florida-based crime syndicate.

Murrin suddenly found himself back in the world of Greville Wynne. It all seemed to fit.

> On November 6, 1981, Patrick Diamond and Susan Elizabeth Diamond of Upper Church Street, Douglas, formed Oyston Limited, whose directors included Glendevon Limited and Amulree Nominees Limited, registered at Room 601, Shell House, 24, Queen's Road Central, Hong Kong.
> Oyston Investments Ltd, a company, with registered office as Department 15, 80, Queensway, London W2, was set up on July 20, 1983, in the Isle of Man by Select Company Formation, of Douglas [Charles Philip Robinson and Mrs Gill Cochrane], controlled by Albany Managers Ltd, of The Quarter, Anguilla.
> In October 1984, Albany Managers Ltd resigned as director of Oyston Investments Ltd and directors Abdul Sattar Khan [London], Sultan Mahmood Beg [Dammam] and Ashad Nizam Shah [Karachi] took over the £100 company.
> Abdul Khan made an annual return for Oyston Investments Ltd., registered in London SW10, and paying the fee in June 1986 with a cheque drawn on The Bank of Credit and Commerce International, [otherwise known as the *Bank of Cocaine* and Colombia].

Murrin passed on his discoveries to David Thomas, a customs officer in Liverpool fighting the runaway drug smuggling that boomed on Merseyside in the hard Thatcher years. On April 12, he asked David Thomas about the two Oyston companies:

Murrin: Was that stuff any good to you or am I going to...

Thomas: It's amazing. I don't know how you managed to come by that... It's well worth having.

Murrin: It was worth it, wasn't it?

Thomas: Mmm.

Murrin: I know you can't tell me anything, but if I get any more, do you want it?

Thomas: Yes. Yes. Any of that sort of background, you don't know what it turns up until you actually have a look at it.

Murrin: Right. I've got enquiries going on at the moment. The company in the Isle of Man, I can't make head or tail of it, you'll probably make more of it than I will.

Thomas: Yes.

Murrin: But when I originally looked at that, that was the only company called Oyston Limited. Now when I went back to look again, there was another company, Oyston Limited, different registration number. And that original company I can't find in the microfiche in the library. So I don't know what has happened to that. There's either a name change or something..."

Later:

Thomas: Mr Hatton seems to be prospering.

Murrin: Sorry?

Thomas: Mr Hatton seems to be prospering. There was a paragraph in the paper this morning that he's opening an office, applying for permission to open an office in Liverpool or somewhere.

Murrin: Yes. Well a lot of his money has come from Spencer, I believe. We seem to be heading for a situation like they have in the States. Or is it already here?

Thomas: It's been here in a small way for a while, hasn't it, really?

Fired up by this, Murrin called Paul Halloran of *Private Eye*:

Murrin: You say you think this character is involved in money laundering?

Halloran: Yes.

Murrin: Have you got anything to strongly indicate that?

Halloran: I've got lots of indicators.

On April 13, 1987, Murrin called Tim Mitchell, the Westminster researcher for the Tory MP Philip Oppenheim, who was concerned about the propriety of Oyston's investment relationship with the Derbyshire County Council pension fund.

Murrin: I think that you will find that the Inland Revenue investigations are a focus of public attention fairly shortly.

Mitchell: You think so?

Murrin: Oh yes.

Mitchell: What about the situation of the PAYE investigation?

Murrin: What about it?

Mitchell: Is that public knowledge? That took place? Or what? Is it just simply that you heard that his employees got back-dated tax demands?

Murrin: No. You must understand, the sources I have are employees of Royal Insurance. I have seen the tax demands made by the Inland Revenue on the employees. I dealt personally with the Inland Revenue officers, both the Special Office and the Executive Branch.

Murrin met Mitchell at the House of Commons a week later.

On April 13, Bill Harrison alarmed Murrin with an astonishing story about how he believed that Oyston's previous criminal activities might have included involvement in the death of Harrison's caravan site manager Norman Leech, as long ago as 1978.

The bodies of Leech and his personal secretary had been found naked and gassed in a caravan on Harrison's lucrative Marton Mere site. Harrison's hatred for Oyston and a colleague named Crowther is obvious in the taped conversation:

Murrin: Yes, he told them he had sold the estate agency for twenty

Harrison: So why did he say that? It's a different price every time anyone opened their mouth. Where did he get the money from, if he didn't get it from the estate agency? He's got it from other sources? Well no.

Murrin: This brings us back to the Isle of Man company again.

Harrison: It brings us back to something illegal.

Murrin: Yes, doesn't it?

Harrison: Yes, criminal activities. And I think back to him telling me to get rid of Mr Leech.

Murrin: Yes.

Harrison: And I think back to him, you know, telling me to get rid of Mr Leech in my caravan park company: "Get rid of him. Let me sit in his chair. I need that cash. I want cash. For what I want to do, I must have a lot of cash."

Murrin: And Mr Leech was found dead.

Harrison: Mmm. never really figured that, you know. Who told you?

Murrin: No, well, we may be opening up a lot of old skeletons.

Harrison: I never, I never understood why a man who was so associated with Calor gas, you know. He'd been looking after the park for six years, he had nurseries, you know, before that, with gas heating and whatever. He was familiar with gas.

Murrin: Such a fundamental error isn't it?

Harrison: Not to open the vent.

Murrin: Yes it's like a driver not sort of putting the thing into, using the clutch, to get into gear. Isn't it almost?

Harrison: Well not opening the vent... that was one mistake, you see that... it smelt. And the other thing was that there was some Claymore Whisky, an empty bottle there. Well he didn't drink that. He was a gin and tonic man and the lass, she was Martini.

Murrin: Did they find a lot of alcohol in him?

Harrison: No.

Murrin: No.

Harrison: But of course when you take in carbon monoxide it knocks a lot of the effects are similar to other things.

Murrin: Oh I see.

Harrison: After a time. And another thing he had was his left arm, or I think it was his left arm was totally burnt all the way through, yet he was lying on the bed 15 feet from the fire, you know, out of the fire's range. It wasn't as though he had been knocked out, lying on the bed or settee in front of the fire and it had burnt whilst he was unconscious. It wasn't like that. The arm was burnt right through. The flesh was off, the undertaker had to pad it up with cotton wool to make him balanced and another thing, I don't know, and I knew him a long time and I never saw him with grey hair, it was dark hair mottled with grey, more dark than grey, only in his coffin he was snowy grey as me. That was a faffle, he was only forty-nine you know. Several things didn't add up, forget the grey hair thing, but I do think about the no vent and the stupid drinks that were there and the photograph, there were some photographs of them starkers, two of them well it was a Polaroid. I think you can put them on automatic can't you? I don't know if you could then or not

Murrin: I don't if you could then. But you can.

Harrison: Well it was ten years ago. So why, you know, peculiar circumstances, I'd say. Another thing there was forty thousand missing. You see that was another thing. He was supposedly doing a deal with someone and my niece said that she saw him at Blackpool airport. He was supposed to be buying a property in Lytham for his son to set up in business the day after. His son was doing the deal that day. I don't know but he was at the airport. My niece didn't know about that but my niece saw him. Well I thought, Isle of Man, you know.

Murrin: That's the most obvious place.

Harrison: But as I say we are going off the track and it was Double O who said, "I need cash." Anyway, he didn't get it, but he certainly threw a lot of coal on the fire during the time I was having the aggravation and Crowther certainly did write me a letter, which I still have. I mean he tried to buy the park, - quiet sale, - also he would take Greyfriars as well. They thought I had bought a home you see, to abscond in America but I had in fact decided that there was an election coming up in next year and I thought at the moment I can buy a holiday home, it is permissible if I pay the dollar premium. [We had the Labour lot in]. If I paid the dollar premium, so I decided to pay the dollar premium, and bought this place in America as a holiday home. One of the reasons was my daughter was engaged to a lad out there who lived near Miami and I wanted her to have security, didn't I? A place that was patrolled with guards and what not. But you see Crowther heard about it, he knew about it before I got back and sent me this letter.

Murrin: Which you've still got.

On April 24, news broke that Oyston had sold the remainder of the family estate agency to Royal Insurance 'in a shock deal worth more than £10m'. Oyston was reported to be left 'with a feeling of bereavement'.

Murrin wrote letters on April 27 to Paul Halloran, Sir Peter Blaker and Robert Atkins MP, speculating accurately that 'T1' [Oyston] had sold the whole of Oystons to Royal Insurance because Royal

> is trying to distance itself from T1 due to ongoing Revenue inquiries.

Three days later Murrin wrote to Atkins and Blaker:

> I have had an accountant consider the position of the sale and he states that it is possible that if the evasion is of an extremely serious nature the Revenue may have gone to the minority shareholder and given them the option of taking over the majority holding or having the business shut down by the Revenue.

He asked Atkins and Blaker to approach Bill Harrison and

> find out what the ceiling is on the overall budget.

On May 1, he wrote a letter to Stephen Long at the Inland Revenue Special Compliance Office in Liverpool stating:

> Corrupt business interests in Bristol are now operating in Preston. One name involved is Harris, believed to be an associate of Frank McGrath. There is too much talk of a silent partner and shady business dealings involving drugs for it to be ignored.

Two weeks later, Oyston made national news when he was revealed as the last gasp rescuer of the struggling left of centre tabloid newspaper *News on Sunday*. He had been its biggest shareholder since a disastrous launch in April. On May 13, he took control in a rescue plan supported with cash from the Transport & General Workers Union and the Derbyshire County Council pension fund. Derbyshire were investing in Oyston's activities up to their five per cent legal limit of twenty million pounds.

The county's maverick Labour leader, County Councillor David Bookbinder was a one-time market trader who had grown up in a Manchester doss house. Bookbinder was now singled out for punishment by the Thatcher government for his 'loony left wing' policies. Thatcher said he was 'my least-liked local authority leader.'

Erlend Clouston in the *Guardian* described Bookbinder in 1988:

> Now that Derek Hatton and Ken Livingstone have, one way or another, left the scene, Mr Bookbinder is said to be the local authority scalp that Mrs Thatcher most craves in next year's elections. The prospect of a scrap with Mrs Thatcher does not appear to bother Mr Bookbinder. He is one of life's natural scrappers. Imagine a Jewish samurai warrior crossed with Edward G. Robinson and you are imagining David Bookbinder.

To avoid being rate-capped by central government, Bookbinder cut budgets where it hurt the middle classes [village libraries and school music lessons] sparing favourite projects, like persuading Toyota to build a 600 million pound car factory in Derbyshire, stabilising school meal charges and investing the county council pension fund in some of Owen Oystons's more colourful projects, which included a bizarre plan in the last years of the Soviet Union to invest in the Blue Bay Crimean 'leisure complex' near Yalta.

With Bookbinder and the T&G deeply involved in *News on Sunday*, the Labour leader Neil Kinnock and his election guru, Brian Gould MP, hoped that *News on Sunday* would not collapse before the general election. Oyston was their man of the hour.

Everyone knew Oyston was rich and at that time hardly anyone in public life, except perhaps Paul Halloran of *Private Eye*, knew of his implacable and dangerous enemies; Bill Harrison, Robert Atkins, Mike Murrin, Chris More and the latest conspirator to have entered the inner circle of the group, Sir Peter Allan Renshaw Blaker, the future Lord Blaker of Blackpool.

During an *annus mirabilis* in 1987, Oyston sold Oyston Estate Agency Ltd. to the Royal Insurance group for about thirty million pounds, bought and rescued Blackpool Football Club, lost, and later in the year regained, the control and chairmanship of Red Rose Radio, Red Dragon Radio and Radio Aire and briefly rescued *News on Sunday* by persuading the trades unions, councils and other investors who had sunk 6.5 million pounds into the company to let him run the paper.

Almost all the leftish investors lost money on *News on Sunday*, including the TGWU, AEU and Nalgo unions, the councils at Wolverhampton, Southwark, Lambeth, Brent, Cleveland, Haringey and Lothian. So did the actress Julie Christie and the author Ken Follet. But Oyston pulled a rabbit out of the hat for David Bookbinder in Derbyshire. He bought Derbyshire's worthless *News on Sunday* shares for £350,000 and then re-invested the money, allowing Bookbinder to announce a thirty per cent profit on the investment in *News on Sunday*.

Oyston seemed to be fireproof and Murrin had written sadly to Robert Atkins MP on June 15:

> I have been told on many occasions that T.1 has protection from highly-placed individuals. If this is the case then it is unlikely that I will be able to dislodge him, it would require action to be taken by individuals or organisations with influence and real power.

Shooting his trawl net one more time, Murrin handed out some of Sir Peter's money in small amounts to the noted financial journalist Martin Tomkinson at the *Digger* [£130.00] and to Paul Halloran at *Private Eye* [£166.91 in expenses] with one thousand pounds going to the detective Chris More at the CILS agency.

In a fateful act in June 1987, the Tory opposition leader at Preston, Councillor Joe Hood, told Michael Murrin that an Anglo-Iranian building firm called Tustin, with Californian connections, was about to be chosen "improperly" as a developer for Preston Dock on the recommendation of a council official named John Field. Once again, an irresponsible politician had given Murrin false information. Spreading rumours to Michael Murrin could be very dangerous.

This particularly scurrilous rumour prompted Murrin to make allegations against Tustin that would become part of a police investigation that eventually cost £25 million. Field and Hossein Ghiassi of Tustin, who had been a fugitive from the Iranian revolution, were completely cleared after a crown court trial.

Their prosecution was part of a huge abortive police operation, known as Operation Angel. After unlawful police raids on Preston town hall and the homes of a number of Preston councillors and financial investigations all over Europe, the police team charged 21 people, including Preston's chief executive, its deputy chief executive and its deputy Labour leader, with corruption, conspiracy or theft. But after six years and nineteen police raids, the only people convicted were four small businessmen and two minor council officials, all but one of whom had already been reported to police before the operation began.

When Murrin booked Paul Halloran into the Crest Hotel at Preston on October 26, he wasn't prepared to tell the *Private Eye* man where all the money was coming from but he assured Halloran that he could have investigation funds 'subject to very reasonable conditions'.

With Oyston pinned down in December by the ongoing Inland Revenue investigation, Murrin and Bill Harrison were delighted by the appearance in the Irish-owned *Digger* magazine, of a story by Martin Tomkinson alleging that Oyston had been feathering his own nest at *News on Sunday* under the headline **'NEWS ON SUNDAY. OYSTON'S SURVIVAL KIT'**

On December 18, 1987, the *Digger* re-printed internal memos stolen from Oyston Estate Agency. Tomkinson reported that Inland Revenue investigators had spent ten weeks at the Oyston offices in Blackpool and quoted from a memo to Oyston that had been written by his office accountant:

> It is my opinion that in the eventuality [a PAYE tax audit], the Inland Revenue would have a field day in the face of such naïve tax evasion. The point here is that faced with such a history it would be far preferable to be "legitimate" rather than still carrying on in the same vein. This is the point, Owen, I worry about most. We will not, as I have said before, serve your interests best by adapting the existing system or trying to invent other dubious schemes.

Two Westminster MPs, Dale Campbell-Savours [Workington], serving on the parliamentary accounts committee, and the left-wing lawyer Brian Sedgemore [Hackney South and Shoreditch] started looking into Oyston and his links with David Bookbinder and Frank McGrath, the Preston councillor working for Oyston's Blackpool Football Club and whose Red Rose shares were now said to be worth one and a half million pounds.

Backed by new funds from Harrison and Blaker, Murrin opened a deadly attack in another House of Commons committee in January 1988 when Philip Oppenheim MP started asking awkward questions about Oyston's involvement in the Derbyshire County Council pension fund.

Murrin wrote to Philip Oppenheim, saying the documents from Oyston's offices referring to 'blatant and naïve tax evasion' had been sent to the Inland Revenue Special Office in Liverpool. He told Oppenheim he suspected Oyston was the real owner of the Manx money laundering firm Oyston Ltd.

After Martin Tomkinson had delighted the conspirators with another *Digger* story about the fate of Derbyshire's cash under the headline **'OYSTON PROFITS IN DEAD NEWS'** Mike Murrin offered Tomkinson three thousand pounds to write a book with the provisional title **'OYSTON: THE MAN AND THE MYTH'.**

CHAPTER 8

Left Wing News and Offshore Money

When reporters from Robert Maxwell's *Sunday Mirror* and Rupert Murdoch's *News of the World* arrived in Whitworth Street, Manchester on the night of April 26, 1987, they had orders to beg, buy or steal an early copy of the launch edition of *News on Sunday*.

The editors of the big red tops knew that a popular Sunday newspaper with left wing views might be a dangerous competitor in the days before a general election.

But they need not have worried about losing readers to this new paper. When it dropped on the Manchester back bench of the *Sunday Mirror* on its first publication, night editor Peter Hollinson looked at a splash story about the sale of human kidneys in Brazil and asked in amazement, 'Is that all there is?' Hollinson was not the only one to ask that question. The sales fell from half a million to two hundred thousand in two months, a collapse later described by Peter Chippindale and Chris Horrie in their book *Disaster! The Rise and Fall of News Sunday – Anatomy of a Business Failure.* [26]

Although a recalcitrant workers' collective controlled the paper, two key investors, Owen Oyston and the Transport and General Workers Union, led by its general secretary Ron Todd. were lured into an attempt to stave off its collapse until after the forthcoming general election.

---

[26] *Disaster! The Rise and Fall of News Sunday*, Sphere, London, 1988

Oyston had already lent ten thousand pounds to help the Labour leader Neil Kinnock, a promising underdog standing against Margaret Thatcher. He told Charles Stewart of the *Lancashire Evening Post*

> The paper is a very exciting prospect with good potential but which suffered a disastrous launch. It is a radical alternative newspaper which is not afraid of criticising any government. It will campaign on issues like my hobby horses, the disease of unemployment and the terrible problems facing industry in the North.

In a pre-election frenzy, Rupert Murdoch's *Sun* was screaming its support for Thatcher with outrageous headlines like **'WHY I'M BACKING KINNOCK, BY STALIN.'** The Kinnock supporters were mightily relieved when Oyston took financial control of *News on Sunday* in May 1987.

Oyston took this risky decision in the very week that Mike Murrin was telling the tax inspector Stephen Long about the existence of a racketeering firm called Oyston Limited that he knew had been controlled by a money launderer in the Isle of Man. Murrin wrote to Long on May 1:

> I am now moving into new, top quality sources and hope to have more information in due course. The information referring to drugs keeps coming through. It is from different, unrelated sources and I do keep cross checking as and when I can. There is too much talk of a silent partner and shady tax dealings involving drugs for it to be ignored. If the tax information has proved accurate, then the drugs information is of similar quality.

On May 25, Murrin told Paul Halloran of *Private Eye* that his 'target number one' or 'T.1' was likely to be forced to repay a million pounds to the Inland Revenue. Paul Halloran had been smelling money ever since Murrin had told him in March that:

> I have now secured a small amount of further funding to enable me to proceed with my enquiry. If you are interested in the story, then perhaps the most effective move would be for you to decide what area you are particularly

> interested in and for me to utilise the cash I have in hand to secure information, i.e. bank account details etc.

On June 15, just after getting five thousand pounds from Peter Blaker, Murrin wrote to Robert Atkins MP:

> I have been told on many occasions that T.1 has protection from highly-placed individuals. If this is the case then it is unlikely that I will be able to dislodge him, it would require action to be taken by individuals or organisations with influence and real power.

He wrote next day to *Private Eye*, suggesting that Oyston was blackmailing a property dealer:

> Source says Oyston stated he had compromising photos of Crowther. Possibility of blackmail has been mentioned since Day One.

He told Sir Peter Blaker:

> An alternative funding source really needs to be lined up but I can only leave that to you. My own network of intelligence is now building up and I would expect results after the summer.

For the rest of the year, as Oyston battled with politicians, journalists, printers, lawyers and bankers to keep *News on Sunday* alive, he was fighting two other expensive business battles.

At Red Rose Radio in July, a group of rebel shareholders combined to remove Oyston as chairman, despite the fact that Oyston owned 25 per cent of the company. Under the Red Rose chief executive David Maker, the shares had risen from ten pence to £1.25 in ten years, making good money in recession years for Oyston and his galaxy of political friends and celebrities. Losing the chairmanship in a coup meant that Oyston had to spend big money to fight back for control of the firm he had founded.

Red Rose had recently captured a pair of weaker radio stations in Yorkshire and South Wales, but David Maker had annoyed Oyston by launching a shaky free newspaper known as the *Red Rose Advertiser*. The Red Rose rebels included David Maker and a wealthy Blackpool coffee importer, Raschid Gibrail. They announced on August 1, that Oyston had resigned 'to concentrate on his interests at the left-wing *News on Sunday*.' This announcement was intended as a damning *fait accompli*. Beating it needed money that had to be raised and deployed with the skill of Oyston's able accountant Michael Connolly and the cunning of one of Oyston's much-criticised 'political' shareholders, Councillor Frank McGrath, a mathematics teacher and deputy Labour leader of Preston.

It took them eight months and £7.5 million to win back control of Red Rose. They were fortunate that firm was growing so fast that Oyston soon found he was running the biggest chain of radio stations in the country, partnered in radio station deals with Richard Branson and in glossy 'county' magazines in the West of England with Robert Maxwell.

Oyston mounted a last minute financial rescue for his local football club, Blackpool FC, involving a commitment to finding money every week for the next twenty years. It would be a cause that often looked more hopeless than *News on Sunday*. Blackpool had won the FA Cup in 1953 with Stanley Matthews and Stanley Mortensen but they had fallen so fast through three divisions in the space of twelve years that by 1983 they had been forced to apply for re-election to the Football League.

Their famous Bloomfield Road stadium, one of the oldest structures in the Football League, was unsafe in high winds. After one unusually bad performance, Oyston had been reduced to offering the despairing fans free tickets to the next match. On the evening before the match, the police checked the weather forecast and phoned Oyston to call off the match.

> I told them I could not possibly call it off. With all my free tickets offers on the table, it would have to be a police decision to call it off, not mine. The police wouldn't take that decision and they left me to face a sleepless night. All night long the wind howled, but still I took no decision. At last, early on Saturday morning the wind dropped and saved the day. [27]

An accountant recorded Oyston's frantic expenditure in this critical year. The accountant was preparing a personal income tax return that would later be corruptly sold to Bill Harrison and passed on to Michael Murrin. The Oyston tax spreadsheet eventually ended up in the hands of journalists, including Martin Tomkinson at the *Digger* and Paul Halloran at *Private Eye*.

> Gifts to staff: GBP 170,000
> County Councillor Louise Ellman for Labour Party: GBP 2,000
> Loan to David Maker: £50,000
> Gift to journalist Julian Allitt: £2,000
> Loan to accountant Robin Oakley: £32,000
> Payment to News on Sunday: £350,000
> Loan to Councillor Harold Parker: £15,000
> *Daily Telegraph* for printing: £24,148
> Central Lancashire Printers: £22,646
> Svenska Finance [*News on Sunday* computer]: £ 1,2111,400,00
> Growfar [Derbyshire County Council pension fund]: £150,000

In late blasts on their battered trumpet the News On Sunday journalists diced with the law by riding on the Sunday Times bandwagon during the Spycatcher affair.

[27] Interview with author

News ON SUNDAY

THE PAPER OF THE PEOPLE August 9 1987 35p

As Churchill put it...

‘Perhaps it is better to be irresponsible and right than to be responsible and wrong’

News ON SUNDAY FIGHT FOR FREEDOM

OUR MESSAGE TO LAW LORDS...

THE News on Sunday will not be silenced in its fight for justice.

On Tuesday the Attorney General's office wrote to this newspaper to say that criminal contempt proceedings were going to be taken against us for an article in last Sunday's issue headed "Spy secrets that Thatcher tried to hide."

The article was an extract from "Spycatcher," the book written by Peter Wright, former assistant director general of MI5.

It is the best selling book in America — and people are allowed to bring it into this country to read it but newspapers are banned from telling their readers what it contains.

We have no regrets for publishing extracts from the book. We do not think we are guilty of any offence. We believe that it is unjust for the Law Lords to rule (by 3 to 2) that British newspapers cannot report so called "secrets" which are an open book for the Kremlin.

The letter from the Attorney General's office says that the criminal contempt proceedings will be served on News on Sunday "during the next few days."

We await them with interest.

We have a defence to the Government's case. We want to test that case in court as soon as possible in the interest of free speech. But the law is ponderous.

■ THE LETTER from the Attorney General's office

A lawyer close to the government told us that we will be lucky to go to trial by Christmas. This is unacceptable.

It imposes a continuous gag. The Law Lord's restrictions — the most repressive in Britain for years — must be challenged and challenged quickly.

We say the Law Lords are wrong. We have a case to put. We ask for justice. And soon.

See pages 2,3,4,5 & 10

The *News on Sunday* defied Margaret Thatcher on August 1, 1987, by publishing an extract from *Spycatcher*, the banned memoirs of the renegade former MI5 officer Peter Wright. The Thatcher government had already started contempt of court proceedings against newspapers for partial leaks from the book. The Fleet Street editors were facing the threat of unlimited fines and prison sentences when *News on Sunday* appeared in Manchester with Spycatcher extracts. Under the headline 'spy secrets that Thatcher tried to hide' they described a Law Lords ruling as 'a law made to be broken'. The Attorney General warned them that criminal contempt of court proceedings were imminent but by Sunday morning the paper that used to describe itself as "no tits, but a lot of balls" had bounced back with 'our message to the law lords' printed alongside a picture of Winston Churchill giving a V-sign to sailors in Aberdeen harbour.

By May 1989, when Mr Justice Morritt fined the *Sunday Times*, the *Independent* and *News on Sunday* £50,000 each for contempt of court, *News On Sunday* was defunct. The paper's last editor Brian Whittaker was already working at the *Guardian* but joined the other two editors in offering 'unreserved apologies' to the court and Oyston was still around to pay the government's legal costs of around £100,000.

The paper collapsed in November, leaving Oyston to face the political and legal music, pay the bills and persuade Norsk Data to buy back their new computer system. One of the bills settled in October by Oyston's supply firm, Growfar Limited, came from a certain Peter Martin of 24, Mosley Street, Manchester. Martin had invoiced *News on Sunday* £2,292 for supplying 'models', good-looking girls supplied to a left-wing newspaper whose advertising agency, BBH, had coined the aggressive sales slogan: 'No tits but a lot of balls.'

Peter Martin CAVENDISH PRESS

Mike Murrin got wind of this angle from a disappointed left-wing journalist who had tracked Peter Martin down to a model agency off Piccadilly Gardens. He telephoned Martin Tomkinson of the *Digger* and invited Paul Halloran of *Private Eye* to visit Preston. Murrin even agreed to pay Halloran's hotel bill.

Late in 1987 Martin Tomkinson's magazine, the *Digger*, put forward the unlikely suggestion that *News on Sunday* would be **'OYSTON'S SURVIVAL KIT'.** They did however accurately reveal that the Inland Revenue had just spent ten weeks at Oyston's Blackpool offices. the *Digger* reproduced damaging internal memorandums about income tax originally composed and then sold to Bill Harrison by a corrupt accountant.[28]

Bill Harrison was so pleased with the *Digger,* despite hearing that its editor and owner John Mulcahy was losing interest in keeping it going, that the Blackpool property dealer considered financing the magazine through Michael Murrin. A series of anonymous encouraging letters received at the *Digger* office echoed Harrison's conversational style. Martin Tomkinson, a very experienced financial journalist, hinted in a letter to Murrin:

> The basic situation with Mulcahy [my boss and managing editor] is that he wants out. He's fifty-five, thought he could conquer the English market with a snap of the fingers, a lot of Irish charm and not much folding money.

On a cue from both Murrin and Sir Peter Blaker, Philip Oppenheim MP, told a Commons committee that Oyston's involvement with the Derbyshire County Council pension fund was:

> a despicable way for a county council to look after county pensioners' or ratepayers' money

After Paul Halloran's visit to Preston, Murrin wrote to Bill Harrison at Greyfriars and suggested funding Halloran's research into Oyston:

> My advice is that you should also offer a carrot i.e. £x if the target is brought to court and £y if he is jailed.

Martin Tomkinson could also smell money, when he wrote on January 22, 1988:

---

[28] Richard Arnold was an accountant employed by Oyston. After Stephen Long of the Inland Revenue Special Office in Liverpool visited Michael Murrin's home on March 21, 1986, Murrin arranged to meet Richard Arnold in Stockport on April 8. Murrin then visited Bill Harrison's Progress Mill offices to see Harrison hand over £2,000 to pay for sight of the 1984 salaries and expenses of senior employees and directors of Oyston Group.

> I have now got over the euphoria of a rare Arsenal away win and am deep into Brother Oyston. To date I have made four appointments with people who have knowledge of our friend for next week. I am doing this on the basis that funds are available for my time and effort and for the entertainment of such persons.

On March 11, when the *Digger* claimed that Oyston had lent Councillor McGrath the money to buy highly profitable shares in Red Rose Radio, Murrin was ready for a scrap. He wrote to Tomkinson on March 17:

> I am now of a mind to say let's go and get the bastard and aim for the jugular. I am quite prepared to take the man on head-on, whatever the odds. I feel that deeply about it.
>
> I have pursued this enquiry with such tenacity because I honestly believe that Oyston may be involved in corrupting local politicians, blackmail and drug abuse.

Tomkinson replied on March 24, revealing that the *Digger* was up for sale and could be bought by Murrin's backers:

> If your friends are sufficiently keen, I would be prepared to come up to the North West and get stuck into Oyston... We'd have to have some very clear ground rules, e.g. some sort of limitation on time and costs and aims on your side — cash up-front, paid weekly, and agreed expenses sums on time.

A day later the *Digger* attacked the complicated Derbyshire County Council pension fund deal that was costing Oyston so much money, by announcing:

OYSTON PROFITS IN DEAD NEWS

Murrin wrote to Tomkinson on March 31:

> I am able to offer you the following agreement: I am to commission you to write a book which, in effect, will be a biography of Mr Oyston. In addition

> to a total fee payable of £3,000, you are to receive 5% of any royalties earned if / when the book is published. A provisional title for the book is to be 'Oyston, the Man and the Myth' with an alternative title being, 'The Oyston Affair - the Inside Story'.

On the same day, Murrin sent copies of documents stolen from Oyston's offices to Philip Oppenheim MP, describing them as evidence of the *blatant and naïve tax evasion* which had been discovered by the Inland Revenue Special Office. A few days later he sent Sir Philip a copy of Andrew Jennings's libellous notes for the BBC *Watchdog* alleging corrupt links between county council leader Louise Ellman and Owen Oyston.

Early in April, Mike Murrin bought himself one share in the Royal Insurance group, for a planned personal intervention at the annual general meeting of the public company which was the source of Oyston's huge personal wealth.

On April 14, Murrin offered stolen Oyston documents to John Robertson of the Inland Revenue Enquiry Branch in Liverpool. He reckoned this would make it impossible for the chairman of Royal Insurance to deny at the forthcoming annual general meeting of Royal that the estate agency they had just bought for untold millions was under investigation by Inland Revenue.

> A week prior to going to the Royal Insurance a.g.m, I phoned up the guy at the Revenue and asked him if he wanted it. He said, 'Yes' and he was keen to have it.

It was to be Murrin's finest hour.

CHAPTER 9

Murrin's Finest Hour

On April 21, 1988, Mike Murrin arrived at the annual general meeting of Royal Insurance with a devastating question for Sir Anthony Tuke, the deputy chairman of the biggest insurance company in the world. Had the Royal known about the Inland Revenue tax investigation at Oystons when they bought 36 per cent of the company?

Sir Anthony brushed the question aside:

The board is not aware of an investigation. These are serious allegations.

But within minutes, pressure from the City forced Royal's head of corporate relations to retract Sir Anthony's denial. Roy Randall admitted that Royal were not only aware of the problem but had now decided to buy Oyston outright, paying off the Oyston family with Royal shares, rather than cash. Five months later, in the record market slump of Black Monday, October 19, 1988, the value of the Oyston shares in Royal crashed by £4.5 million.

Michael Murrin's day out in London had not only cost Oyston the four and a half million lost on shares. He had destroyed Oyston's plan to use cash from Royal to expand the estate agency. Next day, when the *Lancashire Evening Post* reported on 'Oyston chain's tax probe' the newspaper marked the end of Owen's stellar career as an estate agent.

Murrin discussed his coup with Robert Atkins MP, now **a** minister for industry and aerospace at the Department of Trade & Industry. Atkins was still unaware that Murrin was using a tape recorder. Despite his government position, Atkins told Murrin, on tape, how he had suggested to his own department that the DTI inspectors[29] could be ordered to investigate Oyston:

> I have, between you and me, talked to my colleague at the DTI, who is responsible for the City, and he is prepared at this stage, if there is any real evidence, to put the boys in... the DTI inspectors.

After the unexpected humiliation at the Royal annual general meeting, Owen Oyston made another enemy by pulling off a deal, three days later, to prevent Mrs Thatcher's favourite strike-breaker, Eddy Shah, from getting his hands on a chain of glossy magazines.

Shah thought he had shaken hands on a deal struck with Alan Katz of Arthur Andersen, a receiver appointed by the Royal Bank of Scotland to sell *Lancashire Life, Cheshire Life* and *Yorkshire Life*. Katz admitted that he had most certainly 'shaken hands on something' with Eddy Shah, a man famous for defeating print union flying pickets at the 1983 Battle of Winwick Quay. Shah's victory had been achieved with massive support from Margaret Thatcher and cohorts of policemen drafted into Warrington by the Cheshire Constabulary.

The deal went wrong when Eddy Shah was at home in bed. During the night the receiver decided to strike a new deal with Owen Oyston. The ingenious accountant Michael Connolly telephoned a banker at the weekend and rustled up an £800,000 bank draft for the receiver before Eddy Shah was awake.

As soon as Murrin heard about this cheeky coup, he telephoned Eddy Shah and told him all about Oyston's troubles with the tax man:

---

[29] Murrin tape 19 transcript

Murrin: You've got to remember they're looking at over a hundred companies and there has been a systematic evasion of tax. Now there are far more serious allegations going around.

Shah: Yes.

Murrin: Far more serious.

Shah: Is he going to jail?

Murrin: That depends on how much help I get.

Shah: Yes.

Murrin: I'm a bit loath to speak over the phone because, but let me say.

Shah: I mean my argument on this one is more with the Receiver.

Murrin: Well look Mr Shah, let me say that... I have a tape-recording of one of his employees telling me that he boasted of having compromising photographs of a business associate which he used to manipulate that associate.

Shah: Right.

Murrin: I the made checks on the business associate and I found he has some funny habits you know. He likes dressing up in lady's underwear and being whipped and this sort of thing.

Shah: Ha ha ha.

Murrin: You're not photographed.

Shah: I don't either, sorry. Ha ha ha. My wife, actually, her underwear wouldn't fit me. Ha ha ha.

Murrin: Well this guy loves silk underwear. So we're talking about, oh, allegations of blackmail and other more serious allegations.

Shah: And are the Inland Revenue people aware of this?

Murrin: Oh yes. It's gone far further than the Inland Revenue.

Shah: Good. My argument on this one is with the Receiver, you see.

Murrin talked to Bill Harrison about cancelling advertising.

Harrison: People are beginning to believe in you?

Murrin: Well, I mean, one chap who advertised in the *Lancashire Life* magazines, as soon as Oyston took over, he cancelled his advertising.

Harrison: So did my son-in-law.

Murrin: Right, well this guy…

Harrison: That's Livocks Furniture, they were the biggest advertiser.

Murrin: Of which furniture?

Harrison: Livocks.

Murrin: In Blackpool?

Harrison: My son-in-law.

Murrin: Your son-in-law owns that?

Harrison: Yes. It's thirty five thousand a year they spent.

Murrin: Why did he cancel?

Harrison: Because he doesn't like his politics. He's always voted Conservative, and he likes a Conservative attitude.

On May 23, 1988, with his customary instinct for flying into danger, Oyston arrived by private jet in Gibraltar for a week of talks about a radio station deal with chief minister Joe Bossano. It was just eight weeks after the Special Air Service troopers had shot dead three unarmed Provisional IRA operatives in broad daylight in Winston Churchill Avenue on the Rock.

Oyston was travelling with a new friend, Peter Billington Martin, a former Manchester policeman and successful private detective. Martin also ran Model Team International, the biggest model agency in Manchester.

Two of Oyston's daughters had enrolled for modelling lessons at Model Team in 1987 and when Oyston, divorced at the time, called to collect his daughters, he encountered Martin. A few weeks later Model Team supplied models to a *News on Sunday* 'champagne-only' shindig at the 1987 Labour conference in Brighton. The *News on Sunday* journalists were told that not drinking champagne in the *News on Sunday* conference suite might constitute a 'sacking offence.'

When Peter Martin and Oyston were checking in at the Holiday Inn in Gibraltar, Model Team's agency manager, Melanie Hardy, was checking five of the agency's top girls into the Gibraltar Beach Hotel after a scheduled flight from Manchester.

Melanie Hardy was a chic, ash blonde from Leigh in Lancashire. She had been one of Peter Martin's lovers since she was 19. Oyston took Lindsey Butler, Susan Burrows, Alison Brown and Dianne Boroviak across the Spanish border for a day trip to Marbella. He suggested they might look out for his sports boat, named Ojo II, currently loaned to Terry Smith, the boss of Radio City, a Liverpool commercial station targeted for a takeover. There was no sign of the boat however, it was later discovered to have been wrecked on a beach.

In Gibraltar, Peter Martin turned nasty when he discovered that Melanie Hardy had fallen in love with a local boy called Michael. Martin hit back with a disastrous series of spiteful tricks that eventually blew back on him in the form of a very long prison sentence.

Melanie Hardy described what happened after Gibraltar:

Peter showed me letters from Michael to me that he had intercepted and transcripts of our telephone calls that he had recorded.

I tried to finish with Peter, but he resisted and threatened to have Michael arrested for possession of drugs when he was crossing the border into Spain. Michael had nothing to do with drugs, but Peter said he would have him framed.

He tried to break us up, but later in 1988 I got away and managed to live in London with Michael for a year. I was managing at least three model agencies for Peter and Owen Oyston. Owen had told us in 1987 that he would be taking over the Model Team agency. We were all invited to a big dinner at his castle near Lancaster.

There were fifteen girls at the dinner. It was a big affair and Owen announced he had bought out Model Team and that Peter would continue to run it for him.

Owen is a very charming man. He was very charming that night. There had been a lot of trouble about the girls not being paid. At one time Bobby Ball, of the comedy act Cannon and Ball, put thirty thousand in the firm and we had heard he was taking us over. But after a few weeks Bobby Ball left his office in our building and we never saw him again.

This time Owen said he would make sure the girls were properly paid for their work in future.

He was charming and full of fun. The girls had to go across a stage in the baronial hall and through Owen's bedroom to get to the ladies. There was a stuffed alligator in the way. The girls were so nervous that they insisted on going through his bedroom in threes. He was full of jokes.

In May 1988 when Peter and Owen flew by private jet to Gibraltar, I flew out to Gibraltar on a scheduled flight with five other girls. Owen and Peter stayed at the Holiday Inn.

We girls stayed at the Gibraltar Beach Hotel. Owen was there to meet a very important government politician, Joe Bossano. Three months later, Mr Bossano came to Manchester. He was talking to Owen about basing a radio

> station in Gibraltar. Owen had sex with three of the girls in the one week we were there. [30]

Mike Murrin was now circulating a 22-page 'press release' entitled 'Statement - Preston Dock Redevelopment, Red Rose Radio and Cable Television' which included some dangerous phrases:

> There had been constant reports of Oyston being involved in prostitution and blackmail.
>
> My sources within the Oyston organisation were telling me that Revenue officers were actually working in the Oyston head office and going thought the company records. I was later told all Oyston employees had received demands for unpaid tax and national insurance contributions. I was also told Mr Oyston was forced to sell his remaining shares in the business to Royal Insurance who already had a minority stake. The reason was that Royal was determined to distant itself from Oyston who, they thought, could face criminal proceedings by the Inland Revenue. I also understand the Royal Insurance executives who introduced the company to Oyston were either retired early, moved or sacked.

To a pair of prominent Conservative members of Parliament, Mrs Edwina Currie and David Waddington, Murrin sent one of his distinctive distillations of information gleaned from John Huber an American drugs expert at the US Embassy in London, who explained to Murrin how 'Oyston Limited' was linked to the drugs money launderer Patrick Diamond.

Mrs Currie had also asked a parliamentary question about the Derbyshire County Council Pension Fund. On May 23, Christopher Chope MP, on behalf of the Department of the Environment, assured Mrs Currie that

> ...the Government has been concerned about reports that some local authorities have invested superannuation fund moneys in ventures which

[30] Interview with author October 5, 1994.

were most unlikely to show a profit. We are considering what do about this for the future.

Sir Peter Blaker offered Murrin advice about how to handle David Waddington, MP for the Ribble Valley:

> Don't land him in the soup. He's your MP. He's also the Government Chief Whip. He's potentially useful because if he sees that that this is something that should be investigated, then he's the sort of chap, he's a barrister, a QC, an able man, so he is potentially very much to be cultivated at the appropriate time.
>
> I think that looking at it from Waddington's point of view, if you accompany the sending of the affidavit to him, or the affidavit, being the long statement of which I saw a partial draft, right, I think if you accompany it with publicity you may put him off. I think a much better tactic is to get him interested. You must avoid the risk that he thinks you're a crank.
>
> Once you make it clear it's about malpractice by the leader of the Labour Party on the county council, by the leader of the Preston district council and his principal assistant, and by a leading Labour press media tycoon, you will have his interest. [31]

Twelve days later, on June 20, Murrin struck again with a new press release titled 'Royal Lies' sent out to newspaper offices all over the country, giving his home address in Preston:

> It must be an extremely serious matter if the deputy chairman of a company of the stature of Royal Insurance sought to misinform, mislead or deliberately give an untruthful answer to a question raised by a shareholder at the annual general meeting.

Murrin reproduced excerpts from stock market flotation documents and letters stolen from Oyston's offices. He argued that Royal's purchase of Oystons had been unwise and that the Inland Revenue problems had not gone away.

---

[31] Tape recorded by Michael Murrin

When 'Statement - Preston Dock Redevelopment, Red Rose Radio and Cable Television' arrived in the mail at the *Lancashire Evening Telegraph* office in Blackburn, Eric Leaver, chief feature writer, passed the lethal document to this author and on June 27, just before midnight, I knocked on the door of 21, Goodwood Avenue, Fulwood.

Murrin produced some 'crown jewels' especially Oyston's income tax correspondence. This most unusual activist urged me to call John Robertson at the Inland Revenue Enquiry Branch in Liverpool and offered me the telephone numbers of a string of his informants. The list included Bill Nabb, a solicitor, Richard Arnold, a former in-house accountant at Oystons, and Sheila Catlin, a former Oyston employee.

In the small hours of a summer night Murrin showed me his copy of Owen Oyston's personal gift list for 1987. He named several Preston councillors said to be financially involved with a Liverpool man known as Bob 'The Dog' McGorrin[32] who was named as the key drug dealer on Merseyside during the Old Bailey trial of Tommy 'Tacker' Comerford. Murrin said 'Bob The Dog'

> is linked by Councillor Derek Hatton[33] to property developer Ted Spencer and the deputy Labour leader of Preston, Frank McGrath.

Murrin pressed the button on his tape recorder so that we could listen to the unmistakable New Zealand accent of the *Private Eye* staff reporter Paul Halloran, asking for cash from Murrin's mysterious backers.

---

[32] Thomas Comerford, 1932-2003, https://en.wikipedia.org/wiki/Tommy_Comerford

[33] Deputy leader of Liverpool City Council, 1983.

I want a blank cheque made payable to me; cash up front. I want access to your informants.

Tread softly, was my immediate idea. For Mr Murrin was treading on my dreams. I'd been an *Eye* reader since the very early sixties, ever since a beautiful woman had walked into a junior common room in Oxford and sold me a copy of *Private Eye.* It was issue number four, printed on yellow paper.

It was broad daylight on a summer morning when I walked out of the Murrin home, determined to do my bit for the *Eye* and tell the magazine's co-founder Richard Ingrams about Paul Halloran. That would have to be done before anyone could set about dealing with the tax affairs of Owen Oyston or 'Bob The Dog.'

After telling *Private Eye* about the alarming activities of their staff reporter I telephoned the Labour MP for Workington, Dale Campbell-Savours. I had witnessed Dale's early days in politics. He was an ingenious and unconventional member of Ramsbottom urban district council and quite unfairly known at the *Bury Times* as 'Dale Raving Bonkers.'

Photograph by ROGER SCRUTON

On July 6, without alerting Oyston, Campbell-Savours set down notice of an early day motion in the House of Commons, asking Oyston to state whether Oyston Ltd, registered in the Isle of Man and controlled from Hong Kong by Patrick Diamond, had any connection with Oyston Estates Agency Ltd. He also put down a parliamentary question:

> to ask Mr Chancellor of the Exchequer, if all investigations into the tax affairs of Oyston Estates Agency Ltd. and related companies are complete.

Oyston was profoundly shocked when he was named in the Commons. There had been no warning. A former parliamentary lobby correspondent of the *Lancashire Evening Post* telephoned Campbell-Savours from Claughton Hall. Julian Allitt complained that Red Rose Radio should have been consulted about the early day motion and assured Campbell-Savours that any suspicions about Oyston would be unfounded.

Campbell-Savours agreed to meet Oyston at the weekend and Oyston travelled to Cumbria with his ex-wife Vicki and promised a 'worldwide investigation' to find out who was behind the two 'Oyston' firms discovered by Murrin.

Things were tense. A friendly Tory told Oyston that he was being watched by the security services. Campbell-Savours complained that he and another MP were tailed by a man in a red Ford Sierra through heavy London traffic:

> We were followed by a suspicious red car from Marsham Street to The Embankment. At a café on the M4 a man at the same table looked very strangely at us. The same red Ford Sierra diesel was filling with fuel at the M4 service area when we called there. [34]

My copy of Michael Murrin's scurrilous 22-page press release 'Statement - Preston Dock Redevelopment, Red Rose Radio and Cable Television' had

[34] Interview with author

reached me unexpectedly by post, but I did know something about recent events at the offices of Owen Oyston's newly-acquired glossy magazines. I had worked at their Preston office in 1987 before the collapse of its parent company. Peter Martin, owner of the Manchester model agency Model Team, been attracting attention at the Preston office, in connection with a golf course advertising subsidiary called Advertee. Someone there said:

> Martin boasted about getting £50k per annum as Oyston's toe rag. He says he gets calls telling him to take models at night to Oyston in London.

As far as Paul Halloran was concerned, I knew full well that in my world of hard news 'dog don't eat dog.'[35] nevertheless I well and truly snitched on him in a note to Ian Hislop, the new editor of *Private Eye*:

> Oyston has put high tech *News on Sunday* and other publishing assets in hands of Peter Martin, the owner of a Manchester model agency called Model Team International.
> Two Oyston publishing executives said the Model Team girls had complained to them that they never get the tuition they paid for, just Oyston sex outings.
>
> Former *News on Sunday* executive says Oyston suite at the Labour Party conference in Brighton was 'full of Brighton whores, day and night. Champagne and all bills paid by Transport and General Workers' Union. [36]

Two days later, on the very day Oyston secured an injunction forbidding Murrin from publishing his scurrilous 'Docks' document, Martin Tomkinson, a *Private Eye* asset since 1972, wrote to Murrin at 21, Goodwood Avenue:

[35] Flat Earth News by Nick Davies, Chatto & Windus 2008. https://www.theguardian.com/books/2008/feb/03/society

[36] Rosthorn note to Hislop, July 11, 1988.

> I'm taking the risk of committing this to paper but you might feel it sensible to destroy it after you've read it. I leave it to your common sense and discretion...
> The *News of the World* are already interested in Oyston's sexual antics and I am fuelling that interest.
> With all this going on, and Campbell-Savours's involvement, I think it is well-nigh impossible for Oyston to gag any inquiries. He is far too publicly involved [Red Rose, cable TV, Derbyshire] either to go missing or to be able to sit out the whole affair.
> However, that being said, the media, as you know to your cost are at best fickle seekers after the truth. We cannot wholly rely on any of them or Campbell-Savours to stay the course. Which brings me to my own involvement with you...
> Researching my book on Poulson took over 2 years but that was done part-time...
> The only missing ingredient at the moment is funds. [37]

Martin Tomkinson teamed up with me to snoop around the Model Team International offices in Piccadilly, Manchester. We talked to one of Peter Martin's business rivals, a Manchester gumshoe trading as 'Lancastrian' who had featured in a book about private detectives.[38] When we asked the gumshoe about Peter Martin and his early career as a policeman, he warned us that Peter Martin was manipulative and dangerous. How right he was.

In return for the help so freely offered by our informant, all we could offer Mike Murrin in return was a photocopy of a supply chit from the collapsed *News on Sunday*. The chit referred to a payment to Model Team for 'Peter – models' but it didn't tell us anything we didn't know. What we did not know was that Murrin had already asked the effective but expensive private detective Christopher Guest More to connect Owen Oyston to Model Team.

---

[37] Letter: Tomkinson to Murrin, July 13,

[38] *Watching the Detectives* by Graham Nown, Grafton Books, 1988.

Chris More told a reporter in 1996:

> Murrin contacted me to ask me to get information about the model agency. We all thought Murrin was a nut case. He was talking about kids being provided for sex. We made a search to find out who was involved in it. Double O was in there somewhere, whether officially or by hearsay I can't recall. Then there was a lot of shit regarding rumours that it was a front for girls on the game. I didn't substantiate those rumours. Murrin was not paying me. I was not even trying. We passed the information on to him. [39]

Murrin broke the news to Sir Peter Blaker:

> Did I tell you we've located the model agency in Manchester? Sources who are saying that he's involved in prostitution.

On July 12, 1988, one day before flying to Soviet Crimea on Derbyshire County Council investment business, Owen Oyston hit back at Murrin for the first time. The libel lawyers Peter Carter-Ruck and Partners had their speedy court order, restraining Murrin from further circulating the 'Preston Docks' document. They managed to serve the writ at 21, Goodwood Avenue but just one day later Murrin was meeting his secret paymaster Bill Harrison. The property developer wanted Murrin to do something about a competitor, an Anglo-Iranian firm called Tustin Developments. Harrison briefed Murrin:

> The Commission for the New Towns had been selling land on the Red Scar industrial estate. The estate agents said the land had been sold in May. But it wasn't sold until the end of September, apparently. I thought that was rather annoying. [40]

Murrin launched an aggressive poster campaign against Tustin on behalf of a group of residents who were angry about flooding at their Swansea Park

---

[39] Adrian Darbyshire, January 1996.

[40] Letter to author.

estate near Preston Docks. He taunted Tustin with so many provocative window posters that Tustin eventually issued a libel writ against the residents.

Murrin told me that Mrs Thatcher had been staying overnight during Conservative party conferences at Blackpool in Greyfriars Hall at Preston, the home of his secret paymaster Bill Harrison:

> Even when it became known publicly that she was at Greyfriars, and she had to move out, another two cabinet ministers moved in to stay with him during the party conference. Harrison will have told them how Oyston, Harold Parker, McGrath and Askew ruined him as a public figure.[41]

Wherever Oyston went that summer he was being followed. If the security services really had been interested in him, they need only have kept tabs on the dozen or so reporters, private detectives and American business spies who were chasing this cash-rich tycoon. We were just groping in 1988, but we couldn't resist provoking City gossip.

On one disastrous occasion I shared an early morning London car ride with a stockbroker. In a business meeting just one hour after listening to me in the car talking about the Inland Revenue investigations at Oystons, the broker found himself hearing media analyst Chris Akers proposing that the brokers should act for Oyston in a public flotation of Red Rose Radio. But after my friend's unexpected question about whether 'our boy has had his collar felt for tax?' the brokers declined to act.

I had just sent a memo about Oyston's apparently dangerous political liaisons to Roy Greenslade, features editor of the *Sunday Times*, when Murrin arrived at their London office, offering 'material on council corruption' to their chief reporter Peter Hounam.

---

[41] Letter to author July 11, 1988.

Peter Hounam then called me to ask about an interview in Sheffield with Paul Smelt, an Oyston Group accountant in *News on Sunday* days who had told me about Richbold Ltd, a firm which appeared to own Peter Martin's firm Model Team Management. Paul Smelt told me he had been trying to give accountancy help to Peter Martin's business partner, Melanie Hardy, the former model who had been running the agency at that time.

Fleet Street was slowly getting interested in Owen Oyston and his money, so the *Sunday Express* sent their celebrated profile writer Lynn Barber to Claughton Hall, where she counted 157 broken windows:

> Inside, the house was as cold as a catacomb. A maid explained Mr Oyston would be late, and took me to wait in the Great Hall – a room of hangar like size and emptiness where the wind howled through the many broken windows and rain water dripped into a bucket. In the middle of the room, several old desks and table tennis tables had been jammed together to form a parody of a dining table and the maid explained, with understandable alarm, that they were expecting 26 Chinese to dinner. Mongolians, I hoped, complete with furs.
>
> When Mr Oyston finally arrived, 45 minutes late, my teeth were chattering so hard I could barely speak, and Mr Oyston also seemed undisposed to talk so I just stared at him for a while. Was he dressed as Buffalo Bill, or as a Cavalier? His Stetson hat was distinctly Buffalo Bill, but the long curls, manicured nails and pointed beard were more Cavalier.
>
> Rather tetchily, I asked him why he was 45 minutes late. He said, 'I was late today because . . . I'm divorced, do you know that? And I just got back from the Soviet Union.' There was a long pause during which I struggled hard to see the sequitur, then he added, 'And I have been with my ex-wife and we love each other and we are looking to reconstruct our life together, because we can't live apart.

Oyston re-married Vicki on August 1, just before his daring late night television appearance as a 'socialist entrepreneur' confronted by the notorious *rentier* Nicholas van Hoogstraten in a discussion about 'Money' on Channel Four's rambling and unscripted programme *After Dark*.

By August 19, Vicki was being 'investigated' by the private detective Peter Martin, who was lurking around Claughton Hall and observing her movements in Lancaster. In Manchester, Martin hired the Lancastrian detective agency to report on Vicki's movements. Their file on the surveillance disappeared after a break-in at their office, a room above a barber's shop outside Manchester Victoria station.

Bill Harrison telephoned Murrin:

> I think our man, I think he will know, I think he will have known for some time that he is being looked into... and I think you will get him now.[42]

Pinkertons, the legendary American detective agency [We Never Sleep] were hired by Murrin. He sent a thousand pounds from Sir Peter Blaker's dirty tricks fund to settle a Pinkerton invoice for work on Oyston.

Kroll Securities in New York had been hired by merchant bankers in London. They contacted Murrin in October with a request for information on Oyston and paid for Murrin and a local Tory solicitor to meet them in their Curzon Street offices in London.

Martin Tomkinson, an experienced financial journalist[43] who acquired lists of Owen Oyston's personal payments settling the embarrassing debts at *News on Sunday*, ridiculed Murrin's idea of hiring Pinkertons. In a letter to Murrin, he noted that Kroll's client, an American cable television firm, had already dumped their deal with Oyston. They 'one hundred per cent threw out Oyston' wrote Tomkinson:

---

[42] Tape recording, August 1988.

[43] *Nothing to Declare: The Political Corruptions of John Poulson* (with Michael Gillard) John Calder, 1980

Any euphoria about Kroll has now worn off and I'm writing to establish some new, and binding, ground rules. First and foremost, I hope you really do appreciate this thing is now 100% for real. You and I have just fucked up a ten million plus deal for Oyston [or so it seems]. This does not happen every day and from now on things can only get dirtier.

CHAPTER 10

Miss World, Piccadilly Radio and the Sunday Times

On January 18, 1989, Chris Akers, media analyst at Citicorp Scrimgeour Vickers, enthusiastically tipped shares in the Miss World Group, currently 46.6 per cent owned by Owen Oyston.

Murrin told his usual contacts that Akers had been bribed. Akers had worked at Saatchi and Saatchi when he was only 19 years old. After working for banks in Canada and London he would eventually make chairman and chief executive of Leeds United Football Club. But according to Murrin's most unreliable reports, Akers had been simply bribed to talk up Miss World by receiving gifts of land from Oyston.

In fact, Akers had been dead right about Miss World shares:

> The recent merger of Miss World and Red Rose radio brought together two of the UK's most successful entrepreneurs, Eric Morley and Owen Oyston respectively. The former's experience as Chairman of Mecca and Belhaven couple with the latter's expertise in property and radio will be brought to bear on developing Miss World Group into a 'property-based leisure and communications group'.
>
> There are few truly international brands which can transcend national boundaries and overcome language difficulties but we would strongly contend that 'Miss World' is one of them. [If Mickey Mouse is worth a billion dollars to Walt Disney then there is no reason why, if the Miss World trademark is successfully exploited it cannot be contributing millions rather than hundreds of thousands to the enlarged group's profits in the future].

Akers forecast a revenue rise of 18 per cent and introduced the City to the Miss World directors: Owen Oyston, 54, journalist Julian Allitt, 43, and accountant Michael Connolly, 47, were joining Eric Morley, 70, the tycoon who had run the country's first bikini beauty contests at the Festival of Britain in 1951. Morley had bought himself a one third share in Miss World for a million dollars in 1978.

The fourth director was Eric's wife, Julia Morley, the organiser of the beauty contests. By 1989 she had become the butt of savage criticism from militant feminists. When Thames Television dropped her annual finals at the Royal Albert Hall from their TV schedules Julia Morley simply moved the event to Hong Kong. One month after Akers tipped the shares, Miss World won a fierce takeover battle for Piccadilly Radio in Manchester, making Oyston chairman of Britain's biggest chain of commercial radio stations.

In his autobiography, *Jew Made in England*, the racy Cheshire-born publisher Anthony Blond described the first board meeting chaired by Oyston at Piccadilly. Blond had been a founding shareholder in both *Private Eye* and Piccadilly Radio and had planned Manchester's first commercial radio station by the Aga stove in the Knutsford farmhouse of the Manchester solicitor Neil Pearson, with assistance from Pearson's eccentric wife Ruth and 'endless cups of tea' served by her daughter, only ever introduced to Anthony Blond as 'H'.[44]

---

[44] Timewell Press, Pinner, 2004

JEW MADE IN
ENGLAND
ANTHONY BLOND

Ridiculous. At the first board meeting attended by Owen he proposed that the fees of the non-executive directors be halved. When the motion was unanimously passed, Owen buried his face in his hands and almost sobbed, 'Oh, now I feel *so* mean!'

It was difficult to dislike the man but some people managed to. I was summoned by the takeover panel of the London Stock Exchange to answer the rumour that he had tried to bribe me. I told the two Wykehamists – clones of the couple at MI6 who had asked me to spy on a Russian many moons ago – that I wouldn't say he had, and I wouldn't say he hadn't; but that if they pushed me formally I would deny it. I tried to explain to these polite young gentlemen that, though an utter bounder, Owen was not in the prayer-book sense 'a bad man'. He had attracted hostile attention (particularly from one financial journalist on the *Sunday Times*) as much for his exuberance and lechery as for appearing to operate on the windy side of the law. He was also woefully naïve, having asked his PR man to take him to tea at the Ritz to meet society ladies of loose morals. I think that must have let me off the hook, for the inquisitors laughed. I also like to think that Neil would have been proud of me. Owen Oyston was subsequently imprisoned for rape. Along with certain sections of the media, I was convinced he had been framed.

Neil died, but not before he had seen Piccadilly Radio become the most successful station outside London, turning over its capital ten times a year. He once introduced me to each of the sixty or so employees with the words, 'This is the man without whom you would not be here.' Some of the senior figures looked alarmed. We made some provision for his widow, Ruth, but she also died. I like to think of H making endless cups of tea in the kitchen of that eighteenth-century farmhouse.

It was now Murrin who was on the ropes. On May 25, 1989, a judge made Oyston's gagging injunction on Murrin permanent. Murrin had to apologise unreservedly to Oyston for publishing allegations found to be 'entirely without the slightest foundation.' Murrin was desperately short of money, working night and day in his fish and chip shop at Longridge, near Preston. Oyston would often pass by, on the way to a new Paul Heathcote restaurant, and unaware that Murrin was still breaking the permanent Carter-Ruck injunction by posting fresh corruption allegations on a permanent wall newspaper inside the Stonebridge Chippy.

Two months later on July 25, a very heavyweight newspaper came calling. Peter Hounam, chief reporter of the *Sunday Times* sent a telemessage to Goodwood Avenue, asking Murrin to telephone him at home or at his office. The Insight Team wanted help with a front page story that proved utterly disastrous for Oyston. It broke in the *Sunday Times* on September 17, 1989, just as American directors from the South-Western Bell company were arriving in England intending buy out Oyston's cable television interests for cash. The story devastated Oyston's reputation and forced down the sale price of his shares:

Revealed: socialist tycoon's deals with a Labour chief

> IMPROPER behaviour and legally doubtful financial transactions involving the funds of a county council, a prominent local government leader and a millionaire businessman have been uncovered by The Sunday Times Insight Team.
>
> The deals, placing at risk millions of pounds of public money, include complex share investments and plans to build a holiday resort in the Soviet Union.
>
> In a series of share transactions between Owen Oyston – one of the biggest commercial radio operators in Britain – and the pension fund of Derbyshire county council, led by David Bookbinder, Oyston saw the value of his investments leap by as much as £1m at the fund's expense.

> In another, Bookbinder, facing Tory calls for his resignation, seriously misled a council meeting by claiming that an associated share deal with Oyston had produced a profit of £95,000 when the shares were worthless...
>
> Yesterday Christopher Chope, the environment minister said: "The department is examining ways in which the regulations on local authority pension funds could be changed to prevent their inappropriate use. The Sunday Times investigation is timely and the results will help us in our review."
>
> A firm of international accountants, expert in local government auditing, said it would have been obliged to investigate the legality of the pension fund deals and the Crimea project had it been Derbyshire's accountants.[45]

'Bizarre deals of a council leader and the media tycoon' were examined on page 17, which quoted Derbyshire's defiant leader David Bookbinder.

> People need to know that if they are getting into the ring with me, they will end up with a bloody nose.

Bookbinder's threat of a bloody nose proved justified, for one week later, in a second devastating story the *Sunday Times* appeared to have libelled Owen Oyston. His expensive 'learned friends', Peter Carter-Ruck and Partners, quantified the libel as worth 'about 1.8 million pounds' in damages. Those damages would be aggravated by the fact that South Western Bell had taken advantage of the sudden collapse of Oyston's reputation and forced him to lower his price for the cable television shares 'by many millions'. Oyston told a *Red Rose* journalist at the time, 'Things look black for me'.

[45] *Sunday Times*, September 17, 1989

He said later:

> The timing of the *Sunday Times* article was the most critical thing in my commercial life, it was timed just before the biggest deal with Cable, the biggest I've ever conducted.

Oyston was further alarmed to learn from the *Sunday Times* that Sir Peter Blaker, a cable television competitor, had been funding Michael Murrin's dubious activities in Preston.

Secret inquiry into local council links

> A FORMER Tory foreign minister has admitted he was so concerned by Owen Oyston's links with local government politicians in Lancashire that he helped fund a secret investigation by a ratepayer's activist and a private detective.
>
> Sir Peter Blaker, MP for Blackpool South, was one of Oyston's rivals for a cable television franchise. But he said he paid out nearly £5,000 because of his concern that local government was in danger of being brought into disrepute.
>
> Blaker paid the money into the account of a London firm of solicitors, who then paid it to the activist Michael Murrin. Robert Atkins MP for the neighbouring Ribble Valley [sic] and now transport minister, supported the inquiry, but contributed no money.
>
> Their concern centred on the relationship between Oyston and two prominent Labour figures in Preston: Harold Parker, leader of the borough council and Frank McGrath, his deputy.
>
> Five years ago Parker was found to be on Oyston's payroll, with cash going into three bank accounts, while Oyston was heading a Lancashire county council-backed redevelopment scheme for Preston docks.[46]

After unmasking two of Oyston's enemies, Peter Hounam used six further paragraphs to list the business activities of town councillors Harold Parker and Frank McGrath, using facts gathered by Michael Murrin from pilfered bank records and stolen income tax records.

---

46 *Sunday Times*, September 24, 1989

McGrath now owns a £1.3m stake in Oyston's Miss World group, a Preston hotel, three houses and a development site in Blackpool. He is also a director of a Miss World subsidiary, Red Rose Radio. He began with £600 seven years ago which he used to buy shares in Red Rose. Now, because of his acquisition of shares and property, he owes banks and building societies more than £540,000.

The libel followed this headline:

Investigation into share dealings of Miss World group

QUESTIONABLE share deals involving the Miss World group and the pension funds of a county council are being investigated by the Stock Exchange and the City's Takeover Panel after their disclosure by the Sunday Times Insight team...

The City inquiries will consider whether Oyston and Derbyshire were acting in association to influence the share prices of the two companies...

Insight has established that the Derbyshire pension fund bought and sold shares in both Miss World and Piccadilly Radio on more than 50 occasions in the five months preceding the takeover battle.

This has led the Stock Exchange and the Takeover Panel to consider if the Oyston-Derbyshire link was significant in Derbyshire's decision to trade in Piccadilly and Miss World shares.

The *Sunday Times* had hired professional city analysts to find patterns in Oyston's stock market dealing. But their 'bought-in' research was defective. Although *Insight* published a simultaneous explanatory letter from Oyston, this libel would eventually cost Rupert Murdoch's media company a million pounds in damages and costs.

In the published letter, Oyston complained that:

> The article revealed that Sir Peter Blaker MP funded the activist Michael Murrin, against whom I have a permanent injunction. The emphasis you placed in these allegations should be viewed alongside the fact that you subsequently state that I had been cleared.
>
> It was only in the last paragraph of a story headlined "Secret Inquiry into Local Council Links" at the foot of page 17 that you report that Sir Peter and Robert Atkins MP had, after their investigation, found no evidence of any wrongdoing by anyone.
>
> In conclusion I am at a loss as to why you should have seen fit to publish such an article which reflects so badly on Derbyshire county council and discredits me.

Despite six libel writs, the paper was still spoiling for a fight:

> The Sunday Times unreservedly stands by its story and is continuing to investigate all the issues raised.

And they were not alone. Philip Oppenheim MP was facing a libel writ from Derbyshire County Council and David Bookbinder. Oppenheim asked Murrin for information to defend his case but eventually apologised to Oyston.

Murrin's local MP, David Waddington QC, who had been Margaret Thatcher's home secretary, wrote to the Director of Public Prosecutions at this time, asking whether police were investigating Oyston and the Labour politicians. The DPP, Sir Allan Green QC, replied on November 1:

> Thank you for your letter of 5 October 1989 about the allegations which appeared in the Sunday Times newspaper of 17 September and which concerned Lancashire businessman Owen Oyston, David Bookbinder, of the Derbyshire County Council, and Harold Parker and Frank McGrath of the Preston Borough Council.
>
> I have now received reports from the Chief Crown Prosecutors for Derbyshire and for Lancashire / Cumbria, and am able to tell you that the Crown

Prosecution Service is not aware of any police investigations being carried out in either of these areas.
I understand that there was a substantial investigation by the Lancashire police into the activities of Mr Oyston, Mr Parker and Mr McGrath over four years ago, but that no evidence of any criminal offence was revealed.

The *Sunday Times* attacked with another story:

Takeover Panel investigates claim that tycoon offered Ferrari to shareholder in battle for radio station

THE City Takeover Panel is investigating allegations that Owen Oyston, the flamboyant millionaire, won a £40m battle for control of a commercial radio station by illegally arranging to "buy" the votes of an important shareholder. Oyston is said to have agreed to supply an £80,000 Ferrari and other inducements if the investor, with a critical 2.8% of voting shares changed sides.

Under a big picture of Oyston, lounging in a white suit by the red Ferrari at Claughton Hall, the accountant Michael Connolly was quoted as saying, 'There was no deal', contradicting the Sunday Times informant, the chairman of Media Sales Bureau, who had described a car journey with Oyston to Manchester Airport:

At first they offered us Oyston's own Ferrari, then they agreed to buy us another one, provided it cost no more than £80,000.
From our point of view, the whole deal was a straightforward business transaction. We had shares Oyston wished to secure. Our price was an honourable agreement which would help the development of our business. The problem is Oyston never kept his side of it.

The *Sunday Times* accurately forecast that the Takeover Panel Ferrari story would cost Oyston his position as chairman of the combined firm, now known as Trans World:

The allegations are of particular concern to Guardian and Manchester Evening News Group, holding 16.7% of Trans World. Harry Roche, group

> chairman, said yesterday he had heard of the alleged deal last week and taken legal advice. He added, 'I shall be raising the matter at Wednesday's board meeting.'

On October 12, the Panel on Take-overs and Mergers undermined the *Sunday Times* by clearing Oyston and Connolly:

> We have found no evidence of any breach of the Code on the part of either Miss World or Derbyshire County Council... For the sake of completeness, I should record that most of the dealings in Miss World and Piccadilly shares conducted by Derbyshire County Council and its pension fund during the period from September 1988 to March 1989 were simply stock lending transactions. This has been independently corroborated.

Oyston was cleared of running a 'concert party' and was able to announce that profits were up 131 per cent. But it wasn't enough for the City. Harry Roche of Guardian Media had decided to combine with another shareholder and remove the man in the big hat from his £100,000 a year chairmanship of Trans World Communications plc. With 20% of the shares, Guardian Media were able to combine with Emap and block the booming company's access to bank loans.

Things started to go wrong when Guardian Media, holding twenty per cent of the shares and combining with Emap, blocked access to bank loans for the booming firm, now known as Trans World Communications. Two days after station chief Julian Allitt had sacked fifteen long serving radio engineers, one of Oyston's old friends mounted a counterblast. Tim Hudson, a millionaire cricketing disc jockey, turned his Sunday night record session into an attack on the management of Piccadilly. With no engineer in the studio to turn him off air, Hudson broadcast a wickedly incessant critique of Oyston's management ability accompanied by appropriately chosen pop records that included *Go Now* by the Moody Blues, *It's All Over Now, Baby Blue* by Bob Dylan and *Eve of Destruction* by Barry McGuire.

Tim Hudson, who was said to have invented the phrase *flower power* in his Californian radio days, taunted the absent station managers. One of them had to drive through the streets of the city listening in horror to his car radio as he tried to reach the studio and shut down the last ever Tim Hudson Show.

Despite owning 22% of Trans World shares, Oyston resigned as chairman on July 30, 1991, just after reporting a £2 million loss. Once again Oyston had been denied market value for his shares and once again he was on the ropes.

CHAPTER 11

Operation Angel

In March 1990 Peter Martin persuaded Oyston to put some money into his model agency. Oyston dined with Melanie Hardy, Victoria Brooks and five of the models and Peter Martin ostentatiously signed some cheques at the dinner table. There was an Oyston cheque for £13,000 in favour of Model Team's London agency, Count 8, now to be known as Options. The girls got the idea that Owen Oyston would be funding Model Team.

Owen and Vicki Oyston went to Tuscany on holiday that summer. They were seen publicly as the Labour Party's leading private financial supporters and seated with the promising Labour party leader Neil Kinnock and his wife Glenys at the *Palio di Siena*.

Oyston was planning to sue Sir Peter Blaker, the wealthy Conservative MP for Blackpool South, for conspiracy to defame. He needed therefore to acquire evidence from Blaker's penniless co-conspirator Michael Murrin. The preferred tactic was to offer an olive branch to the struggling agitator from Goodwood Avenue. Murrin was invited to visit Claughton Hall but the invitation was handled just as badly as Oyston's disastrous interview with the journalist Lynn Barber.

Murrin arrived at Claughton Hall [pronounced by Lancastrians as *Claffton*] on Sunday, October 14, 1990, only to find no Oystons in residence. He drove home in his old Datsun Sunny, quite baffled by events until back home he got a phone call from Owen and Vicki. They had been trapped on the wrong side of a level crossing at Hest Bank. Could Murrin meet them at The Tickled Trout Hotel near the M6 interchange at Preston?

There were some big questions at this first meeting. Would Murrin transcribe his tape recordings for Oyston's lawyers? Would he agree that his only payment would be for transcription services and stationery? Would he divulge the name of his secret backer? Would that be William Harrison?

The case in prospect, an action against two former Tory ministers for conspiracy to defame, was going to cost millions, but legal restrictions meant that Murrin would be advanced no more than fifteen hundred pounds before starting the transcription of sixteen hours of tape recordings at a measly £12.50 an hour. Murrin agreed to transcribe the tape recordings but refused to betray Harrison. Oyston remembered later, 'He just toyed with me and kept Harrison's name from me.'[47] Murrin also telephoned a warning to Harrison that some stolen material had already been handed back to Oyston.

Murrin handed over 36 cassettes of tape recordings, proving that the two former government ministers and their mysterious financial backer had raised about fifty thousand pounds to buy stolen information, bank statements and Oyston's personal income tax statement for 1987.

Word that Murrin might be changing sides reached Peter Hounam at the *Sunday Times.*

Hounam: From what Vicki is saying to you then, they're in dire trouble?

Murrin: No, no, no. That is not true. No, that's not right. No, she was saying that... it had hurt them very badly in an emotional sense

[47] Interview with author

> and it had affected the family. Now you've got to remember what I've done to him Peter. He walks into a bloody merchant bank in London and the first question they ask him is: 'Before we do talk business Mr Oyston, have you been involved in running drugs from Hong Kong? I mean Jesus Christ! You know I hurt the guy didn't I? Not that I was the one who put the information into the merchant bank but, I mean, it was pretty successful campaign wasn't it?[48]

Murrin complained to Lord Waddington in March that he was now being threatened for passing the tapes to Oyston. Christopher Guest More, the private detective who had sold Inland Revenue records to Bill Harrison, was annoyed. He needed to know just how much Murrin had blabbed to Oyston. Murrin told this author:

> [More] asked me whether I had talked to Oyston. When I said, 'He says he won't pay me.' More suggested to me that I should tell Oyston to hire Frank Dobson, another private detective friend of More, who would conduct a big inquiry in which some of the proceeds would be given back to me.
> I suggested this to Oyston, but Oyston refused to employ Dobson. In fact, Dobson was later paid by the *Sunday Times* to investigate Oyston. More asked me if I wanted him to alert his own client, William Harrison, to developments.
> More said Oyston would have to pay more money to More to finish his struggle. He said to me, on tape, 'Get in there quickly and grab some.' Another suggestion from More was that I should go to the police and report I was being blackmailed by Oyston.

Sir Peter Blaker called Murrin, complaining in smooth tones that he simply could not understand how the *Sunday Times* had learned of his own

[48] Tape recording

activities. On Murrin's tape recording he seems relieved to hear that Harrison's identity was still being hidden from Oyston.

On October 16, Peter Hounam, under pressure from Murdoch lawyers, called Murrin to ask whether Murrin would be giving evidence for Oyston in his libel case against the *Sunday Times*, or whether Murrin might try to 'sting' Oyston for money:

> I think if you are planning to set him up, you've got to try and get him to, obviously you don't want to disabuse him of your importance, you want to blow it up out of all importance, likewise you should go for a substantial sum.[49]

Hounam said that if Murrin decided to 'set up' Oyston, he would have to be 'decisive' and go 'wired up' to the next meeting with Oyston: 'It's got to be the coup de grâce.' Hounam then told Murrin about progress made by the *Sunday Times* Insight Team, chasing Murrin's Inland Revenue tip about corruption around Derek Hatton, the deputy leader of Liverpool Council. The former Merseyside firefighter had been expelled from the Labour Party in 1986 for belonging to the banned Militant Tendency Marxist grouping.

Hounam told Murrin that a police prosecution of Hatton that had been planned to start before the 1987 election had been stopped 'from on high' but that Hatton might soon be charged with an offence. Twelve days later, the *Sunday Times* claimed that the Merseyside Police Operation Cheetah was uncovering political corruption connected to the drugs business.

Murrin wanted to take credit for triggering Operation Cheetah. He told Lord Waddington that although legally barred from discussing Oyston with Peter Hounam of the *Sunday Times*, he had nevertheless been the source of

---

[49] Tape transcript, October 16, 1990.

the information that led to Operation Cheetah, the investigation into Derek Hatton:

> I did, however, agree to meet Mr Hounam and was able to provide information concerning alleged corruption in Liverpool. The information I gave was as follows:
> 1. An informant told me that a Mr E. Spencer was involved in paying bribes... in return for planning consents and preferential treatment re: land deals.
>
> 2. Mr Spencer was put under 24hr surveillance by Liverpool drugs squad because of his association with Mr Bobby McGorrin an alleged drugs dealer. Mr McGorrin was associated with the Hughes twins described as a 'couple of Liverpool thugs'.
> Mr Hounam then started making inquiries in Liverpool and on page 12, col2 par6 of the *Sunday Times* it states, 'it was this paper which prompted the fraud squad investigation by presenting the results of its own inquiries to the Merseyside police force in March this year...' In telephone conversations [which I have recorded] Mr Hounam confirms the information I gave him has led to Cheetah.[50]
>
> I published a press release the next day, saying that I had been invited to attend Stanley Road police station in Liverpool and make a statement concerning the source and content of the information provided to the *Sunday Times*. This request was complied with.

Those Inland Revenue officers who had rashly gossiped with Mike Murrin about corruption on Merseyside had unwittingly triggered two enormous police investigations. They had even invited Murrin to inspect a file at their offices in Liverpool.

Michael Murrin passed his copies of the stolen income tax records of the Preston councillor Frank McGrath and the tax records of Mrs McGrath to Merseyside police detectives for use in the ultimately abortive anti-corruption operation known as Cheetah.

---

[50] Tape recording October 29, 1990.

These documents, undoubtedly protected by the Official Secrets Acts, were later passed from Liverpool to the Lancashire Constabulary for use in a second abortive corruption case, again inspired by Murrin, and directed this time against Councillor Frank McGrath. Both police forces paid no heed to the obvious fact that the stolen documents were themselves evidence of crimes under official secrets legislation. Merseyside's abortive Operation Cheetah is said to have cost fifty million pounds.[51]

Operation Angel broke cover on August 7, with heavily publicised raids at Preston town hall and at the homes of the leaders of Preston's Labour Party, Harold Parker and Frank McGrath. The operation was to last for six years and would involve two chief constables, three commerce branch chiefs and 36 detectives who eventually visited Germany, Spain, Jersey and the Isle of Man at a cost of £25 million.

The only persons convicted of any offences in Operation Angel were four small businessmen and two minor council officials. All but one of those convicted had already been reported to police by council officials before Operation Angel began.

Lord Justice Nolan eventually found that all nineteen searches of homes and offices had been unlawful. In March 1992, when Frank McGrath and his solicitor Colin Marland were arrested in an investigation into land deals, Lord Nolan ruled that the Chief Constable of Lancashire had 'no such rights' to retain the documents that had been unlawfully seized from McGrath. All those charged under Angel with fraud, corruption or conspiracy to defraud saw the charges dropped by the Crown Prosecution Service or were eventually found not guilty in court.

---

[51] Between 1990 and 1992 the Merseyside police fraud squad made three spectacular raids involving up to 280 officers. They arrested 40 people but, charged only seven. Derek Hatton and three co-defendants were in 1993 acquitted of conspiring to defraud Liverpool City Council. Jonathan Foster, The Independent, March 13, 1993.

Frank McGrath, businessman, former councillor
Arrested in January 1992.
Charged with deception, conspiracy to defraud and theft.
Cleared in December 1994.
Colin Marland, solicitor
Arrested in January 1992.
Charged with conspiracy to defraud.
Cleared in December 1994.
Robin Hill, property developer
Arrested in 1991.
Charged with deception.
Cleared in October 1994.
Tony Owens, former Town Clerk.
Arrested in June 1993.
Charged with conspiracy to defraud.
Case dropped in 1995.
Hugh McClorry, former Deputy Town Clerk
Arrested in June 1993 charged with conspiracy to defraud.
Case dropped in April 1995.
John Field, former Borough Architect
Arrested in October 1993.
Charged with corruption.
Cleared by the courts in May 1995.
Hossein Ghiassi, property developer
Arrested in October 1993.
Charged with corruption.
Cleared in May 1995.
Karen Heald
Charged in October 1992 with conspiracy to defraud.
Cleared in November 1993.
Richard Boyes, quantity surveyor
Charged in October 1992 with conspiracy to defraud.
Cleared in November 1993.

Arthur Proctor, property developer
Charged with conspiracy to deceive in
October 1992. Fined £2,500 and ordered to repay
£2,645 to Preston Council.
Howard Parker, businessman
Arrested January 1992.
Charged with defrauding Preston Council.
Jailed for 12 months, reduced to nine months on appeal.
Frank Jones, former Head of Council's Unemployment
Resource Centre
Charged with theft June 1992.
Conditional Discharge in December 1993.
Hugh Sneddon, businessman
Charged with theft June 1992.
Conditional discharge in December 1993.

For political reasons, the civil servants at the Crown Prosecution Service concealed the names of two of the informants behind Operation Angel. Defence lawyers were simply shown a police computer printout with obliterated names. One of the defendants, a local government officer, had been served with a copy of a formal and signed witness statement. He noticed that part of the address of the anonymous informant corresponded with a blocked-out address on a Home Office HOLMES computer printout. Informant R2AX could therefore be identified as Lord Blaker.

In another report, the informant behind report R6C was identified by counting blanked spaces on a computer printout that exactly matched the letters in the name of Robert Atkins, prime-minister John Major's sports minister, organiser of his campaign for the party leadership after the fall of Margaret Thatcher and one of the few politicians ever invited by John Major to a New Year's Day lunch at Chequers.

These clumsy attempts to conceal the identities of Atkins and Blaker called into question the political impartiality of the Crown Prosecution Service. Worse still, the information offered in the reports from Atkins and

Blaker was inaccurate. What the documents did show was the heavy political pressure from Westminster that was pushing the ostensibly non-political Crown Prosecution Service in Manchester into re-opening a previously closed corruption investigation into the Labour council at Preston.

In the R2AX document, Det Insp Michael Needham of the Lancashire Commerce Branch reported receiving a telephone call from Lord Blaker on February 4, 1992, with a string of allegations; against a building firm called Tustin Developments Ltd, against Preston's borough architect John Field, against Howard Parker, son of the Labour leader, against Owen Oyston and against Preston's deputy Labour leader, Councillor Frank McGrath:

> OYSTON and MCGRATH in the past have been offering shares in various small companies to officers of Preston Borough Council.[52]

It was significant that the CPS officials did not extend anonymity to the local Tories in Preston who were being interviewed by the very same detectives and had passed on similarly inaccurate stories about their Labour colleagues. The documents named a woman Tory councillor who had insisted on telling a detective that he would find that a carpet in the deputy Labour leader's house matched a carpet in the town hall.

Councillor Joe Hood, the Tory leader on Preston Council, was named as an informant. Interviewed by Det Insp Michael Needham on October 1, 1991, he:

> queried Owen Oyston's involvement in the former Lancastria Co-op known as Lancastria House, when Owen Oyston wanted to use this building as an estate agency and then sold out his interest in it. Mr Hood stated at this moment he would not like to make a written statement regarding his concerns, but if required for a prosecution he would do his civic duty.

---

[52] HOLMES computer printout, disclosed to defendant

The statements gathered from the Tory politicians in both Preston and Westminster were not only spiteful, they were completely inaccurate. When it came time for the Crown Prosecution Service to withdraw charges against Deputy Labour leader Frank McGrath at Liverpool Crown Court, Mr Justice Forbes determined that all charges were 'concluded in Mr McGrath's favour.'

McGrath, who had been a millionaire in 1987 from personal investments in Oyston radio stations had been charged with defrauding the Midland Bank of £1.89 million.

In the early stages of the case, he and his defence team were excluded from court to permit an ex parte application from the Crown in which Michael Shorrock QC persuaded Judge Denis Clark to give public interest immunity protection to a number of 'sensitive' police documents so that they would not be disclosed to McGrath.

Document D-909 on the PII list was described as "Merseyside Police file re McGrath"

The plan to keep D-909 a secret might well have worked but within a few weeks, someone, perhaps accidentally, managed to send to McGrath's solicitor just what the judge had not ordered - a complete court transcript of the ex parte PII hearing.

As soon as McGrath read this transcript, he perceived that back in the days of Margaret Thatcher his political opponents had been studying his income tax returns.

The transcript showed how prosecutor Shorrock had explained D-909 to the judge:

> 'It is old. It has nothing to do with the matters under investigation in this case. It is a sort of money profile of Mr McGrath. It is clear that this information is gathered by the Merseyside police by accessing the Inland Revenue... which, I suspect, is a source which the Merseyside police certainly would not want disclosed. Because if one looks at it,

it looks as though they looked at his tax records and his tax returns, and letters he had written to the Revenue.'

The judge announced: "D-909 is a money profile. I will not tell you from whom the information was garnered but it is in the public interest not to disclose from whom they obtained the information.'

But when the transcript fell accidentally into McGrath's hands, the Crown's junior counsel, Anthony Russell, had to write to the defence, on January 27, 1994, and reveal that the judge had been seriously misled. D-909 had not come from the Inland Revenue at all.

"They told us the Inland Revenue information had been obtained from a third party, known to the police and not to the Inland Revenue", McGrath recounted recently.

> On November 23, 1995, I received a five-page document, anonymously through the post, which I believe to be D909, or part of D909. A careful reading of the document demonstrates that they have had access to my Inland Revenue files. The final sentence of page five suggests that someone has been paid for obtaining this information. I am in no doubt that a person unlawfully obtained my tax records from the Inland Revenue and is guilty of theft and offences under the Official Secrets Act.
>
> 'I was already aware of the activities of Michael Murrin, a private investigator who was employed and financed by prominent Conservative politicians, including the MPs Sir Peter, now Lord, Blaker and Robert Atkins, now Sir Robert Atkins. Michael Murrin recorded his telephone conversations and following a compromise in a civil action brought by Owen Oyston against Michael Murrin, these tapes were made available to Owen Oyston."[53]

McGrath's legal aid certificate specified 'an action for damages for conspiracy to injure' against the chief constable of Lancashire, the chief constable of Merseyside, Lord Blaker, Sir Robert Atkins, Michael Murrin, William Harrison, Mrs Thatcher's host during Tory Party conferences, and

---

[53] Letter from Frank McGrath to author.

Christopher Guest More, the millionaire private detective, who had just been named as a defendant with Lady Grantchester in the Littlewoods Organisation racketeering case.

After *Private Eye* magazine revealed that Bill Harrison and Lord Blaker had paid at least £30,000 to fund investigations by Murrin and More into the affairs of Owen Oyston, Frank McGrath and Harold Parker, Frank McGrath said, 'The Inland Revenue have confirmed to me that they have never produced any information concerning my affairs to any police force. I allege that the tax records were obtained unlawfully and that both the Merseyside and Lancashire police forces must have been aware of this.'

Hossein Ghiassi, the Iranian-born boss of Tustin Developments Ltd., cleared of corrupting the borough architect, commented outside Liverpool Crown Court in May 1995:

> Preston has suffered because of petty internal wrangling, personal vendetta and political expediency.

Operation Angel prosecutions for mortgage fraud over a house in the dockland development hung for three and a half years over the Labour leader's daughter, Deborah Parker. Ms Parker, 34, a BBC television news reporter, was summoned with the approval of the Director of Public Prosecutions in July 1993, with her boyfriend, Detective Constable Chris Robinson, who was then suspended from duty. Debbie Parker, who had once been married to Barry Askew formerly the crusading editor of the *Lancashire Evening Post* said courageously:

> As far as I am concerned, this is connected with Operation Angel, whatever the police say. It is nothing more than a vendetta and anyone connected with the family seems to be fair game. My boyfriend has been targeted because of his relationship with me and I have been targeted because my name is Parker. Who will be next, my two-year old son?

All the outstanding Operation Angel prosecutions were abandoned by the end of 1997. But Debbie Parker's brother, Howard Parker, was jailed for twelve months, reduced on appeal, for defrauding the council on home improvement grants. His nine-month sentence was the heaviest penalty imposed in any of the Operation Angel cases. It was imposed in respect of a home improvement procedure that was later made legal by the British government. His father Harold had managed to serve as Mayor of Preston during its famous Guild Year in 1992, when he was still under investigation by Operation Angel. When he died in 2009, after 44 years on the council, a contributor to the *Lancashire Evening Post* comments page wrote that Operation Angel

> lasted from 1992-96 and Harold's financial and personal life was investigated over and over again. In spite of this, he was never convicted of any offence. If he had done anything wrong it would have been detected. If Operation Angel should have been mentioned – it could have been to say this man was a victim of a police investigation that cost millions and only proved that Harold had done nothing. Harold also paid a price – as anyone who knows him - both in terms of health and financial well-being. Perhaps Operation Angel should have been mentioned – because I am pretty certain Harold would still be alive today if that event had never taken place.

Arif Patel, 29, a former Preston sock manufacturer, flew back from India to answer charges of cheating a Department of the Environment urban renewal programme by submitting false invoices when he was 22 years old. This was proclaimed in the press as a success for Operation Angel, but the case involved a council development official who had already been reported to police by the council before the Angel investigation. Judge Denis Clark at Liverpool Crown Court imposed an eight-month sentence suspended because of Patel's previous good character, guilty plea and repayment of £12,500 to the borough council.

The gradual disclosure of the police documents looked like the opening of the Stasi files in East Germany. Labour politicians discovered exactly what baseless accusations of villainy had been laid against them by their fellow town councillors. Tempers ran high and the auditors KPMG advised

Preston Council to appoint an outsider to take the vacant post of town clerk. They suggested Geoff Driver, a local authority chief executive with a stormy past at Kirklees and Plymouth.

Driver turned up for the two-day interview procedure, walked out on the second day, but telephoned later to say he had changed his mind about walking out. He got the job on a 5-4 committee vote over the head of Preston's existing deputy chief executive Hugh McClorry. Three weeks after starting his new job, Driver recommended that Hugh McClorry be suspended from his post as deputy chief executive.

Hugh McClorry had been one of the original victims of Operation Angel. Lancashire detectives had arrested him and charged him with conspiring to defraud the Department of the Environment of £650,000. The Crown Prosecution Service dropped the charge. Nevertheless, Preston Borough Council sacked him unfully for 'fundamental, irremediable incompetence' in conducting a council land deal. Hugh McClorry won almost maximum compensation for the unfair dismissal. He obliged the council to declare in public that there had been 'no incompetence and no misconduct' in his work. He became town clerk of Kendal.

Four months later, the leader of Preston Council, Valerie Wise, daughter of the left-wing Westminster MP Audrey Wise, ordered Geoff Driver to leave the town hall, take a holiday, or be suspended. Driver stayed at home under suspension until December 1995, refusing to hand over witness statements for the planned proceedings against Frank McGrath.

On his return to the town hall in 1995, Geoff Driver accused the assistant director of legal services, Mrs Shirley Harrison, of corruptly failing to proceed with legal action against Frank McGrath. When Mrs Harrison filed a complaint about sex discrimination to an employment tribunal, Driver complained to the Office for the Supervision of Solicitors that the sex discrimination case had been made in corrupt collusion with Hugh McClorry.

In 1995, at the age of 50, Driver negotiated a £400,000 retirement package announced in May 1996 by the new Labour leader David Borrow:

> He goes in the interests of the authority, his own interests and in the interests of the people of Preston.

These bitter disputes lasted for more than two decades. David Borrow, a future MP, was obliged to accept KPMG's report that his Labour party had mismanaged land deals involving £200 million. Joe Hood, the leader of the Tories and a key informant to Murrin and the police insisted, 'Mr Driver has been hounded out of Preston.'

Geoff Driver soon turned up in the council chamber, barred from talking to the press, but openly passing notes to the Tory councillors until one morning in November 1996, when Councillor Tony Reid, a left-wing pacifist politician in a large cardigan, interrupted a council meeting to announce:

> A few minutes ago, I was making my way to the public gallery to speak to someone I know. Geoff Driver, formerly the town clerk, came down the stairs. We did not speak. But he came up to me, grabbed me by the jumper and pushed me against the glass. He threatened to thump me. He said I was thirty seconds away from being hit. He said if I mentioned his name again in this town, he would put me in hospital. I think it's a joke really. I have made legitimate criticisms of the town clerk. If I do end up in hospital, I would like the council to know how it happened.[54]

Councillor Reid had blamed Geoff Driver, consultants KPMG and the Attorney-general for the hideous cost of Operation Angel. Yet three years later, Geoff Driver was elected as a Conservative member of the council he had served as chief executive. As chairman of the Ribble Valley

---

[54] Author's contemporary note.

Conservative Association he was chosen in preference to Audrey Scott, the woman who had first introduced Mike Murrin to Robert Atkins.

The cost of the enduring hatred in Preston was still being paid in 2001 when a Liverpool employment tribunal found that Geoff Driver had maliciously waged an 'unremitting vendetta' against Shirley Harrison, when she was deputising after Hugh McClorry had been unlawfully suspended. Driver was found guilty of victimising Mrs Harrison under the Sexual Discrimination Act:

> All of her actions that he has questioned and criticised are manifestly defensible on professional and rational grounds. To challenge and debate them in the hurtful, relentless manner he has adopted suggests a deep personal motive. What has she done to him to make him see corruption when on a rational basis she is only practising her profession? She has accused him of sex discrimination – that accounts for his treatment of her.[55]

Driver insisted he had been 'cleaning up the council in the aftermath of Operation Angel.' In 2009, he took power as leader of Lancashire County Council for four years until the Conservatives lost control in 2013. There were at least 21 instances of interference by Preston Conservatives in the traditionally non-political fields of Inland Revenue, local government audit and criminal investigation between 1983 and 1996.

Lawyers defending the deputy Labour leader of Preston, Frank McGrath, heard that a list of the six starting points for Operation Angel had been compiled confidentially by a member of the Angel investigating team, Det Supt John Jameson. The lawyers pressed Ray Wildsmith at the Crown Prosecution Service in London to release the list and discovered that the vast police operation had originated with the BBC *Watchdog* TV documentary of 1983, itself instigated by Mike Murrin.

---

[55] Sexism claim victory rocks the town hall, *Lancashire Evening Post*, December 11, 2001.

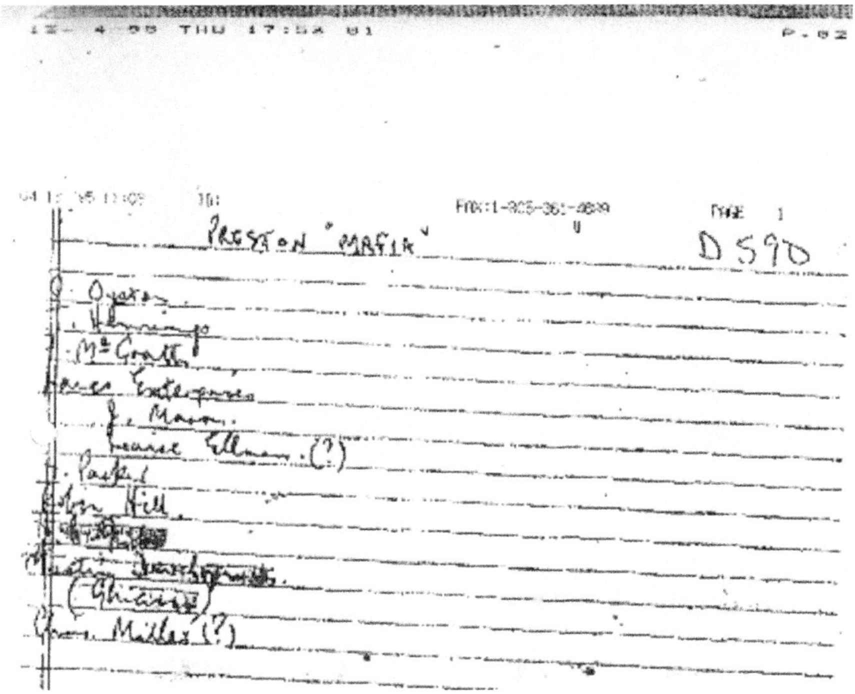

PRESTON "MAFIA"

D590

O. Oyston
E. Hemmings
F. McGrath
Louise Ellman (?)
H. Parker
Ron Hill
Miller (?)

Preston Mafia guidance note

The CPS handed over to the defence an astonishing police guidance note, entitled *Preston Mafia,* composed by the borough treasurer of Preston, Ian Threlfall, for a secret meeting at Lancashire police headquarters in January 1991. Owen Oyston's name was name was top of the 'Preston Mafia' list, along with the names of Eddie Hemmings, the Center Parcs and Scottish & Newcastle tycoon, Labour councillors Harold Parker and Frank McGrath, and Louise Ellman, leader of Lancashire County Council and future Labour MP for Liverpool Riverside.

When the Operation Angel team raided Preston town hall on August 7, 1991, Mike Murrin had sent messages to the Press Association, Reuters and the *Lancashire Evening Post* warning that previous investigations at Preston had been sabotaged by police leaks. Murrin recommended that

> One senior officer named in the attached note should be removed from the current investigation.

On August 27, he went further and declared that the officer who should be removed for forewarning the politicians and officials targeted in Operation Angel was actually the Chief Constable of Lancashire, Brian Johnson. Three days later, the chief sued Murrin for libel. Murrin told this author:

> Time ran out on me. I have no money to defend the writ, even if I could defend what I wrote. I had to close the shop. I think the villagers know why. I've been fighting a campaign against the local politicians for eight years. It's put me through the bankruptcy court and libel courts once. It wrecked my marriage and I ended up in hospital with total exhaustion. The last straw was last Saturday, when the joiner got worried about me ever being able to pay him. He let himself into the shop and took away my new display counter. It's finished me. I'm signing on the dole tomorrow. I will have to go bankrupt this time.

Murrin believed that Robert Atkins and Lord Blaker had intervened on his behalf. At Goodwood Avenue, Murrin taped himself telling the journalist Paul Halloran:

> Blaker and Atkins saw the Chief Constable. They were already in the process of seeing the Chief Constable concerning the leaks coming out of Hutton. Now after I had published that letter, I had Blaker on the phone to me very upset. Why did I bloody do it? What possessed me? He went off like a bomb and all. This sort of thing. He said that he and Atkins had seen the Chief Constable and would be most surprised if the Chief Constable were responsible for any leaks back to Oyston. You have got to remember that I had Oyston asking me to go and see the Chief Constable because, and this is a quote from Oyston, 'He's a friend of mine.'
>
> So the upshot was that Blaker went on to tell me that provided I didn't repeat what I had put in my letter the case would be dropped. I would hear no more about it. All right? As far as I was concerned the case was dropped. I have now received a summons to appear in court in February in London to be assessed for damages and costs.

Feeling abandoned by the other conspirators, Murrin asked this author to tell the *Sunday Times* that he was thinking of handing over his tapes to Oyston. He suggested revealing Bill Harrison's secret part in the conspiracy, 'Why don't you try to be the first to blow old Harrison out into the open?' This prompted a telephone call from a phone box near Greyfriars Hall in which Bill Harrison linked his campaign against Oyston to the death crash:

> It is very possible that Owen Oyston, as a principal advertiser with the *Lancashire Evening Post*, had considerable influence on the paper's coverage of my daughter's case. He was certainly friendly with the editor of the paper.[56]

The editor had been Barry Askew. He had shared the Journalist of the Year award for the investigation of Harrison's influence on the chief constable and later edited the *News of the World*. When he learned that it was Harrison who had funded Murrin, Barry Askew told this author:

> Until August 1991, I had no idea who had funded Mike Murrin's investigation. It has been the most amazing and persistent private investigation of a man's affairs.
>
> I was the man who brought Harold Parker and Owen Oyston together. Years later, Mike Murrin tracked me down to ask the most pertinent questions about Oyston's relation with Harold Parker and Frank McGrath.
>
> Both men had joined with me in winning the local radio franchise for Red Rose Radio. It was a lovely operation. We had Russell Harty and Clive Lloyd on board. Later, unwisely, when I was short of money, I sold my shares at par to Frank McGrath. He went on to become a millionaire. I had fallen in love with Debbie Parker.
>
> I accepted an offer from Rupert Murdoch to take the editor's chair at *The News of the World*. I took it partly because it gave me the chance of living with Debbie Parker in London, where she had gone to study. I fell out with Rupert. I caused a public fuss when he killed our world exclusive, uncovering the De Lorean swindle. By then I was drinking heavily, a problem which later became very serious.

---

56 Telephone conversation, Harrison to author.

I came back to live with the Parker family in Preston. I got very close to Harold Parker. I was awash with money and keen to get involved with him and Frank McGrath in schemes for shopping malls in Southport. We had all been stunningly successful for Owen in using our influence to win the Red Rose Radio franchise and I could not see why we could not go on to have our own success in the aftermath.

Harold Parker was perpetually in financial trouble. He had a gas cylinder filling business which was going badly wrong. One night when we were on holiday, Harold broke down. He told me that he was becoming suicidal about his business affairs. He could see no way out. The man was at the end of this tether.

I lent him a thousand pounds and invited him up to see Owen Oyston at Claughton Hall. I was a regular visitor up there for rough-shooting parties and horse-racing expeditions. We were often at the races, following a string of talented two-year-olds lined up for Owen by Jack Berry, his local trainer. There is no doubt that Harold was saved by Owen. He told me he was actually working for him. Soon afterwards their relationship was exposed by the BBC *Watchdog* programme and Harold was shattered when he was confronted by the BBC and the *Daily Star*.

On September 23, Det Insp Michael Needham and Det Chief Insp Gudgeon of Operation Angel interviewed Preston's Tory leader Councillor Joe Hood who dished out an allegation that Harold Parker, the Labour leader, was questionably employed by Hemm Inns Ltd, a company controlled by Trevor Hemmings of Center Parcs and Scottish and Newcastle, a man on the infamous 'Preston Mafia' list. Hood said he was concerned about Tustin Developments Ltd. at Swansea Park and at the Red Scar industrial estate, where ten acres of land had been sold to Tustin at a ridiculously low price. He questioned the development of Ribble Village by R.H. Estates Ltd., a firm run by Robin Hill, described by Hood as a 'former bankrupt with no experience.'

In a grotesque atmosphere, the Lancashire Tories tried to make political capital out of the floundering Operation Angel. Robert Atkins, the MP for South Ribble, put a planted parliamentary question to his friend, prime minister John Major, about corruption and mismanagement in Preston.

Nigel Evans, the MP for Ribble Valley, visited Conservative Central Office to persuade Dr Brian Mawhinney to call at Preston and add the town to his campaign against 'loony left councils'. A stunt, in which Mawhinney was going to tip coins of the realm into Preston Dock was cancelled at the last minute.

On May 27, 1994, a letter from a little-known organisation for controlling regional politics from London, the Government Office for the North West, reached Michael Murrin. It may serve as a 'smoking gun' to illustrate the hidden hand of central government in Britain.

> Dear Mr Murrin,
> Thank you for your letter of 17 May to Mrs Corbett about Preston Docks. The Government Office for the North West is taking a very close interest in Operation Angel and is in regular touch with the Police and Preston's Town Clerk, Geoffrey Driver. I spoke to Mr Driver yesterday and he tells me has acknowledged your letter and is looking into the allegation that the site has not been properly de-contaminated.

On October 8, 1991, on the afternoon of the second day of their libel battle with Oyston, the *Sunday Times* threw in the towel. Things had been looking bad at lunchtime. The editor Andrew Neil wanted to fight on regardless. But Andrew Knight, Rupert Murdoch's newly-appointed editorial director at Times Newspapers, spoke to Murdoch long distance and overruled the editor. Editor Andrew Neil explained the power relationship later:

> Andrew stroked Rupert's ego and Rupert regarded him as a genius.[57]

Apologising before Mr Justice Otton in open court, the *Sunday Times* accepted their analysis of Oyston's share dealings had been faulty and that he had not rigged the market. Outside the High Court, Oyston said the libels had knocked £1.8 million off his shareholdings but meeting his costs of more

[57] *Full Disclosure* by Andrew Neil, Macmillan 1996, p19

than a hundred thousand would mean the case had cost the *Sunday Times* a million pounds. They would have to print a very prominent apology, complete with a fine portrait of the man they had traduced. It was a night for celebration in London.

Sunday Times apology to Owen Oyston

THE following statement was read before the High Court last Monday when four actions relating to articles published two years ago were settled by agreement between the parties.

Mr Owen Oyston's counsel said: "Mr Oyston is a nationally known businessman and the former chairman and chief executive of Trans World Communications. Over the last decade, he has developed numerous interests in commercial radio and cable television.

In the autumn of 1989, The Sunday Times printed three major articles which contained false allegations against Mr Oyston. The first was an Insight article published on September 17 under the headline, "Bizarre deals of a council leader and the media tycoon". The council leader was Mr David Bookbinder of Derbyshire county council; Mr Oyston was the tycoon.

The subject matter of the article was a joint venture between Mr Oyston and the Derbyshire county council pension fund in which the fund invested £2m in shares in Red Rose Radio plc, which it acquired from Mr Oyston. The article also dealt with the plans made by Mr Oyston and Mr Bookbinder to develop a multi-million-pound tourist resort in the Soviet Union with financial backing which might have included the funds of Derbyshire county council.

This article was widely understood to allege that Mr Oyston's relationship with Mr Bookbinder was corrupt. This implication was emphasised, in their eyes, by a separate boxed article on the same page which dealt with Mr Oyston's financial relationship with Mr Parker and Mr McGrath, the leader and deputy-leader respectively of Preston borough council. The Sunday Times said that Conservative MPs, Sir Peter Blaker and Mr Robert Atkins, had been so concerned at these links and at the danger of local government being brought into disrepute that they had helped to finance a secret inquiry. In fact, as The Sunday Times stated, that inquiry produced no evidence of wrongdoing by anyone.

The defendants have at no time sought to defend these proceedings by suggesting that Mr Oyston was guilty of corruption in his relationship, either with Mr Bookbinder or with Mr Parker and Mr McGrath, and they join in this statement to make that quite clear. They also accept that none of the dealings between Mr Oyston and the Derbyshire county council pension fund were of a corrupt nature in any way. In short, they acquit Mr Oyston of any such misconduct.

The second article attacking Mr Oyston appeared in The Sunday Times on September 24, 1989. This was headlined "Investigation into share dealings of Miss World group" and stated that questionable share dealings involving the Miss World group and the pension funds of Derbyshire CC were being investigated by the Stock Exchange and the City's Takeover Panel after their disclosure by The Sunday Times. It was said that the inquiries would focus on a suspicious series of share transactions by the council prior to the takeover by Miss World of Piccadilly Radio: in particular, whether Mr Oyston and the council were acting in association to influence the share prices of the two companies and create a false market.

This second article was based on an analysis of the council's dealings over a period of months in the shares of the two companies. However, unknown to The Sunday Times, the majority of the share dealings concerned were what is called "stocklending". When stocklending takes place, the shares are dealt with at arm's length by market makers and the owner of the shares has no control over the time when or the price at which the shares are sold. The defendants accept that they were at fault in their analysis of the share dealings and that Mr Oyston did not rig the market. This was confirmed by the result of the Takeover Panel's investigation, which acquitted Mr Oyston of any impropriety. The defendants accept that this finding was correct.

The Takeover Panel also investigated the allegations made by The Sunday Times in its third article of November 26, 1989, and found them to be without substance. In this article the newspaper alleged that Mr Oyston had won the takeover battle for Piccadilly Radio by illegally offering financial inducements (including a Ferrari car) to a critical investor who then changed sides. The defendants now acknowledge (as the Panel found) that this allegation against Mr Oyston was unfounded.

The defendants have now agreed to join in this statement and to pay the plaintiff a substantial sum by way of damages. Since they will also be indemnifying Mr Oyston in respect of all his legal costs, it has proved possible to settle these actions to the satisfaction of both parties."

The Sunday Times's counsel said: "On behalf of all the defendants in the four actions, I confirm that they accept what has just been said. It was never the intention of The Sunday Times to suggest that Mr Oyston was corrupt or had engaged in any kind of corrupt relationship or dealings. They take this opportunity to make that clear and to express their apologies to Mr Oyston for the distress which the articles have caused him, his family and friends."

Owen Oyston: a nationally known businessman

Sunday Times, 1992

On the very night of Oyston's legal triumph in London there was trouble brewing at the Midland Hotel in Manchester. In the Edwardian Baroque terracotta palace, where Mr Rolls first met Mr Royce, Peter Martin, self-styled 'corporate affairs director of the Oyston Group' was extracting five thousand pounds from a desperate businessman.

Kevin Cullis, a civil engineering contractor from Wolverhampton, had been lured to Manchester and persuaded to hand over £4,750 in cash with a cheque for £250 in favour of a firm appropriately called Phasechance Ltd. This was to be a pre-payment from Kevin Cullis for having a crack at bidding for civil engineering contracts with Oyston Cable and Southwestern Bell.

Kevin Cullis

This was no more than a cheap swindle by Peter Martin and a pair of sharp Manchester wheeler-dealers working for a firm called Trade Reports. A police report described the swindle:

> At this time MARTIN introduced himself as the Acquisitions and Mergers Manager for the Oyston Group and had offices at Strand Mill, Preston. He explained that the Oyston Group were interested in placing a tender for the installation of cable TV systems throughout the North West of England and that they would require someone with civil engineering experience to assist them. It was further explained that an initial investment of £5,000 would be required from CULLIS and other parties including THOMPSON and MARTIN. At the time CULLIS' business was in financial difficulties and he had to sell his private car to finance the deal. In September 1991 he again met MARTIN at the Midland Hotel, Manchester, where MARTIN explained all was proceeding as planned. CULLIS never saw his money again, nor any proceeds from his supposed investment. CULLIS visited MARTIN's office on one occasion in March when MARTIN made further promises in relation to the business venture.

There was absolutely no business to be won from South Western Bell, the damage from the *Sunday Times* libels had already forced Oyston out of the cable TV business. Peter Martin was playing some dangerous games.

Michael Thompson was not just swindling Cullis. He told Cullis that he was planning to swindle Owen Oyston. Cullis, who was still pestering for some return on his hard-won five thousand pounds, was asked to go to London with Michael Thompson. Thompson said he had an appointment at the *Sunday Times*. Cullis said[58] the meeting lasted an hour and a half but when Cullis asked Thompson to pay back the five thousand pounds he had given to Peter Martin, Thompson told him the cash

> had been given to a young tart, to set up Owen Oyston and force him to buy a business, against his will.[59]

Oyston was celebrating the libel win over the *Sunday Times*. He invited Mr and Mrs Murrin and their children to join him for tea at Claughton Hall.

---

[58] Kevin Cullis interview with author.

[59] Kevin Cullis interview with author.

Vicki Oyston took a photograph of her husband and Mike Murrin standing on the steps and the Murrin family surveyed the fine herd of American bison that roamed the wooded hillside below the hall. Oyston decided to lend £1,500 to Murrin so that his former tormentor could repay some cash loaned to Murrin by the detective Chris More when Murrin had been facing a bankruptcy petition.

When the *Sunday Times* published their prominent apology to Oyston, Murrin commented:

> It's all pretty strange. Two years ago, he was suing me for libel in the High Court. Now we are talking in a friendly way about me helping the TV researchers. There is at least one hour-long documentary planned. We discussed the whole thing over a cup of tea. It was all very friendly, but Mrs Oyston was there, and she found it hard to conceal that she thinks I ruined part of her husband's life. I think she is very bitter about what I did to spy on her husband and his many deals. But I have a clear conscience. I did what was right. I followed leads which indicated serious corruption. The investigation cost me twenty-five thousand pounds, but I did not keep a penny of the money. In fact, I am nearly bankrupt.

CHAPTER 12

Mike Murrin and the Model Agency

In the autumn of 1991 two reporters tried to reveal the identity of the man who had paid for the disastrous covert investigations conducted by Michael Murrin. Lancashire County Council were demanding an investigation into what they called 'The Oyston Affair.' Murrin tried to persuade Bill Harrison to break cover and go public, arranging for this author to wait in a car in the driveway of Greyfriars Hall as Harrison's solicitor spent two hours over coffee in a Victorian conservatory persuading the property developer to change his mind.

But Chris Blackhurst, city editor of the *Sunday Express,* noticed that two important Conservative MPs had broken cover in the *Lancashire Evening Post*:

> Sports Minister and South Ribble MP Robert Atkins issued a statement on behalf of himself and former Foreign Office Minister Sir Peter Blaker in response to the Lancashire County Council demand for an investigation into "The Oyston Affair."[60]

On a Friday afternoon, in good time for a Sunday morning exclusive, Chris Blackhurst asked this author to 'doorstep' Greyfriars Hall. Would Harrison admit funding Murrin? At the second time of asking, Harrison gave his reasons for getting Tory MPs involved in his savage campaign:

---

[60] *Lancashire Evening Post*, October 11, 1991

> It is very possible that Owen Oyston, as a principal adviser with the *Lancashire Evening Post* had considerable influence on the paper's coverage of my daughter's case. He was certainly very friendly with the editor of the paper.
> My daughter is now married with children and I do not want her name brought into all this. If a principal advertiser wants XYZ doing, then that is how it happens. The investigation of the case against my daughter proved it to be groundless.
> It is fifteen years since I last spoke to Oyston. It all happened so long ago, but I did meet Michael Murrin when he started investigation work for the Ratepayers' Association. I cannot speak for the MPs who have been named, but as far as I can gather, the investigations were carried out under Mr Murrin's directions.
> I am very pleased that enquiries into public affairs in Preston are still going on, all these years after Mr Murrin came to me with his suspicions. Of course, Owen Oyston loves publicity. His name is never out of the papers. His deals are always being talked about. They always involve local politicians.

Harrison's reasons were obviously personal and certainly not in the public interest. Harrison's statement would have badly damaged Atkins, Blaker and all the conspiratorial Lancashire Conservatives had not Chris Blackhurst's story been killed by the newspaper late on Saturday press night. In Fleet Street tradition the story that had lived for a few hours as a galley proof did not die, it would resurface in the glossy pages of *Esquire* magazine.

On October 13, in a letter published in the *Lancashire Evening Post,* Mike Murrin relished listing his many Conservative helpers:

> Mr Kehoe is wrong to say that none of the Conservative councillors on the Preston Borough Council knew of, or had involvement in my investigation. I had extensive contact with Conservative councillors over a number of years: Audrey Scott, Marjorie Horam, Philip Worrall, Ron Ball, Jack Heatley, Joe Hood, Dorothy Chaloner, Alec Gittins and Mr Jordan.

Despite his desperate personal circumstances, Murrin simply could not give up the great game and loved taping himself talking to reporters:

Murrin: Yeah, now what I have, this is totally off the record, what I'm telling you, right what I did do, what I have done, is to see whether or not I would be in some way offered something, now all the way through, there have been tentative hints, you know, lines thrown out to see whether the bait is taken, well of course, I have never risen to the bait 'cause I've said all the way along, I must never ask for anything, right? Now when I was down in London, with erm, erm, er Carter Rucks at one meeting with erm, Julian Allitt, erm, it came to the point of the tapes, can we have the tapes, and I said well, some of them, erm, at some stage and they said we need them all transcribed, erm, we will pay you to transcribe them. Right? So I, at that point, I accepted money to transcribe the tapes, now I purely accepted the money to transcribe, I did not take the money for the tapes, all right?

Rosthorn: Yeah, quite.

Murrin: Erm, now what I'm worried about with Harrison is that my objective behind the whole thing, as you know, has been to expose political corruption if it's there, right? And to bring out into public er, view and erm, to a proper form of enquiry the allegations that were made concerning corruption. Now my prime motivation behind doing that has been because I was being told that there was an element of money laundering and drugs trade behind it, right? And that has been proved in Liverpool, very heavily into drugs in Liverpool, and the erm, the Special Branch are involved down there as I understand it and the same links in the form of Spencer, were coming in to Preston. Now when I went to Bill Harrison, I said to him - Mr Harrison I'm running an investigation - now he got erm, you know, he was not sort of very impressed with the car I drove and the way I looked I suppose and he decided to, that he could do better than me, right? He buggered it up and then I came back into the picture but I have always worked with Bill Harrison, as with the others, on the strict understanding that I'm pursuing my own enquiries and on the strict understanding that I'm pursuing those enquiries because of my concerns of organised crime or crime-related individuals becoming involved in politics and becoming entwined with politicians, right? Now Harrison's feelings towards Oyston as far as I was concerned was irrelevant, totally irrelevant. Now what I'm concerned about is, I don't want a picture going out to the public of a vendetta having been waged against Oyston with me having been used to run that vendetta by Harrison because that would not be a correct picture.

Rosthorn: Right, yes.

Murrin: Now Harrison gave me the money because I'd told him that I believed that there was drugs behind the allegations of corruption in Preston and that's why he gave me the money and he gave me about five grand.

Rosthorn: Have you got any kind of a paying in slip that could prove that?

Murrin: No, I haven't got a paying in slip, but he won't deny it.

Rosthorn: How was the money paid over, into your bank?

Murrin: No it was paid over in cash.

Rosthorn: Did he ask for a receipt?

Murrin: No.

Rosthorn: And then what did you do with that?

Murrin: No, but he won't deny it, I haven't got a paying in slip, but he won't deny it.

Rosthorn: How was the money paid over, into your bank?

Murrin: No it was paid over in cash.

Rosthorn: Did he ask for a receipt?

Murrin: No.

Rosthorn: And then what did you do with that?

Murrin: Well this is the other point, all the money I received, every penny I've received including the receipt from Oyston, has all gone to cover legitimate expenses, a lot of it went to pay Chris More, erm, there was something like 200 company searches there was somebody I paid to go through those searches and list all the details from them, so every last farthing went on running the enquiry. I received not a penny of personal benefit. Now if you look back through my credit history...

Rosthorn: I've repeatedly quoted you on that so...

Murrin: Well I've got a file here, four inch thick of county court judgements, bankruptcy petitions and final notices so I mean I haven't had a bloody ha'penny out of it.

Rosthorn: It seems to me that it might be possible for you to tell Bill Harrison that you're not going to let Oyston have these tapes to do what he wants with, which he'll be very relieved to hear.

Murrin: Well he, he, look the other point is erm Andrew, right, Bill Harrison trusts me, he trusts me totally, now he knows what I've done. I met him on Sunday, this last Sunday, now he trusts me totally you see and I, you know, I've got a great respect for the guy really, erm, far more so than people like Atkins and I don't want him being put up front and having a erm, er, being the puppeteer with me being the puppeteer orchestrating a vendetta against Oyston, because that is not the way it was. It was not that way at all. You see I've given Oyston those tapes, I gave him those tapes to coax him into court and they did. They became the cornerstone of his case Erm, but I made sure that I had a letter saying they could only be used in litigation so basically, he's got all the information but he can't use it, which must be a very frustrating situation to be in.

On October 25 the magazine *Private Eye* was first to reveal Bill Harrison's part in the campaign against Oyston. The *Eye* reported that Murrin was transcribing forty hours of tapes of his conversations with his backers and informants and handing them over to Oyston. In November, Murrin sent copies of the tapes of his conversations with Robert Atkins MP to Dale Campbell-Savours, the Labour MP for Workington. Under the headline 'Your Favourite Tories On Tape' *Private Eye* published transcripts of Blaker and Atkins talking to Murrin, including the damning remark from Atkins about getting 'the boys' at the DTI to look at Oyston.

Chris More, the detective who had worked for both Murrin and Bill Harrison, gathering tax information on Oyston, McGrath and Parker, tried to defend his position. Murrin had previously sent him some looted documents for safekeeping. Chris More refused to hand them back, claiming that he was owed £450 by the penniless agitator and harassing Murrin with malicious telephone calls. More even refused an offer of cash from the journalist Paul Halloran, who was by now acting as negotiator for Owen Oyston.

On January 2, 1992, Murrin went to see an assistant chief constable of Lancashire at the police headquarters at Hutton, just outside Preston. Det Chief Supt Bill Hacking asked Murrin to try and recover the documents that were being held by Chris More, so they could be passed to the Operation Angel police team who were very close to arresting the "millionaire councillor" Frank McGrath.

Early in the morning, just five days later, the police arrested McGrath, 41, and his solicitor Colin Marland. The solicitor was a prominent local Tory who had chaired Robert Atkins in an election victory celebration and had stood unsuccessfully for the council as a Tory in 1990. Mrs Emma McGrath, whose own income tax records had been bought and sold by her husband's political opponents, was headmistress of St Mary and St Andrew's Catholic Primary School. She told the *Lancashire Evening Post*:

> It is a fairly shocking thing to happen. But I think we have been expecting it since they have been investigating him for some time.

Paul Halloran, the *Private Eye* reporter who had once asked Murrin to pay him for investigating Oyston, was now investigating the conspirators against Oyston. Researching a *World in Action* TV news programme on the conspiracy, he arranged for Murrin to meet Mark

Hollingsworth, a journalist who later collaborated with Halloran on a celebrated biography of Margaret Thatcher's wayward son.[61] Murrin told Mark Hollingsworth about his contacts with Lord Waddington, Mrs Thatcher's home secretary between 1989 and 1990:

> I have seen him on three or four occasions, one meeting at his constituency office in Clitheroe. He said to me that what I was doing was a public service, at another at his surgery in Preston, he said that the whole affair stank.[62]

Murrin told *World in Action*, 'I have drawn up a statement which was handed to the police. I could bring you a copy of that. That gives a chronological view of what happened.' He gave Halloran and Hollingsworth an idea of just how much money had been sloshing around during the Oyston libel case. Murrin said the *Sunday Times* solicitors, Biddle & Co, had paid Chris More's firm one thousand pounds a day for eight weeks and a London private detective, Frank Dobson, five hundred pounds a day for enquiries in Lancashire.[63]

Chris More was keen to stop Murrin and Paul Halloran from spilling the beans to *World in Action* but decided to meet Halloran in Manchester and hand over the documents for the agreed £450. When Halloran arrived by train to meet Murrin in Preston, Chris More had wired up the Deep Pan Pizza House with hidden microphones, to monitor conversations between the New Zealander, now working for Oyston, and Murrin, the unpredictable political agitator who had instigated More's legally dangerous looting of income tax secrets.

Murrin suspected that Chris More had been working for both sides in the libel battle between Oyston and the *Sunday Times*: 'There's a story going

[61] *Thatcher's Gold: Life and Times of Mark Thatcher*, Simon & Schuster, 1995.

[62] Tape recording by Murrin

[63] This author was also paid by Biddle & Co. for research and assistance.

around that you approached Oyston for money at the same time as you were dealing with Biddle.'

More: What's this about the Inland Revenue?

Murrin: Oh, the Inland Revenue were after me... where I got my information from. They were concerned whether someone had been bribed in the Revenue and I said, 'No.' I said, 'It's, er, erm, it would have come from the accountants.'

More: Course it's come from the accountant's office.

On February 19, More blamed Murrin for wrecking a 'very, very involved plan' which was 'knackered completely' when Murrin failed to 'accidentally' include in papers destined for the eyes of Owen Oyston some details of a criminal allegation made against Paul Halloran in Amsterdam. When the penniless agitator asked for help with a fresh investigation, More said:

> If I am to proceed, I want ten grand, and I want to see it.
> I have someone else interested in backing me.
> If I accept them as a client, whatever I do in regards to Halloran, and anything else that comes out of it, will not come to light.[64]

More wanted to negotiate directly with Oyston. He asked Murrin for telephone numbers but lost control of affairs on March 2, when *World in Action* screened The Dirty War, using Murrin's tape recordings to illustrate the venom behind the plot mounted against Oyston by Murrin, Atkins and Blaker. Murrin certainly appeared as the villain of the piece, but in case anyone was questioning the honour of the men who had arranged his funding, the MPs Atkins and Blaker covered their tracks by putting down a parliamentary early day motion, claiming that The Dirty War had been

[64] Tape recording by Murrin

> wholly misleading in that, *inter alia*, the investigation into the affairs of Mr Owen Oyston was, at all times, that of Mr Michael Murrin.[65]

The *World in Action* executive producer, Ray Fitzwalter, admitted to this author, years later, that 'It was not one of our best efforts' and the carefully constructed TV news story blew back unexpectedly and catastrophically on Owen Oyston.

On March 20, reporter Mark Killick from *World in Action* called Murrin:

> Michael, there's a woman we've got in contact with who's got some information on Owen Oyston. A Miss Hardy... Manchester... She's reluctant to talk to us and wants to talk to you.[66]

Melanie Hardy

[65] House of Commons, Early Day Motion 841, March 10, 1992.

[66] Murrin tape recording

The chic, ash-blonde model agency manager who had been the teenage girlfriend of Peter Martin had watched *World in Action*, The Dirty War. Melanie Hardy said to Murrin:

> Michael, that TV programme was very unfair to you.

Miss Hardy proposed an immediate meeting in Manchester, but soon cancelled. Her former lover Peter Martin called on her with a warning that Murrin might be an agent for Oyston. It would be June before she could meet Michael Murrin. Meanwhile, the agitator lived in the eye of the storm. The aborted *Sunday Express* story on the conspiracy resurfaced in April as a skilful five-page exposition by Chris Blackhurst in editor Rosie Boycott's *Esquire* magazine, across five pages and alongside a glitzy interview with Ivana Trump at Mar-a-Lago in Florida:

> **A seamy saga of smears, death and vendetta. Or how two Tory MPs, a fish and chip shop owner, and a Blackpool wheeler dealer with a secret grudge tried to ruin a socialist millionaire.**
>
> The more Harrison thought about the *Post's* campaign, the more he detected the hand of Oyston, his former business associate. Oyston was a major advertiser with the paper and a friend of Askew. He came to believe that Oyston had encouraged Askew to vilify Parr – and also his daughter.
>
> Even today, he is convinced it was Oyston's doing. "It is very possible that Owen Oyston as a principal advertiser with the *Lancashire Evening Post* had considerable influence on the paper's coverage of my daughter's case."
>
> When asked for evidence that Oyston had encouraged the paper's campaign, all he will say is: "That was the way it was put to me at the time." As to who it was who told him, he won't specify: "Lots of people."

Without hard evidence from Harrison, the claim seems bizarre. True, Oyston and Askew were friends – they went riding and fell-walking together – but Oyston seems genuinely bemused by the idea that he influenced the exposé of Parr. Sitting at home, with his wife Vicki nodding agreement, Oyston revealed that far from being Parr's enemy, he had defended the chief constable to the newspaper. Harrison, he maintained, had got it all wrong.

But that did not stop Harrison from getting his revenge. In later years, Oyston's life became a nightmare. "It was like imagining the worst dream you can ever have", he says, "But the difference was, this was reality."

Esquire reported Robert Atkins saying he was shocked that Murrin had taped his telephone calls:

> Absolutely appalled beyond belief. It is unbelievable behaviour. Conversations you have with people are not always articulate and don't always make sense.

Chris More, a man who had much to lose over the trading of income tax secrets, asked Murrin, 'Is Harrison considering taking legal action against them?' He urged Murrin to sue Carter Ruck and their client Owen Oyston, for releasing the tapes to journalists.

Murrin was now trapped in no man's land between the big battalions. There seemed no sign of the police following up on their arrest of McGrath by striking out against Oyston. Det Chief Supt Hacking told Murrin that Operation Angel was proving 'immensely complicated':

> All that Hacking said to me was, 'You've been at it 12 years and we've been at it 12 months.[67]

[67] Interview with author

It seemed that everyone in journalism now wanted to deny that their informant had ever been the man from the Longridge chip shop. Paul Halloran warned Murrin that the *Sunday Times* had written to *Esquire* denying that Murrin had been Peter Hounam's informant on Derek Hatton. Hounam complained about *World in Action* to the Broadcasting Complaints Commission. Paul Killick called Murrin:

> We are currently having a row with Peter Hounam over our programme. Peter's view is that you had nothing whatsoever to do with any of the three articles that the *Sunday Times* published. [68]

Murrin insisted that:

> They automatically went through the stuff I had sent down on Oyston in Preston and I had moved on and had received some information concerning Derek Hatton in Liverpool and I gave that to the *Sunday Times* and they checked that out. If it hadn't been for the information I gave, concerning Liverpool, the police enquiry in Liverpool wouldn't be going ahead now.'

Murrin told this author:

> If Oyston has got to fire his shots at anybody, or go for anybody because of the damage that has been caused to him, it's not Harrison, it's me, because I did him the damage and I set about planning to cause him maximum damage.

He was defiant:

> The police are not only going to have McGrath, but they are going to have Parker, and if they get Parker, they have Oyston.

On May 19, Murrin agreed to take part in a *Hard News* TV investigation into the allegedly dirty journalism being practiced by Peter Hounam and the freelancers Martin Tomkinson and Andrew Rosthorn. Murrin told Lynn Ferguson, a Channel 4 reporter:

---

[68] Tape recording

> If you look at the articles that the *Sunday Times* did on Liverpool you will see that there is a quote in there that the drugs involvement in Liverpool is so great that there is an involvement by Special Branch because, and I believe I am right in quoting, it has implications for national security.
>
> I gave them specific items of information concerning Derek Hatton and other individuals in Liverpool. They went down, Hounam went down, and checked out the information I gave him. He found it to be accurate.

On June 16, Murrin managed to meet his new informant. On the fifth floor of Four Ways House, Tariff St, Manchester, he met Melanie Hardy. He was back home in Preston by teatime and typing up his report:

> Miss Hardy said she had had a long affair with Mr Peter Martin and had been persuaded by him to register as a director of three companies; Askews Ltd of New Bond Street, London, Model Team Agency Ltd of Portland Street, Manchester and Count 8 Ltd, which may now be trading as Options
>
> Miss Hardy went on to say that Oyston was closely involved with Peter Martin and had put money into Model team and Askews although his name does not appear on any company documentation. The amount put into each business by Osyton is reported to be £30,000. Model Team then provided services for Oyston companies and issued invoices which were not paid.
>
> Martin is alleged to have also carried on business as a private detective and to have been employed by Oyston in this capacity. On one occasion Martin was employed to maintain surveillance on Oyston's wife... Miss Hardy was extremely frightened.
>
> Miss Hardy has said she is facing bankruptcy proceedings from American Express in connection with a company credit card. She claims that Martin forged her signature on the application form for the card and also forged her signature on other company documents. It is my intention to ask Miss Hardy to make a statement to the police. I will suggest this at the next meeting.[69]

[69] Murrin typed report June 16, 1992.

On June 18, Murrin called on the head of Lancashire CID at police headquarters in Hutton. He told Det Chief Supt Hacking about Melanie Hardy. Hacking duly reported to the Assistant Chief Constable and to Det Supt John Jameson of Operation Angel:

> Miss HARDY had some grievance against OYSTON and an assistant of his named Peter MARTIN. She made allegations to MURRIN that MARTIN had committed various criminal offences in relation to Manchester companies in which they were both involved. The criminal offences were forgery of share certificates and other documents.[70]

Hacking put Murrin in touch with the Greater Manchester Police commercial fraud squad. They would 'deal with it'. Within the hour, Murrin was back in Manchester with Melanie Hardy, writing a three-page report on the financial relationship between Peter Martin and Oyston.

> During 1987 Peter Martin claimed he was owed £150,000 by Owen Oyston. Martin was in severe financial difficulties and had been forced to re-mortgage his house. Oyston refused to settle the debt but offered Martin between £5,000 & £10,000 if Martin would sign an agreement that the payment was in full and final settlement of the monies outstanding. Martin did sign the document but then consulted a firm of solicitors in St Helens as to the legal position as the agreement had been signed under duress.
>
> Rostim Ltd was formed to take over the business of Askews. The original business was run by two sisters, Valerie and Gloria, together with their brother Tony Askew. The sisters are described as tough and the brother is described as a very decent man. Oyston put money into Rostim Ltd and the amount is believed to be £30,000 which was described as a personal loan to Valerie Askew. Two share certificates were issued to Miss M. Hardy, one was No. 1 for one share at £1. The second certificate was No 3 for 14,999 shares at £1 each, both certificates were issued on 5/1/90. Mr Martin handed Miss Hardy certificate number three and said, "You are holding these for Owen Oyston."

70 Home Office HOLMES computer printout

> Dusone Ltd was formed to take over the business of Count 8 Ltd and proceeded to trade as Options... a table was booked at an Indian restaurant in London... Among those present at the meal were Melanie Hardy, Peter Martin, Owen Oyston, Lisa Warsfold, Tracy Steel, Kate Fletcher, Nigel Plummer, Sally Nicholson and Victoria Brooks. The models said they would not work for Options until they had been paid arrears due from Count 8. Oyston instructed Martin to sign cheques for the amounts owing.
>
> Martin provided Oyston with women during 1987 and 1988. Martin is noted for his involvement with women and has been known to interfere with underaged girls and has had sexual relations with them. Martin provides women for sex to businessmen in Manchester.

Murrin filed a report to the police on June 18 and telephoned Peter Hounam at the *Sunday Times*. Hounam was still in the dark when he telephoned Murrin as he set off for Manchester by train:

Hounam: Who are we meeting?

Murrin: Well let's not say any more over the phone.

Murrin taped himself asking Peter Hounam to get the *Sunday Times* to carry out company searches on the Melanie Hardy / Peter Martin model agency companies. He passed those searches to Lancashire police.

Murrin and Hounam discussed the forthcoming *Hard News* investigation. It would prove to be the very last *Hard News* programme ever screened. Peter Hounam asked Murrin whether Paul Halloran, the initiator of the programme, was actually being paid by Oyston. Would Carter-Ruck or Oyston 'take the rap' for breaking the agreement to use Murrin's tapes only for legal action against the *Sunday Times*?

Armed with the fresh information from Melanie Hardy it was now Murrin who was calling the shots. In a single day, June 22, he called Melanie Hardy to arrange her meeting with Peter Hounam, called Paul Halloran to discuss arrangements for meeting Owen Oyston in London in July, and took a call from Chris More, the detective who was on the road shadowing Peter Martin for an unknown paymaster.

Next day Murrin and Hounam joined Melanie Hardy for a second briefing about Peter Martin; about the £10,000 that Oyston lent him in 1991, about his night club business partner Chris Quinton [Coronation Street's Brian Tilsley], about an illegally held hand gun and about his recent detective work for the West Midlands engineering firm Triplex Lloyd. Murrin's report on the meeting reached Lancashire police next morning.

He sent the police a company search on Triplex Lloyd on June 29 and pointed out that Melanie Hardy said Peter Martin had been introduced to Triplex Lloyd by Derek Zissman, a senior accountant at KPMG. Zissman was a financier well known to Oyston and the brother of Sir Bernard Zissman, the Conservative Lord Mayor of Birmingham.

Murrin might well be penniless and restricted by powerful libel injunctions from both Owen Oyston and the Chief Constable of Lancashire, but he was now passing to Lancashire police the information that would one day land both Peter Martin and Owen Oyston in jail:

> Hardy has stated that at the time of the Piccadilly takeover, girls from Peter Martin's model agency were provided to Oyston who used them as inducements to shareholders and or businessmen.[71]

On July 5 he wrote to Det Insp Frank Whitehead of the Greater Manchester Police Fraud Commercial Squad:

> There were constant reports of Oyston being provided women by Martin and of Oyston providing women to politicians and business associates. The use of "children" was also the subject of one report. I request a full investigation into the allegations made concerning Martin and Oyston.

---

[71] Murrin report to Lancashire Constabulary

The next day Det Insp Malcolm Robishaw of the GMP fraud squad called Murrin:

> The matters that you have been writing to Insp Whitehead have been passed to me for action.

Robishaw asked Murrin and Melanie Hardy, if they could meet him at the GMP training centre, Sedgeley Park, on July 14. Robishaw asked Murrin to bring documents and let him have Hardy's telephone number. Murrin told Robishaw:

> She will be providing the main evidence. She has repeated that to me in the presence of a journalist.

Robishaw interviewed Murrin on July 14. Things went very badly. Murrin was incensed by Robishaw and expressed his feelings in a letter he posted to Manchester on July 15:

> I have set out below some comments which you will, no doubt, find slightly irritating but that is something you will have to stomach, I have had to tolerate far worse during the past ten years.
> Firstly, I would like to point out that, Oyston is / was a very dangerous man. He has immense charm but preys on people's weaknesses. He came very close to becoming very powerful at a national level with his close connections with Kinnock and other national politicians.
> I believe I am right to claim that had I not kicked the stool from under him by exposing the Inland Revenue investigation into his estate agency business [which I initiated] thus forcing Royal Insurance to get rid of him, he could have pulled it off and become a very significant figure.
> The feeding of information into Kroll Associates ensured that he had to dispose of cable TV for next to nothing and Red Rose shares are down to 50p.
> I always pursued this case because of the constant reports of Oyston being involved in drugs, the provision of prostitutes and the bribing of politicians. Everything about the man is sleazy and dishonest...
> Personally, I acted because I felt I had a duty to do so. I am coming to bitterly regret such misplaced sentiments. As I suspected, from the outset the rats have abandoned ship but I have to admire their cheek in asking me to provide them with lifebelts. Unfortunately, I am not in a position to secure your early

retirement but I will not let you get away with believing that I accept any of this negative thinking.
Oyston and Martin should be brought to book and there should be no more excuses, no more inertia and no more bull.

It was Sir Peter Blaker who had provoked Murrin's remark about rats leaving the ship. Blaker had telephoned Murrin just after Murrin had written the angry letter to Robishaw. Sir Peter wanted Murrin to type 'a simple letter' for Blaker's lawyers, a letter that was designed to defeat Oyston's attempts to win damages from Blaker for conspiracy to defame:

Blaker: Do you remember the problem which we discussed?

Murrin: I don't really know. I don't know. I don't know what's going on, you see.

Blaker: Well, nor do I.

Murrin: Mmm.

Blaker: I think that's why it would help if I tell you a little more about... I take it that you are not happy about the publicity that has occurred?

Murrin: Far from it.

Blaker: And as you can imagine I am not either. And I mentioned to you that it would be helpful to me if you could write a letter, a simple letter to... of the kind we discussed when we last spoke, that I could defend myself if I were to be asked.

Murrin: Have you been asked?

Blaker: Yes.

Murrin: By who?

Blaker: By a friend. And what I'm suggesting is nothing more than you can really say, because it would be simpler and shorter. The problem about what you have already written to me is that it contains a lot of material which has not yet been shown to anybody. And there is another factor... I talked to my lawyer about the further publicity at the time. I'm going to see him again soon. Two things in that letter would be helpful and could be used by him with some prospect of stopping... Sorry can you hold on a minute? He could possibly by legal means use such a letter to prevent further publications and that, I think, would be very useful if it could be achieved. But of course he couldn't use the letter of the long kind that you've written, and a lot of other material, for that purpose. He could use the letter for proof that you were... well. He could use the letter of a very simple kind which simply makes the point that the tapes were tampered with and montaged and useless... what you are reported as saying to the West Lancashire Gazette. That is the main point. And that one is the main point which was in the letter which I suggested you might write, repeating what you said in other letters already. If you wanted to add that you confirmed that at no point did I seek to influence your inquiries or pressure you into investigating specific matters, that would also be helpful, but it's not the main point. The main point is...

Murrin: The main point for you... It may not be the main point for me.

Blaker: It's something you want to say isn't it?

Murrin: Well of course it is. I'm...

Blaker: If you want to say that, that helps, it suits me. It's true, amongst other things. So what I want you to copy...

Murrin: Just hang on a minute. *Murrin talks to a child.* Go on.

Blaker: I'm not planning to use this against you and I'm hoping that it could be of use in the interest both of myself and yourself, as you've just explained to me you don't want to see further articles of the kind that have appeared. But I think it's in both our interests that it should be done. I thought that perhaps it might help if I explained.

Murrin: Have you heard of anything else going on?

Blaker: No. How do you see the thing?

Murrin: Well, I don't know. I think that it would be interesting to see if the police come up with anything I suppose.

Blaker: Yes. But of course I'm not in touch. I'm further from the scene of activity.

Murrin: I don't know how true these things are but I understand they will be charging Parker.

Blaker: As I recall, there was... Operation Angel. Am I right in thinking that it involved him? In the sense there was a police...

[*Blaker had actually given inaccurate information about Harold Parker's son to an Operation Angel detective four months earlier*]

Murrin: Oh yes. Raided them. They've already charged his son.

Blaker: Well I don't know. I was not intentionally in touch with these things really My main purpose is to stop further articles and programmes of the kind of which have appeared, which I regard as wholly misleading. I very much agree with what you said in one of your letters that... because... they give a wholly false report of the reality.

Murrin: Mmm.

Blaker: And therefore, I would like to do what I can to prevent them appearing again. And this is the one way of perhaps achieving that result, so my lawyer advises me. So if you feel like writing me a letter of that kind, just, may I just suggest the two points, one, that the tampering, that is the point, that the tapes cannot be relied on and that may help prevent them being used again, and secondly...

Murrin: Well, I think he's already done that.

Blaker: Who's done that?

Murrin: Well, I don't think that any of the Press will use them again.

Blaker: Well one would like to be sure.

Murrin: I don't think they'll use them again.

Blaker: Why do you say that?

Murrin: Because I stamped on it when I saw the article.

Blaker: Stamped on it in what sense?

Murrin: I told them that the tapes were being tampered with.

Blaker: You told the...

Murrin: I told the Press and the magazine, once they were published.

Blaker: Well, you told the Press locally.

Murrin: I told the Press locally. I told the Press nationally as well.

Blaker: You told them nationally?

Murrin: Mmm.

Blaker: Through some organisation that would make sure the Press knew.

Murrin: Mmm.

Blaker: I see.

Murrin: Well, you should do.

Blaker: Yes.

Murrin: Why? Have you had some comeback?

Blaker: No. I haven't I haven't been talking to the Press. I read the report in the West Lancashire Gazette. I didn't read another report anywhere else that they'd been tampered with, so I'm interested to know that you've told the Press.

Murrin: There was one in... I think Blackpool Evening Gazette. The Lancashire Evening Post didn't cover it because I told them before the article was published.

Blaker: But of course there has been national articles, in Esquire and in *Private Eye* and in... then there were two television programmes and they were highly misleading in my opinion. They completely had the wrong end of the stick. I think that they were wholly tendential and one wouldn't want that view to be repeated.

Murrin: Mmm.

Blaker: Anything that can be done, I think, is desirable to do... I'm not sure what you would lose by writing these letters.

Murrin: I'm not clear what I would lose. I'm quite obviously being extra careful. I'm still getting funny approaches and...

Blaker: Of what kind?

Murrin: Of all kinds. I mean you can't do what I've done to the likes of Carter Ruck and not expect some comeback. I fully expect that if Parker is arrested then Old Oyston will be very edgy.

Blaker: Isn't it desirable that I should be able to get my lawyer's advice on what can be done from a legal point of view to prevent further publications on these lines. Surely that reinforces the case?

Murrin: Well it's not publicity that I'm worried about, it's petrol through my letter box.

Blaker: Well naturally I hope that doesn't happen, but...

Murrin: Yeah, but I'm the only one that's going to look after me if it does.

Blaker: Well, highly unlikely, because...

Murrin: There's a lot of things about this case which are unlikely.

Blaker: Yes I understand your...

Murrin: He did not photograph my children for nothing.

Blaker: Well what do you lose by what I've just been suggesting, writing me a letter of the kind that I can discuss with the lawyer?

Murrin: I don't think I need anything.

Blaker: I don't think you do. Both you and I.

Murrin: I've had no contact with Harrison.

Blaker: No. No contact. I haven't had contact with anybody except yourself. These contacts...

Murrin: I'm certainly absolutely furious about the publicity.

Blaker: I echo your feelings about that.

Murrin: I would be very careful about mentioning cable television. That's only my thought...

Blaker: Well there's no need to mention that.

Murrin: Because that could be twisted to say, 'That's why he was involved.' And as far as I'm concerned, you might have had your own motives, but that's not the motives you came across to me with.

Blaker: Oh, really?

Murrin: Huh?

Blaker: That's how it all began as far as I was concerned.

Murrin: What? The cable television?

Blaker: The reason that I was interested in the whole subject was because of the cable television process which I mentioned to you when we first met.

Murrin: That was...

Blaker: That was why I was interested in the subject at all.

Murrin: Well you wouldn't like it to come across that you were seeking to demolish a competitor, would you? No. But that's the way it could be interpreted.

Blaker: Indeed I would welcome an opportunity of explaining why the cable television angle interested me.

Murrin: Why? Because you felt it had been an improper process?

Blaker: Yes.

Murrin: Mmm.

Blaker: Indeed I explained all that to you when we met. I see that it can be twisted if one is not careful. I think it probably better not to mention it in this letter, so I was going to suggest that you might take out any reference to that and I don't know whether you have your draft there, but if you have, I would take out the last two sentences reading, 'There was no conspiracy,' and take your mind off why I was involved. I was going to suggest that anyway, because I think that's a bit of a red herring, and simply limit it to saying, 'I confirm

> that at no point did you seek to influence my enquiries or pressure me to investigate specific matters. The investigation was my own.' And end on that note.

Unknown to Murrin, who was by now seen as a very loose cannon, Greater Manchester Police did carry out a secret investigation into Peter Martin's model agency in 1992, conducted by Malcolm Robishaw and Det Sgt Harry Harrison. The investigation was not revealed until January 1996, when sensitive documents were handed over to defence lawyers at the eleventh hour before Oyston went on trial for raping girls from the Model Team agency.

The names of models who later featured in the 1996 court cases had been listed by Melanie Hardy and handed over to Det Sgt Harrison and Det Con Julie Sharpe, who both later worked on a 1994 investigation that followed a police raid on Peter Martin's home. Harrison's 1992 report, based on interviews with Melanie Hardy and another agency manager called Carole Jones, mentioned allegations about Martin using a grille in the wall at the agency to look at naked models. This allegation, 'borrowed' from the secret investigation, was mentioned by police in their first press releases after the 1994 raid. But the 1992 inquiry concluded negatively. Murrin was seen as almost unbalanced and Melanie Hardy was not prepared to make a complaint against Peter Martin.

Sgt Harrison had asked his two informants, Melanie Hardy and Carole Jones, to gather the names and addresses of girls at the agency. Robishaw reported to Det Insp Anson of Greater Manchester Police on July 17:

> This office has received information from a Michael Hugh Murrin of Preston regarding the activities of businessman Owen Oyston who lives in Lancashire.
> Murrin is also supplying information to Det Chief Insp Maloney, Lancashire Constabulary Commercial Fraud Squad, regarding Oyston and members of

Preston Borough Council. Murrin has a fixation about these matters and in particular has conducted a vendetta against Oyston.

The information Murrin has supplied to this office does not disclose any offences in this force area although some information has been passed to Det Chief Insp Maloney re-relevant Lancashire matters.

A side issue of all these matters is that Murrin has directed me to Melanie Yvonne Hardy b 6.6.62 and Carole Jones b 26 8 43. Both these women are model agents who in the past have been associated with Central Models [latterly Model Team] of 44, Portland Street, Manchester. The agency is allegedly owned by Oyston although he is not shown on paper as the owner.

The manager of this agency is Philip Charles Billington Martin b 3.1.44 [no previous convictions] of 82 Northenden Road, Sale, an ex-Manchester PC. He uses the alias Peter Martin.

Both Hardy and Jones allege that Martin uses his position to influence girls under the age of 16 into having sex with him either at his offices or his home address. These offences allegedly take place on Saturdays and Sundays when model training for young girls takes place at the agency. At these times some out of town girls stay at Martin's home in Sale.

Martin has a common law wife named Tracey Grainey who may also be involved in these matters. It is understood that Martin has made a ventilation cover in his office which directly overlooks the agency changing room. The inference is that he uses this vent to watch girls changing. The information contained in this report results directly from Hardy and Jones. I believe they are truthful but I am also aware that they have personal grudges against Martin and Oyston.

Hardy and Jones supply some direct evidence regarding the allegation, i.e. evidence of what they have seen or heard. However, they are not prepared at this stage to make witness statements as they are in fear of Martin who has a reputation for violence. I ask therefore that if Hardy and Jones are re-interviewed caution and confidentiality are exercised by the interviewer.

The police still had to deal with Murrin's intemperate letter to Robishaw, so Det Chief Insp Anson reported on August 3:

> Murrin is a prolific writer of letters to the police, MPs, ministers, government departments, etc. and has made a series of complaints to Lancashire Constabulary alleging corruption and malpractice by Preston Borough councillors in respect of land deals: however no hard evidence has ever been uncovered which would justify criminal proceedings in respect of his allegations.
> MURRIN is said by detective Chief Inspector Moloney of the Lancashire Constabulary Commerce Branch to have developed a personal vendetta against Owen OYSTON who MURRIN believes has manipulated Preston Borough councillors to his own advantage in respect of land deals in which OYSTON has concealed interests...
> Over the past few years MURRIN has written to Lancashire Constabulary on a regular basis making allegations of corruption against OYSTON and his business associates. These have been investigated but not substantiated.
> In February / March 1992 MURRIN appeared in a Channel 4 television documentary which focused on the leader of Derbyshire County Council, David BOOKBINDER, and his alleged association with OYSTON. There was an inference of, at least, malpractice.

In fact, it was the Granada *World in Action* documentary *The Dirty War* that exposed the Murrin-Atkins-Blaker plot against Oyston and Bookbinder. Viewers had heard tape recordings of Blaker talking to Murrin about having Oyston arrested. Anson's report made it clear that he had been briefed by Lancashire police. Mentioning the TV programme showed that at least one senior officer in Greater Manchester Police knew of the campaign against Oyston being waged by Atkins and Blaker. But not Det Supt Bill Roberts, the head of the team that investigated the Oyston case in 1995.

Bill Roberts swore on oath in the third trial of Oyston that he had been unaware of the civil action being brought by Oyston against the ex-cabinet ministers when he took the decision to arrest Oyston, just three weeks before the civil case against Atkins and Blaker came to court.

The remaining matters in the 1992 investigation were covered by a report from Det Sgt Harry Harrison after his interviews with Melanie Hardy and Carole Jones:

> Interviewed both Hardy & Jones. Nothing witnessed. All innuendo and suspicion. No love lost between Tracey Grainey and Melanie Hardy as they were both going out with Philip Martin at the same time.

Det Sgt Harrison concluded:

> It is all supposition on behalf of Jones and Hardy and I have asked them to ascertain girls' names and addresses who they consider to have been abused by Martin from a friend of theirs who still works for Martin. No further action can be taken until we have any complaints. So we must await further developments from Jones / Hardy. to look into the under-age sex allegations against Martin.

Harry Harrison and Julie Sharpe listed the names, ages and addresses of sixteen girls, said to be at risk by Jones and Hardy. But the police took no further action in 1992 or 1993. The police did not contact the parents of the under-age girls on the list.

Two years later, in September 1994, armed with a fresh complaint about Martin from a mother and daughter, Det Sgt Harrison raided Peter Martin's house. Tracey Grainey went to answer the front door as the police broke through the back door and caught Martin hiding video-cassettes in the loft.

Despite Det Sgt Harrison's work in the 1992 Murrin/Hardy/Jones investigation, his 1992 reports were hidden from the Crown Prosecution Service and from defence lawyers until February 8, 1996, just a few days before committal proceedings began in multiple rape charges against Oyston.

The papers were logged on to the HOLMES police computer on that day by Det Sgt Harrison, the officer who had been involved in both the 1992 and 1994 investigations of the model agency. Consequently, in the three forthcoming rape trials of Owen Oyston there was no mention of the fact that police investigations of the model agency had begun with the reports from Murrin and that the police personnel who investigated Oyston in 1994 had been the officers who had followed up the allegations from Murrin and Melanie Hardy in 1992. Neither Murrin nor Melanie Hardy would appear at any of the many future court hearings in the Oyston Affair.

CHAPTER 13

Oyston versus Atkins & Blaker

Owen Oyston desperately wanted to use Michael Murrin's tape recordings to force Sir Peter Blaker, Robert Atkins and Bill Harrison into a civil court and win damages for defamation. But the tapes were late. By February 1991, Murrin had only handed over a couple of micro-cassettes and it was September 24, 1991, before the tapes that proved the case had landed in the hands of Alasdair Pepper at Peter Carter-Ruck and Partners in London. The tapes supported Oystons's claim against Blaker, Atkins and Harrison, showing how they

> had authorized and paid Murrin to publish numerous and grave slanders of him including that he: had committed such crimes as tax evasion and corporate fraud; had used illegal narcotics and was involved in trafficking; was a blackmailer; was involved in prostitution; had committed acts of bribery and corruption; held orgies; was a paedophile and involved in child pornography and procurement; was involved in organised crime and laundering money.

The slanders were time-barred, outside the three-year time limit for defamation. Carter-Ruck needed leave of the High Court to get an additional period of a year allowed from the date 'on which the Plaintiff knew all the facts, previously unknown to him, which are relevant to his cause of action.'

"Mindful of the looming limitation problem", Carter Ruck went before Master Rose, the Practice Master, for advice on whether they could proceed *ex parte,* without having served writs on the respondents, Blaker, Atkins, Harrison and Murrin. Master Rose consulted colleagues overnight before finding no objection to the application being made *ex parte.* Oyston could now sue them. Unfortunately for Oyston, three of the alleged conspirators, the three with enough money to pay for lawyers, later managed to reverse this judgment, by arguing that Master Rose had erred when he allowed the application to be made *ex parte.* News of this legal battle broke in February 1993, when Murrin announced:

> I am penniless. I have been told I am going to be committed to prison for non-payment of £1113 in business rates. I have lost my shop. All my possessions have been sold by the village auctioneer. All I own is the clothes I wear and the shoes I stand up in. I expect to be jailed for my rates before I can face up to this libel hearing. I didn't really expect to finish up in this situation.

The evidence that proved *conspiracy to defame* would eventually be discussed in Prime-Minister John Major's dining room. It would end the Westminster career of the prime-minister's closest political ally. But it would not allow Oyston to drag his opponents into court,

Oyston was raising the stakes. He certainly had the cash to pay for a legal battle with his wealthy opponents; the privy councillor, the cricketing pal of the prime-minister and the bad-tempered property millionaire from Greyfriars Hall. But Oyston was short of information. He was soon to find in a legal fight at this level, he had too many enemies and too few friends.

Raising the stakes sealed his fate. For one reason, he was living and working too close to the doomed private eye Peter Martin. For another, the solicitors who fought his successful battle with the *Sunday Times* were hit below the waterline by the faulty *ex parte* application.

In August 1993, Mr Justice Ognall set aside Master Rose's decision, ordering Oyston to pay costs and refusing leave to appeal. Oyston bounced back. An Appeal Court judge granted leave to appeal, so that Atkins, Blaker and Harrison would remain facing the threat of public disgrace in 1994.

They remained under legal pressure, even though Oyston complained that his lawyers, Peter Carter Ruck & Partners. were dragging their feet. Lord Justice Henry eventually concluded in 1995 that Oyston's 'specialist libel solicitors' had indeed been 'sailing very close to the wind.'

Carter-Ruck also struggled to handle the unpredictable and utterly penniless fourth respondent, Michael Murrin, the man the solicitors needed to validate the tape recordings. To make matters worse, the private detective Chris More was bugging Murrin's telephones, inspecting his bank accounts and photographing him whenever he tried to make contact with Oyston's new helper, Paul Halloran.

More: Well how did Rosthorn know that this meeting was photographed then? How did he know the details of the meeting?"

Murrin: Well it's not going to happen now.

More: It's not going to happen now. But I think what we must do tactically is to let him think it has. Now we've got a leak here matey. We've got a leak somewhere. First of all, let's clear the decks.

Murrin: Well my...

More: I, I, I, I... Are you listening to me?

Murrin: Mmm.

More: Well I have a score to settle

Someone had warned Paul Halloran that he was being photographed. Was it David Hooper of Biddle & Co, the solicitor for the *Sunday Times*, or was it Robert Atkins, or even Lord Blaker, or perhaps Frank Dobson, their detective?

More: I did something on Friday that I have never ever done before... I offered my services to Peter Blaker and Atkins for free.

On May 24, 1993, Carter-Ruck decided to bring Murrin to heel with a statutory demand, to repay the £1,500 lent to him by Oyston in 1991. The demand misfired, as Murrin hit back by releasing the letter to the *Independent on Sunday*. Under his new banner, Alpha Investigations, Murrin circulated a 22-page financial survey of dozens of Oyston's businesses, alleging convincingly that most of them were losing money, twelve million in a year.

While Murrin made trouble with what would be known one day as 'fake news' Peter Martin managed to entangle Oyston in Britain's most vicious business battle of the day, a titanic dirty tricks struggle between British Airways and Virgin Atlantic.

Using the pseudonym *Peter Green,* Martin attempted to *'sting'* David Burnside, director of public affairs at the newly-privatised British Airways. The 'stinger' and his selected victim were well matched. Burnside, the canny son of a Protestant farmer from Ballymoney, Co Antrim, had been press officer in Northern Ireland for Bill Craig's terrifying right-wing Vanguard Party.

According to a 30-page confidential report by British Airways detectives, a certain 'Peter Green' was claiming to have been hired by Richard Branson's Virgin Atlantic to spy on the BA chairman, Lord King, and assemble evidence to show that David Burnside had been stealing from BA.

Julian Allitt, managing director of Piccadilly Radio in Manchester, passed this false story to Burnside and on April 13, 1992, Burnside travelled to the Tickled Trout Hotel near the M6 in Preston, to meet the mysterious

Peter Green. The chairman of Julian Allitt's firm was Owen Oyston, already a business partner of Richard Branson. Oyston agreed to oblige his new friend Peter Martin by introducing David Burnside to the bogus informant *Peter Green* at the Tickled Trout Hotel.

Burnside was to be shadowed by British Airways detectives. The BA men had been tailing the mysterious Green in a month-long investigation carried out in Preston, London and Manchester under the code-name Operation Covent Garden They observed Burnside as he met Owen Oyston and the mysterious *Green* at the Tickled Trout. One week later they were watching at the Stanneylands Hotel near Manchester Airport as Burnside arrived to join a gathering of journalists, advertising reps and a number of girls from Model Team International, all staged by Peter Martin, posing as *Peter Green*.

A stunning woman called Lisa French introduced herself to David Burnside. She assured him that 'Owen' would be along later and suggested going on to a party. The BA detectives observed Burnside declining Lisa French's invitation. Burnside arranged another meeting with his informant in London, but in the words of the BA surveillance report:

> It was apparent during this meeting, that 'Peter Green', far from revealing anything to David Burnside, was in fact trying to elicit information which would assist him in his inquiry, a pretext form of investigation often used by skilful interviewers.

After the London meeting, the BA team followed *Green / Martin* back to Manchester by train and found themselves in a hair-raising car chase as *Green / Martin* tried to throw off his shadowers by driving his Toyota Supra sports car in the wrong lane under illuminated red crosses in the notorious London Road tidal-flow traffic system.

> He drove this car at speed and against both traffic flow and regulations. He drove in the direction of Sale in Cheshire where he did a U-turn in the middle

> of the road. However, our surveillance showed that he returned to 82, Northenden Road.

The BA men found 'a complex web of deceit'. The Toyota was leased to the Oyston Organisation. *Green* was found to be Peter Billington Martin, a former Manchester policeman, claiming to be hired by Trade Reports plc, a firm run by two Manchester businessmen, Michael David Thompson and John Puddifoot, the pair who had helped Peter Martin extort five thousand pounds from the luckless Wolverhampton civil engineer Kevin Cullis.

The BA team reckoned that Trade Reports plc was owned by Oyston:

> A company, owned by Owen Oyston, was actively working on an investigation into David Burnside and by the admission of one of its staff, into British Airways.

David Burnside lost his BA job after the airline settled out of court with Branson and Virgin in 1993. BA apologised "unreservedly" in the High Court for the "dirty tricks" campaign and agreed to pay half a million in damages to Richard Branson, £110,000 to Virgin Atlantic and Branson's legal costs of £3 million. David Burnside appeared to bear no grudge against Oyston, for he later turned up at a Claughton Hall shooting party. Described in the local newspaper as 'a businessman from Northern Ireland' he was found by a villager asleep in a car at 7:00 am on an August morning with the engine running and the headlights on. Lancaster magistrates heard the intoximeter reading was three times the legal limit. They banned him from driving for three years after the defence said it would be his first drink driving conviction since 1985.

Burnside returned to Northern Ireland and served as both a Westminster MP and a Stormont MP for the Ulster Unionist Party between 2001 and 2009, when he opposed both his UUP leader and the momentous Good Friday peace agreement in Ireland. In 2018, Open Democracy[72] announced that Burnside had been for ten years PR man for Vincent Tchenguiz, the largest shareholder in SCL Group, the company that created Cambridge Analytica, closed down during the Facebook data scandal after 'misappropriation of digital assets, data mining, brokerage and data analysis with strategic communication' during Britain's referendum on EU membership.

Owen Oyston walked tall in the land in 1994, leading Blackpool's most famous footballer Sir Stanley Matthews on to the pitch at Bloomfield Road to announce the construction of a new football stadium with a retractable translucent roof, planned for a greenfield site outside the town. He threatened that the club would 'die' if planning permission for his 'Wembley of the North' were denied.

He stunned the City in February 1994 by deciding to sell his pivotal 24 per cent stake in Trans World Communications and precipitate a battle for control in the booming radio market between his despised partners Guardian Media Group and Emap:

> Trans World, which is headed by John Whitney, the former director-general of the Independent Broadcasting Authority and chairman of Andrew Lloyd Webber's Really Useful Group, has enjoyed a chequered history. If Mr Oyston sells his shares – he is believed to be looking for £20m for them – it would bring to an end a turbulent period in the company's history.[73]

Emap won the battle and Oyston raised about fifteen million pounds.

One day in August 1994, in unexplained circumstances, two of Peter Martin's most successful models arranged a meeting in Ronnie's Café Bar, a smart coffee house operating in the old Kardomah building in Albert

---

[72] Adam Ramsay and Peter Geoghegan, Open Democracy, March 23, 2018.

[73] Independent on Sunday, Chris Blackhurst, February 20, 1994

Square, Manchester. Melanie Hardy, Mike Murrin's 1992 informant, was now a *booker* at a rival agency in central Manchester known as Boss. She fixed up a meeting with Lisa French, the girl from Model Team who had chatted up David Burnside in the attempted British Airways sting at Stanneylands Hotel. Lisa, 20, came from Warrington and her real name was Lysa Rubotham. She was just back from Japan and was still in touch with Model Team. Just how this meeting came to be arranged was never explained, largely because in all the trials and civil court cases that followed the fateful encounter between the two women, despite questions from jurors and judges, the English adversarial legal system ensured that Melanie Hardy would never appear in court.

Over coffee at Ronnie's, Melanie asked Lysa if she would to talk to the police about Peter Martin. Melanie telephoned Lysa later and arranged the first of 27 police interviews between Lysa Rubotham and Greater Manchester Police - fifty hours of interrogation.

Model Team were going to be raided. The aunt of a 13-year old girl attending modelling lessons at Model Team International had complained about Peter Martin at Eccles police station. Det Sgt Harry Harrison and the Family Support Unit of Greater Manchester Police were back on the case.

CHAPTER 14

Videos in the Loft

Det Sgt Anthony Griffiths of Greater Manchester Police raided Peter Martin's 'model house' in Northenden Road, Sale, at 07:20 on September 23, 1994. He carried a search warrant. There was no reply when he knocked on the front door. Peering into the letter box he saw the elegant figure of Tracey Grainey dashing upstairs. He broke a window to open the back door and chased Peter Martin's lover up to the first floor: 'At the top of the stairs, I saw a pair of ankles sticking out of the loft.'

Peter Martin's bare legs were dangling from a trap door to the loft. He was wearing underpants and a T-shirt and covered in black dust. He was holding a box that was not dusty. The box contained 51 videotape cassettes found to have been filmed at the city offices of Model Team and featuring young girls dressing and undressing in the changing rooms. This was exactly what Murrin and his informant Melanie Hardy had alleged to police in 1992. Other tapes showed Tracey Grainey having sex on different occasions with at least nine different men and one beautiful 16-year old girl.

The police managed to identify a number of businessmen who had taken part in 180 hours of videotaped sex scenes. One of the men identified was the former chairman of Piccadilly Radio, Julian Allitt, a former parliamentary lobby correspondent of the *Lancashire Evening Post*. Det Chief Insp Martin Flaherty later told a court that two files were sent to the Crown Prosecution Service with a view to the potential prosecution of Julian Allitt and an Italian restaurateur named Giorgio Balduni.

Tracey Grainey

Thanks to what Det Sgt Harry Harrison knew from his 1992 interviews with Melanie Hardy and Carol Jones, set up for him by Michael Murrin, Harry Harrison knew exactly where to look next. At 12:30 that day Det Sgt John Ashley of the Obscene Publications Unit raided Model Team at 44, Portland Street.

By 3.00 pm, Ashley was interviewing Melanie Hardy in the smart offices of Model Team's rival, the Boss agency. Ashley logged a report on HOLMES, the Home Office Large Major Enquiry System developed in London and Manchester to tackle co-ordination problems on big cases, particularly after the long hunt for the Yorkshire Ripper. A HOLMES computer printout later showed to defence lawyers that Det Sgt Ashley already knew much about Oyston's involvement with Peter Martin. Ashley used Oyston's business nickname, OJO, in a police document. Oyston was clearly going to be part of Greater Manchester's forthcoming investigation, designated that day as Operation Chittering:

> HARDY suspects that girls from the agency were made available to a number of Martin's male friends [including OJO]

Three days later the Operation Chittering team were joined by their new senior investigating officer, Det Supt William 'Bill' Roberts, a man well known for taking scrupulous care over his work, a father of three children with 26 years service who was just returning from his summer holidays.

Melanie Hardy had told Det Sgt Ashley how to get in touch with Lysa Rubotham, using her Model Team name, Lisa French. The police identified Lysa on the first day and computer-coded her as a key witness in the case. Next day, accompanied by a woman police officer, John Ashley met Lysa at Newton-le-Willows police station, near her mother's home. For four or five hours that days he interviewed Lysa at the Thistle Hotel near Haydock Park racecourse.

Det Sgt Ashley reported:

> Lisa RUBOTHAM, born 26/11/73, 20 years of age. Currently unemployed having just returned from Athens where she worked as a dancer. Sergeant ASHLEY and Constable STONE interviewed Lisa at 10am (1000hrs) on Tuesday 27th September 1994 (27/09/94) at Newton Le Willows. Lisa started

as a student model at the Model Team Agency, 24 Mosley Street, Manchester, in 1985 at the age of 11 years having responded to an advertisement in the Manchester Evening News. Initially with a friend from school, she attended weekend classes, where the girls were weighed, wearing nothing other than a towel. The girls had to strip off all their clothes in a changing room that adjoined the studio. MARTIN'S office also adjoined this changing room.
The girls, when wearing only a towel, would be checked physically by one of the class leaders (female) to ensure they were naked underneath the towel. It was apparent to Lisa that from an early stage she was singled out for special attention by MARTIN, who regularly passed comment on her 'beautiful long legs'. At the age of 13 years she was in MARTIN's office when a girl called Karen WALSH lay on the settee and MARTIN laid on top of her - she was surprised at this. Soon after this, whilst still 13 years she was called to MARTIN'S office, introduced to Owen OYSTON and made to stand in front of him in just a swimming costume whilst MARTIN passed comment on her legs. At this time Lisa became aware that certain of the girls were sleeping at Sale at MARTIN'S house. These girls together with Lisa and MARTIN regularly on a Saturday evening ate out at a number of Manchester restaurants. At the end of the evening MARTIN would drive Lisa home and the girls would be taken to Sale by Tracey GRAINEY. From the age of 14 1/2 years Lisa was given tablets by MARTIN to further reduce her weight, apparently diuretics and possibly amphetamines. These she believed were obtained privately by MARTIN from Dr Joseph Barsh KASTANZY?? a Maltese national, with a clinic in Manchester and also a doctor at the MRI. He was a regular visitor to the agency treating MARTIN for diabetes and GRAINEY for some medical problem (heart?). Lisa first stayed at MARTIN'S home in Sale when she was 15 years old. Tracy GRAINEY was also staying there. Soon after getting there MARTIN stripped down to his underpants. Lisa was told to go upstairs to shower and provided with a T shirt - very short to wear and was told not to wear any underwear in bed as it was unhygienic. She was told to come back downstairs before going to bed. She was worried about going downstairs in just the T-shirt and put a dressing gown on. On going into the lounge MARTIN seemed angry when he saw her and said he wanted to see her legs now that she was dieting. She showed her legs through the dressing gown and was told to go to bed. She was told she must leave the bedroom door open in case of fire. Lisa then started to stay regularly at Sale and was told to tell her mother that it was Tracy's house and not to mention that Peter was there. Around this time MARTIN started to touch her bottom and say how firm it was and commented on how firm her breasts were. He asked her whether she liked men with beards and kissed her full on the lips in the

kitchen in Tracy's presence. On another occasion she was at the house, she was wearing leggings when MARTIN passed comment that she had lost so much weight her pubic bone was sticking out and placed his hand on her pubic area. Tracy was present and MARTIN put her hand on to Lisa's pubic area also whilst they discussed it. Lisa was 15 years old at the time. When Lisa was 16 years and 1 week old, she had intercourse with MARTIN at Sale. They only had intercourse on this one occasion. Shortly after this Lisa was introduced by MARTIN to a number of his male friends, who visited the agency. Relationships developed and she would be taken out for meals and bought presents. She naively says that these men were her boyfriends. At the age of 16 years she was seeing four different men, all of whom were over the age of 40 years. These relationships became full sexual ones. She was never allowed to take the men to Sale, where by this time she was living with MARTIN and GRAINEY. She was told by MARTIN to take the men to the Agency at Portland Street and given her own keys. The men that Lisa went with and had intercourse with were: Owen OYSTON, Nino MILANO, Giorgio, Julian ALLIT [sic], Warren HUDSON [sic].

In a later 10-hour interview at St Mary's Rape Crisis Centre in Manchester, Lysa supplied dozens of names of the men and women involved with the agency. The news of the police raid broke next day in an exclusive by Steve Panter on the front page of the *Manchester Evening News*:

SECRET CAMERA ON NAKED GIRLS

Child models filmed through grille

HUNDREDS of child models were secretly videoed as they undressed for fashion-photo sessions. Girls aged 10 and upwards were filmed naked in a mirrored room at a reputable model agency in Manchester. Today detectives set up a major inquiry and were trying to trace the children caught naked on camera...

Det Supt Bill Roberts confirmed: "We have an inquiry under way which is progressing. We want to hear from any parent who has taken their daughter to Central Models in Portland Street, Manchester...
Parents can contact police from Monday on 061 856 7832.

On October 1, the *News of the World* turned Bill Roberts's appeal for parents to come forward into a nationwide story:

Pervert videoed girls, 10 in nude

Filming girls under 17 naked is illegal under obscenity laws.
Worried parents can contact police from tomorrow on 061 856 7832.

The special telephone at Stretford police station rang night and day. Det Chief Insp Martin Flaherty, second in command of Operation Chittering, said to reporter Adrian Darbyshire:

> Two phones were manned from 8am to 10pm and the shortest time between putting a phone down and picking it up again was 13 seconds, but of course not all calls mentioned any allegations of impropriety. On the proforma we asked the question: 'Did anything untoward happen?' and we were able to prioritise the calls that way.
> The other suggestion is that it is all a set-up as part of this conspiracy. But Oyston's name didn't crop up until ten days into the inquiry.

The astonishing news brought Mike Murrin back into battle. On October 3, he arranged for a reporter [Andrew Rosthorn] to interview Melanie Hardy.

On October 5, Miss Hardy told Rosthorn and Nick Pritchard of the *News of the World* that the police had told her not to speak to the press. Nevertheless:

> A beautiful model claims socialist millionaire Owen Oyston is the real owner of the model agency that was raided by police who discovered that girls under 17 have been secretly filmed nude in the changing room...
>
> Ex-policeman and former boss of Model Team, Peter Martin, questioned after a raid in which police seized illegal nude videos of over thirty young girls said, "I am not the owner". Melanie Hardy, his former lover, agrees. She says that Owen Oyston, the man who once controlled Miss World and Red Rose, the largest chain of commercial radio stations in Britain, and who now owns Blackpool Football Club, arranged for her to hold for him controlling shares in at least three agencies that ran strings of models in Manchester and London...

"I lived with Peter Martin for many years. He was a big spender. The girls who worked for the Model Team agency were not being paid properly until he brought Owen Oyston into the firm. There was no doubt in anyone's mind about who was boss. Peter became an indispensable fixer for Owen. He worked for all the many firms in the Oyston empire, at one time or other.

"We were always gathering all the girls on our books for big all-night parties with Owen at the Midland Hotel in Manchester.

"At a dinner at the castle, Owen Oyston was charming and full of fun. The girls had to go across a stage in the baronial hall and through Owen's bedroom to get to the Ladies. There was a stuffed alligator in the way. The girls were so nervous they insisted on going through his bedroom in threes. He was full of jokes.

"My troubles started after I met another man in Gibraltar. He was called Michael. I broke off with Peter Martin. I had been his lover since I was 19 years old. He was very angry with me. After many problems I managed to live with Michael for a year in London, when I was working for Owen and Model Team.

"My troubles got worse when the American Express card I had been given by Model Team went unpaid. Seven thousand pounds was owed to Amex, for flights from London to Manchester and other company expenses.

"To my horror, I discovered that the American Express debt was actually in my own name and they were taking legal action against me in court at Southend. I was facing bankruptcy.

"I asked Peter Martin for help and he just offered me £50 for the train fare to the court case.

"Then I went to Owen to ask for his help. He told me that he could only give me advice. He said he was not to blame, because his name was nowhere on the shares. He said there was no way he could be linked. He could not help.

"I was angry with them both. They had both tricked me.

"In the end, American Express discovered that the signature on the American Express application form did not match mine, so they dropped the bankruptcy action against me."

Just a few yards away from Melanie Hardy's office at Boss, Lysa Rubotham underwent another nine hour police interview in the old headquarters of the Manchester City Police at Bootle Street.

Among thousands of telephone calls generated by the publicity there was a call from a young woman in North East Lancashire, a woman who would later allege that Oyston had raped her. English law requires that she is not identified and is therefore described only as *Miss H*. In her telephone call to the hotline Miss H made no mention of Oyston. Of Peter Martin she said only:

> In 1990 I worked at the agency and I want to tell you about the things he used to do and ask the girls to do. He used to make them love him, so it was natural.

A police officer noted

> No complaint of rape or indecent assault made when she called the incident room, see M101

But late on the afternoon of October 12, by arrangement with the police, Miss H cycled from the factory where she worked to the Lancashire Constabulary police station at Accrington for an interview with Det Con Julie Sharpe and Det Sgt Harry Harrison, the two officers who had examined Mike Murrin's allegations about Martin and Oyston in 1992.

Miss H refused to talk in the presence of Harry Harrison. Consequently, Det Con Sharpe, a university graduate with 11 years police service, conducted a four-hour interview on her own. Det Sgt Harrison said he went to visit his mother in hospital. Julie Sharpe told a court later that she lost the rough notes of the interview, but she came away from Accrington with a signed statement from Miss H, stating that Miss H had not only been raped by Peter Martin at the model agency, but also raped by Oyston in his bedroom at Claughton Hall - in the presence of Lysa Rubotham.

In the statement, Miss H said Peter Martin had driven his car late one night from Manchester to Claughton Hall with Lysa Rubotham in the front seat and Miss H and Oyston in the back. During the journey, Oyston forced

Miss H's head down on his penis. At Claughton Hall, she and Lysa went to Oyston's bedroom where she was forced to watch him have sex on the bed with Lysa before, in fear of Martin who was outside in the car, she allowed Oyston to rape her.

Harry Harrison went back to talk to Melanie Hardy at the Boss agency on October 20 before asking Lysa Rubotham on October 21 to come in for another interview. Detectives Denise Lloyd and Martyn Hughes interviewed Lysa on October 24, at her home in Newton-le-Willows. What now seems uncanny is that they did not put any questions to Lysa about Miss H's October 12 allegation of being raped in bed in the presence of Lysa. Martyn Hughes mentioned the allegation in only one of his 24 interviews with Lysa. When she was asked about it, Lysa said there had been no sex in Oyston's bedroom that night. Det Con Hughes took no statement. He was later criticised for not taking a statement by Anthony Scrivener QC, defending Oyston:

> It does not require a great brain to realise in the circumstances that Lysa Rubotham must be an important potential witness. She should have been able to corroborate what Girl H had alleged. Police interviewed her on 24 occasions after the allegation. On only one occasion did they ask her about the allegation. Det Con Martyn Hughes asked her whether anything improper had taken place at Claughton Hall with either herself or with Girl B. She told him that nothing like that had happened. She was told it wasn't necessary to make a statement to that effect.
>
> She was never asked to make a statement about it. Obviously, a material witness – and when she was asked, she indicated to the police that she would not be corroborating the police's version of it and so [they felt] it was not necessary to take a statement.[74]

In September, the police discovered in Peter Martin's office an emotional. hand-written letter from Kevin Cullis, the luckless businessman from Wolverhampton. Cullis wanted his five thousand pounds back. He exerted

[74] Court transcript

pressure on Peter Martin by threatening to tell Owen Oyston what 'has happened or is going to happen to him.' Just five days after Miss H made her rape allegation against Oyston, the police had traced the letter to Kevin Cullis. They arranged for two Manchester detectives to interview him at home in the West Midlands.

> My wife sat in our front room with me at my request. The detectives were surprised at this. It was clear that they thought I might have had sex with the girls and might have been blackmailed by Peter Martin. The police showed me photos. They told me all the pictures had been taken at the model agency. I told them I didn't recognise anyone, because I didn't.
> They knew of my association with Peter Martin and a man called Michael Thompson, my business adviser. They took notes but I wasn't asked to sign anything. They were collecting evidence on Martin. They'd discovered a letter I had written, about my five thousand. It was a hand-written letter, from the heart, in which I had threatened I would tell Mr Oyston what was going on and what was happening.
>
> When I was asked about my letter, I told the police, 'Mr Oyston is the victim of a sting, believed to be conducted by Thompson and Martin.'
>
> My wife will confirm that I told the police that Martin had used my five thousand to pay a girl to set up Oyston. It shamed me at the time, to have to tell the police, in front of my wife, that our money had been used to pay a young tart to set up Oyston.
>
> Soon afterwards, my business collapsed and we went through a terrible time. The loss of that five thousand pounds put us out of our home. It should have been paid to our building society but it had been paid over as an investment to try and save our business.
>
> With three young children, we were forced out of our house, on to the street, and eventually into a three-roomed council maisonette. I was distracted by these personal problems, but when I heard that Oyston had been arrested for rape, I was surprised that I had not been approached by his defence, especially after what I had told the police.
>
> I did try once to get to speak to him about it. I had been involved in football for 25 years and I knew Sam Allardyce, who was Owen Oyston's manager at

Blackpool Football Club at that time. So I managed to get a door pass for the Birmingham City boardroom and I did get to within a few feet of Oyston, at a reserve game.

I was going to ask for a private talk with him but, quite frankly, at the last minute, the idea of me telling a man like him that my money had been used to entrap him, got too big for me to handle and I bottled out.

It is important to remember that the police approached me for information. They found my letter. I had absolutely nothing to gain by deceiving them. I had no idea a girl had just made a rape complaint against Oyston. In fact, the police told me they suspected Oyston was being blackmailed. After I had told the two detective constables what had been going on and what had happened to my money, they told me, 'We perceive a number of people may have been set up for blackmail and Oyston is one of them'.[75]

The police knew about Thompson and Martin. They remarked that his name had been brought to their attention by others, including Matthew Clarke, a businessman who had been present when Martin introduced the cable project.

They informed me Clarke was in Portugal and had offered to come back and blow the whistle on the whole thing, but was seeking immunity from prosecution. He'd skipped the country when he was on bail from Worcester Crown Court accused of acting as a company director whilst bankrupt. The police said they had declined his offer.

Clarke had warned me about Martin and told me he had found out that Thompson and Martin were using Model Team as an extortion firm. He said Martin and Thompson were trying to put pressure on Oyston.

He said something strange was going on between Martin and Thompson and had established that Martin was a pimp and that the whole set up was a cover for high class prostitution.

---

[75] Interview with author, October 10, 2002.

Kevin Cullis's threatening letter to Martin was never seen by Oyston's trial lawyers. It was listed by police among thousands of items and documents seized from Martin's offices under computer entry 648 HH/24K, where it is described simply as

> a hand-written letter from Kevin Cullis to N1 Martin.

The letter was not disclosed to Oyston's trial lawyers. The police record of their interview with Kevin Cullis was described on the HOLMES computer and logged as DI:R13:

> On Thursday 28th October, 1994 (28/10/94) I interviewed N1 082 Kevin CULLIS. He told me that he was a civil engineer by trade and had worked for Shell Petrochemicals throughout Europe for a number of years, but had more recently been self-employed with his own civil engineering company. For a number of years he has been a close acquaintance of a Michael THOMPSON, who had a company formations business based in offices on Tariff Street, Manchester called Trade Reports. He runs this business together with a John PUDDIFOOT. It was through this acquaintance with THOMPSON that CULLIS first met N1 MARTIN in July/August 1991 when a meeting took place at the Goldthorne Hotel, Wolverhampton, to discuss a business proposition on behalf of the Oyston Group of Companies. At this time MARTIN introduced himself as the Acquisitions and Mergers Manager for the Oyston Group and had offices at Strand Mill, Preston. He explained that the Oyston Group were interested in placing a tender for the installation of cable TV systems throughout the North West of England and that they would require someone with civil engineering experience to assist them. It was further explained that an initial investment of £5,000 would be required from CULLIS and other parties including THOMPSON and MARTIN. At the time CULLIS' business was in financial difficulties and he had to sell his private car to finance the deal. In September 1991 he again met MARTIN at the Midland Hotel, Manchester, where MARTIN explained all was proceeding as planned. CULLIS never saw his money again, nor any proceeds from his supposed investment. CULLIS visited MARTIN's office on one occasion in March when MARTIN made further promises in relation to the business venture. CULLIS never visited MARTIN's home. address or met any of the girls. From my enquiries, CULLIS has committed no offences and is just another person who had been conned by MARTIN's charm. CULLIS has nothing further to add

> which will benefit this enquiry and a further interview is not anticipated. A B Spruce D/C Ml 275

The police interviewed Michael Thompson and his business partner John Puddifoot at Stretford police station on November 9, 1994. In an interview report handed over to Oyston's defence team there is no sign that the two men were asked about Kevin Cullis's five thousand pounds or his warning to police that Thompson and Martin were setting up Oyston. According to police computer log entry D I:R15, the interview was wide-ranging and the two men from Trade Reports plc expressed their wish to assist the enquiry and would assist to prove a business connection between Oyston and Martin.

The police noted:

> both could give evidence of Martin having possession of a hand-held video camera which he produced and discussed with them at a business meeting at a Manchester hotel.

Kevin Cullis is only briefly mentioned in this report and anyone searching for him by computer would have been thwarted by the incorrect spelling of his name as CULLISON. The HOLMES report also stated:

> It became apparent whilst discussing Trade Reports' involvement with MARTIN that THOMPSON had become much more involved than PUDDIFOOT to the point where THOMPSON'S interest became far more than a business interest. THOMPSON admitted regular twice-weekly visits to the Portland Street agency. He acknowledged a relationship with LISA RUBOTHAM. He accepted that he would meet MARTIN at the agency and give lifts back to Sale to agency girls on a Friday afternoon. He also somewhat reluctantly admitted having paid MARTIN £7,500 of his own money to assist in the setting up of a model agency [a company called Phasechance Ltd. was created for this purpose]."

When Owen Oyston was later convicted of rape on the uncorroborated word of Miss H, his defence notably failed to produce any evidence to suggest any reason for the complainant to have invented a rape allegation. The appearance of Kevin Cullis as a defence witness might have seriously damaged the prosecution case. Cullis had documentary proof that he had paid five thousand pounds to the complainant's employer before being told that his money had been paid 'to a young woman to set up Oyston'. Suspicion of sexual entrapment and blackmail would have been supported by the seizure of the videos that showed important businessmen having sex with models at the agency.

Suspicion that there had been a plan to blackmail Oyston would have been further supported by the evidence that large sums of money were paid by some of these businessmen to Peter Martin and that some of the models, when questioned, had made allegations of rape and indecent assault against other businessmen, although the Crown Prosecution Service declined to prosecute.

The accuracy of Cullis's allegations about Michael Thompson trying to force Oyston to buy Trade Reports Plc and Thompson's later threat to punish Oyston for pulling out of the deal is supported by other facts:

1. The police report DI:R13 does not give any reason for the police visit to Mr Cullis, but it does state that Cullis told them about five thousand pounds being paid to Peter Martin at the suggestion of Michael Thompson.

2. Cullis certainly sent a hand-written letter to Martin. It was found in Martin's office by police and logged as 648 HH/24K in the unused material list. It was never seen by the defence.

3. Cullis said the Midlands businessman Matthew Clarke was at the cable TV investment meeting when Thompson and Martin were luring potential investors. He reported Clarke as saying that Thompson and

Martin had tried to blackmail Clarke after Martin videoed him having sex with Tracey Grainey. Some confirmation of this can be found in the police HOLMES computer log under entry DI : R12. Matthew Clarke telephoned Greater Manchester Police and made this same allegation to them on October 10, 1994, before the police had interviewed Cullis.

4. Sharon Cullis swore an affidavit to confirm that she heard her husband tell the police that he believed Oyston was being "set up".

5. Cullis had a receipt, signed by Peter Martin, for five thousand pounds.

6. Cullis stated that his former business adviser, Michael Thompson, was trying to damage Oyston as early as the winter of 1991. Cullis said that after he had handed the five thousand to Martin, and after the *Sunday Times* had lost to Oyston in the expensive libel case, Cullis had travelled to London with Thompson for a visit to the *Sunday Times* offices, by arrangement, for a meeting that lasted one and a half hours.

7. On August 6, 1998, in HM Prison Frankland, Peter Martin admitted to Dale Campbell-Savours MP that he had received the five thousand pounds. Martin claimed not to remember anyone called Kevin Cullis but did admit to the member of parliament that he had received money from a Midlands businessman. He said he had passed the money to Michael Thompson.[76]

8. Kevin Cullis said he was asked to make out his £250.00 cheque to a firm called Phasechance. Police records show that Michael Thompson set up a firm called Phasechance to control a model agency and that Thompson put £7,500.00 of his own money into the business.

---

[76] In the presence of this author

9. Kevin Cullis also described how Michael Thompson turned on Peter Martin:

At this time Thompson had come into my office and brought down a number of documents referring to Peter Martin. I said I didn't want to get involved. He said he just wanted to use my fax machine to get Peter Martin back. He was sending faxes to the Inland Revenue and to the local authority saying Martin hadn't got a licence for a model agency. He faxed two documents to two girls, one of them was in South Wales. I said, 'Why don't you let sleeping dogs lie?' But he was determined to bring Martin down. Something had gone wrong between them. Again, he told me that my money had been paid to 'a little tart'. [77]

Interviewed by Dale Campbell-Savours MP, Peter Martin said that an anonymous letter about him had been sent to the Inland Revenue and it is a matter of record that his model agency had local authority licensing problems.

10. Cullis told how he had tried to recover his money from Martin and Thompson:

I rang Oyston Mill as a last resort in the latter end of '92 or early '93, probably January 1993. I wanted to tell Oyston. The reception girl went deathly silent when I asked for Peter Martin. I was put in touch with Robin Oakley. Robin Oakley said he did not know a Martin. Oakley was icy. Five minutes later, Peter Martin contacted me, threatening me, saying, 'They don't know me at Oyston Mill' I said to him, 'If you don't sort out my money, I'll sort you out.' All I managed to get off Martin was a cheque for five hundred pounds, which he gave to me when he was at Birmingham New Street station with his girlfriend and manager, Tracey Grainey. Martin said my money was long gone. He had given my money to Thompson and it was gone. I couldn't locate Thompson at all. But eventually he rang and said he could not discuss my money on the phone. I met him at Keele Services on the M6. He said he'd got into a spin selling Trade Reports to Oyston. It hadn't

[77] Interview with author, October 10, 2002.

> happened. In confidence, he told me he'd 'got into bed' with Peter Martin and done certain things with Martin and now Martin had a hold on him. Martin was saying Oyston had done him out of £150,000 on the deal. Thompson said he was piggy in the middle with my five thousand. He said Martin was extremely upset and Thompson had made a number of financial commitments and the pressure was building up. Neither had any money. Thompson then said that Martin had paid my money to a girl to set up Owen Oyston.

Peter Martin supported this claim in a letter from prison to the magazine *Private Eye* published on June 30, 1997:

> If she was so frightened of me, why did she visit my office after I had been arrested, but before Oyston or I had been charged with offences against her? On her visit she offered to withdraw allegations against me, provided I supported her version of events. She told me she intended to get a lot of cash from him.

On August 6, 1998, Peter Martin told Dale Campbell-Savours MP:

> It was in October / November 1994. She said she had made a rape allegation against Oyston and she would withdraw the one she had made against me if I would back her up on Oyston.

This appeared uncorroborated, until it was noticed that a message logged on a police computer showed that Miss H had told police she was outside the model agency on October 21 and October 22, 1994, a month after Martin's arrest and during his release on bail, one week after she had first told police Oyston had raped her.

In a message logged on the Operation Chittering HOLMES computer log as "*MESSAGES ON ACCOUNT M233*", Miss H reported to police that she was keeping observations at Peter Martin's agency offices in Manchester, which were 25 miles away from her home in Lancashire. It was surprising, in view of the loathing and fear of Martin that Miss H described to the jury in the later trials of both Oyston and Martin. At Oyston's trial she told the jury:

> You had to do what Peter said. You didn't have a choice. You had to do everything what Peter said. can you imagine if you had upset one of his mates what he would have done?[78]

She told the jury,

> Peter had such a hold on me he wouldn't let me go home anyway. Even at weekends I was told to stay with him. I was terrified of him, he was often losing his temper completely. He was like a psycho.[79]

The jury heard evidence that Miss H was taking drugs and traumatised after she gave evidence to the police at Accrington police station on October 12, 1994. She gave up her job after the police interview and on October 20 she visited her doctor. He recorded 'acute stress' but one day later, at lunchtime, Miss H was twenty-five miles away in Manchester, keeping observations on Peter Martin's Manchester offices. She telephoned the police and told them what she was doing. The police HOLMES log reported:

> On Friday 211094 at midday [Miss H] saw Tracey Grainey park outside Central Models on Portland Street, Manchester, and enter the address. Approx. 2/3 minutes later Grainey re-emerged and drove of[f] in the white Ford Sierra. About the same time on Saturday 221094 [Miss H] saw the white Sierra again parked outside the agency.

Neither Cullis, nor Martin, nor Thompson ever gave evidence at Oyston's trial. In the absence of their evidence, it would have been impossible for Oyston's defending counsel to suggest to the jury that Miss

---

[78] Trial transcript: Day Seven page 617

[79] Trial transcript: Day Eight page 678

H's presence at the model agency that day was deeply suspicious, that the telephone call might have provided a cover for nefarious negotiations with Peter Martin. Miss H's telephone call to the police could have been presented as a necessary cover for a legally dangerous visit to the man accused of raping her.

A jury might not have convicted Oyston on the uncorroborated and disputed word of a single complainant if they had known that the police controlled undisclosed information about blackmail, about hidden links to Oyston's political opponents and undisclosed evidence of money being paid to the complainant's employer.

In an unsuccessful submission to the European Court of Human Rights, Ben Emmerson QC argued that the non-disclosure of Cullis's blackmail warning was 'a clear violation of Article 6 of the European Convention of Human Rights.'[80] In the police report on the interview with Cullis, logged as DI:R13, the police detectives made no mention of the blackmail threat or the use of Cullis's five thousand pounds. Cullis's hand-written letter was logged on HOLMES as "648 HH/24K" without any description of its contents.

The failure to describe the contents of Cullis's letter was compounded by the way Greater Manchester detectives handled an interview with Michael Thompson and John Puddifoot of Trade Reports plc on November 9 at Stretford police station. A report of that interview, logged as DI:R15, included a list of people who had business connections with Peter Martin and Owen Oyston. Thompson and Puddifoot were reported to have offered to 'assist to prove a business connection between Oyston and Martin.' Yet

[80] Article 6 ECHR: In the determination of his civil rights and obligations or of any criminal charge against him, everyone is entitled to a fair and public hearing within a reasonable time by an independent and impartial tribunal established by law.

the report shows no record of the police asking Thompson about the five thousand pounds 'paid to a girl to set up Oyston' and in any case Cullis's name had been misspelled on HOLMES as "CULLISON".

The police detectives noted that Thompson had admitted being involved with the model agency and having an affair with Lysa Rubotham:

> It also became clear from Thompson and Puddifoot that they initially became involved with Martin because they saw business opportunities from the Oyston Group. Very little of substance ever materialised and Oyston's obvious disinterest in them became more and more apparent.

The police asked Thompson and Puddifoot about other women in Oyston's life. They described a 'girlfriend of Oyston who lived in Hull and had turned up with Oyston at the Midland Hotel in Manchester in 1991'. This was Miss J, who had also been mentioned by Lysa Rubotham in a list of 24 girls compiled in an interview on October 27. The officers noted:

> Rubotham will help with further info. She gave the following names as girls who would have had a relationship with Martin and Oyston or had knowledge of such relationships.

Lysa's list included the names of both Miss J and Miss H. A woman detective therefore went to Lincolnshire to check up on Miss J in November. Miss J later insisted that as her interview was ending and the detective was leaving her house, she told the detective that Owen Oyston had raped her at Claughton Hall. The detective did not take a note of that allegation.

But three weeks later a detective took a full statement from Miss J, which led to Oyston being charged in 1995 with raping and indecent assaulting her. Oyston was eventually acquitted of both those charges.

It is clear from HOLMES computer printouts that once Owen Oyston came into the frame for rape, the police tried hard to steer clear of any connections with the widely reported political conspiracy against him. They also had to avoid getting further involved with their original informants, Melanie Hardy and Mike Murrin, whose activities could be easily connected to Robert Atkins MP and Lord Blaker. Neither Melanie Hardy nor Michael Murrin ever gave evidence in court.

Consequently, on December 12, 1994, with Oyston unaware of any allegations, Det Sgt Pinder of GMP logged an order for all officers in Operation Chittering from their SIO Det Supt Roberts. They were to have no contact with Michael Murrin without Bill Roberts's permission:

> N397 Michael Murrin re-knowledge of Martin 'Liaise with SIO prior to allocation'.

Roberts was running the biggest sexual offences case in the history of Greater Manchester Police. He kept the political conspirator Murrin out of Operation Chittering. Peter Martin, on bail in Manchester, knew about the possibility of rape allegations against Oyston, three months before Oyston was arrested:

> Cullis was making plaintive noises about his money. I think he wrote to Oyston at Oyston Mill.
> About November 1994, Miss H came to see me. She looked nervous. She'd been seen by the police. She'd accused Oyston of raping her. She accused me of raping her. I said, 'How can you go to the police now and say Owen raped you? It's bullshit. You were only there a few minutes.' I threw her out when she said, 'I'm going to make some money out of it'.[81]

It was hardly surprising that Miss H appeared nervous. The police knew she had several times travelled 25 miles down to the model agency in Manchester and she had told them over the phone about seeing Tracey Grainey coming and going at the building. They reported:

> A403 known to have been involved with N1 Martin

---

[81] Interview with MP and author: August 6, 1998, HM Prison Frankland.

The police were closing in on Oyston. Just before Christmas, Det Con Alan Fitzsimmons went up the Lune Valley to survey the area around Claughton Hall. On January 5, 1995, Miss H signed a second statement to clarify the dates on which she had worked at the model agency and in Lincolnshire, on January 12, Miss J signed a statement declaring that Oyston had raped her. Oyston flew home to Lancashire from a Caribbean holiday in February 1995.

Before dawn on February 9, a sixteen police officers drove up a rough track through the woods below Claughton Hall. They hammered on the heavy door under the tower where Oyston slept. They carried warrants for his arrest on charges of rape, indecent assault and procuring girls for sex. Det Con Martyn Hughes cautioned Oyston and recorded his reply at 7.17 am that morning:

I am amazed. I am astonished by this.

He asked the policemen if they knew that in three weeks his action for conspiracy and defamation against the Robert Atkins, Lord Blaker and Bill Harrison was due in court. The Manchester policemen said they knew nothing about it and took him away for questioning in Manchester.

CHAPTER 15

'Oyston Held in Sex Probe' – Manchester Evening News

They questioned Oyston at Altrincham police station on February 9, 1995, in the presence of his Blackpool solicitor Sammy Lee and Ken Chadwick the 'in-house' Oyston company solicitor. Detective constables Martyn Hughes and Alan Fitzsimmons handled the interviews and took almost all the 36 hours allowed by law for questioning Oyston before he was charged.

Fitzsimmons: Well gentlemen I think then in that case, I'll move on to the allegation made by Miss A. Do you recall the name [Miss A]? Mr Oyston?

Oyston: I do. Yes.

Fitzsimmons: I'll show you a photograph of Miss A.

Oyston: I know her well. I know her father well. Well, not well, but I know her father, yes that's A, nice girl.

Fitzsimmons: I can tell you then, when Miss A was seventeen, she was recruited to go to the Mosley Street Agency. She'd already undergone some training before. She said you'd met in a restaurant outside of Manchester. Martin had taken her there together with other girls. Before he introduced you to Miss A he told her that she was going to meet somebody who was very important. Now I can tell you that would be in about 1989. Do you recall that meeting?

Oyston: I don't recall it, and I mean he wasn't bringing girls just to meet me. I was meeting him. Sometimes he was on his own. Sometimes it was convenient for Tracey to bring her girls with him. You are making it sound as if they were coming specially for me, that wasn't the case.

Fitzsimmons: Well it appears to us Mr Oyston and we will continue throughout the interview, and all the girls say that they were brought to your table at various places to meet you by Martin.

Oyston: I've had hundreds of girlfriends, Peter Martin has never met with, doesn't know. They're just four girls you say that I knew....

Fitzsimmons: Well no, I didn't say that, there are a lot more than that as I said and I went through the names earlier of two, four, six, nine girls there that don't make anv allegations against you, but were present at dinner with you at various hotels.

Oyston: Well I don't deny that.

Fitzsimmons: Brought to the table by Martin.

Oyston: Yeah, well what's wrong with that?

Fitzsimmons: I'm saying that certainly those girls there...

Oyston: In a public place. There's nothing to hide. I've nothing to hide.

Fitzsimmons: But why would he bring them to your table Mr Oyston?

Oyston: Didn't bring them to my table. I'd arranged to meet him, sometimes he would come with an entourage and sometimes he would come on his own.

Fitzsimmons: He would often pay for dinner?

Oyston: Not often. I can't remember how many times, if at all, but occasionally I'm sure I would and sometimes he would pay, or they would pay I don't know I cannot remember the details of that.

Fitzsimmons: We are on the end of tape number two and we'll have to cease the interview at this. The time now is 12.27pm and the tape is being switched off. If I may then continue – concerning Miss A - as I said, she was taken with others by Martin to a restaurant in, which she can't really name, but she says it's some distance out of Manchester. I must tell you now, again, Miss A has made a full statement to the police in which she alleges rape against you.

Oyston: Excuse me laughing.

Fitzsimmons: Well again that's what she alleges.

Oyston: I've known Miss A for a long time. We've been good friends and until this moment I thought she was a good friend of mine. She only rang a few days ago to the football club to speak to my managing director there. I'm puzzled by this, that she's made allegations like that.

Fitzsimmons: She rang when, sorry?

Oyston: A short time ago, to speak to one of my people.

Fitzsimmons: Did she speak to you?

Oyston: No. I wasn't there.

Fitzsimmons: Did she ask to speak to you?

Oyston: I don't. I didn't pursue it, but one of my people took the message and I can't remember what was said now, but she rang up. It just doesn't fit this. We were good friends. I knew her for a long time.

Fitzsimmons: Well. If I may continue, Mr Oyston, she says…

Oyston: She actually proposed marriage to me, if you want to know. Put that down.

Fitzsimmons: Well, it's there on the tape. It's been recorded. You're saying that she proposed marriage to you. When was that?

Oyston: She did, yes. I can't remember, I can't remember… going back quite a long time ago.

Fitzsimmons: Well, she says that she first met you in 1989, so it would be about then.

Oyston: About that time. Yes.

Fitzsimmons: And at that time, you say you were divorced?

Oyston: Yes. But she's a very nice girl and we had a terrific relationship.

Fitzsimmons: Well, she doesn't say that in the statement, Mr Oyston. She says that when she first met you at the restaurant, she took an instant dislike to you.

Oyston: Right. OK. That's up to her. If she disliked me then why did she continue the relationship?

Fitzsimmons: Well, we'll get to that. Did you have a relationship with her?

Oyston: Yes. I did.

Fitzsimmons: You did? A sexual relationship?

Oyston: Yes. For quite a longish period as I recall.

The detectives questioned Oyston about Miss A's visit to Claughton Hall:

Oyston: I have to tell you this is crazy. I mean, I've known her for a long time. She has never, ever… I mean we've been good friends. I told you she actually proposed to me on one occasion and it just doesn't stack up. I don't know if she's leading you up the garden path or what because these are all models you know, who want publicity and they want to be in the limelight and they want to sell their stories to the *News of the World*.

Fitzsimmons: We guarantee you that none of these ladies that we're talking about wants any publicity from the newspapers.

Oyston: Pleased to hear it. I'm pleased to hear it.

Fitzsimmons: That's the last thing on their minds, we can assure you.

Oyston: Good. Good. I'm pleased to hear it. I hope we don't have any…

Fitzsimmons: Well Miss A says that Martin took her into the house. She thought the house being so large there might be someone else in the home. You said earlier you don't recall Miss A being at the house, but she may have been?

Oyston: Yes. I'm sure she was.

Fitzsimmons: She says that once inside the house Martin said to her, *'Owen will look after you and don't be frightened, you'll be all right. He'll show you round the house and I'll wait in the car'*.

Oyston: I can't remember that. This is nonsense.

Fitzsimmons: She recalls…

Oyston: This is nonsense. I wouldn't ask him to wait in the car. This is nonsense…

Alan Fitzsimmons then told Oyston that Miss A said she was raped on Oyston's bed before running 'hysterical and sobbing' back to Martin's car, where the model agency boss had given her two hundred pounds. Fitzsimmons said Miss A had also complained about Oyston indecently assaulting her a few months later at Peter Martin's house.

Later in the afternoon, when Oyston was being questioned about Miss H, who was actually described during the interview as *Miss B*, one of the detectives, Det Con Martyn Hughes, bent the Police And Criminal Evidence [PACE] rules against putting false questions to suspects. Reading from prepared notes, Hughes told Oyston under caution that Lysa Rubotham had told the police that she had witnessed the rape and that she too had been raped by Oyston. The detectives knew this was not true. They had both interviewed Lysa. Martyn Hughes had specifically asked her if anything untoward had happened at Claughton Hall and a week earlier Alan Fitzsimmons had raided her house looking for a diary. Det Con Hughes later apologised in the crown court for his 'error'. In the four months before Oyston was arrested, the police spent over fifty hours questioning Lysa Rubotham, treating her as a valuable and reliable witness. They met her on 27 occasions but never once asked her whether she had seen Oyston rape Miss H.

Defending Oyston at the eventual trial, Anthony Scrivener QC said

> Mr Oyston asks, you will see, two questions below, he says, "And who was the second girl?" Because the police have been hinting, or more than hinting, that there was a second girl. Then the officer says, "Well I will name that girl as Lysa Rubotham."
>
> Then there is a bit about that. Mr Oyston said, 'Oh, I know her'. And he says, towards the end of the page, 'Are you saying she was the other girl in the car when we were coming back to Claughton?'
>
> 'Yes.' He says, 'It can't be so because I can't believe that with two girls in the car anything like that could go on, it is ridiculous.' Top of page19, Detective Constable Fitzgerald, 'She says you sat in the back of the car with Girl B.' She says, 'You sat in the car....' They have not got any information from Lysa Rubotham about it.
>
> If you want to look at the clincher, the one for which the officer had to apologise, look at page 20, last line, and follow it through to 21.

The bottom line: Mr Oyston says this, 'So what was Lisa doing while I was making love to the girl against her will? What was Lysa doing? She was there observing it?' The officer says, 'She was there in bed.'

You will remember this question. Mr Oyston says, [it is page21 at the top] 'Does Lysa say that?' Answer: 'Lysa says that, yes.' 'What? Against her will?' says Mr Oyston.

The officer says this, 'Let me just say that Lysa and Girl B [Miss H] did not consent to have sex with you, neither of them did.'

Members of the jury, the officers have said it is a terrible mistake, they had no statement from Lysa at all. This was a complete fabrication, a complete fabrication. The impression being given to Mr Oyston was that they had a statement from Lysa who was going to say she was raped, who says she was present watching Girl B [Miss H] being raped. It was a complete and utter fabrication.

I eventually asked the officer, that D.C. Hughes, the same D.C. Hughes who had telephoned Lysa Rubotham on 30th January and when he heard she could not corroborate, and would not corroborate the version being put forward by Girl B [Miss H], and when she offered to make a statement, said, 'No point in it.' The same officer who sat through this interview, nine days later, and allowed these mistakes to be put.

I asked D.C. Hughes, I said, 'So there was no statement in your possession from Lysa where she said that? The answer from him was, 'No.'

Members of the jury, I do not know how knowledgeable you are about things. There is a duty of disclosure nowadays on the prosecution, there have been some miscarriages of justice because of documents held back, not disclosed, so there are rules about disclosure and if they had taken a statement from Lysa that would have had to have been handed over to the defence. They did not take a statement from Lysa.

If you remember for the moment what Lysa Rubotham said. She said that she had last had sex with Mr Oyston prior to January 1992. She left Sale in January 1992. She went to live at her mother's house. She was asked this, 'Were you having an affair with Mr Oyston at that time?' The time when she left. Answer: 'No, I was not.'

> Detective Superintendent Roberts said he had not discovered this error, which I referred to in the interview, until last week, I think he said, after the trial had started.
>
> The fact of the matter is usually people are interviewed at police stations or in their home. Lysa was asked to go to the Haydock Post House Hotel by the police for the interview, on one interview, when she finished off her statement.
>
> She gave the police a statement in a rape centre. She worked out from her own record, because she kept a note, that she had been altogether interviewed for forty or fifty hours but never once about Girl B [Miss H]. When she offered to provide a statement, it was not necessary.

Lysa Rubotham had actually noted in her Filofax diary when she heard on the lunchtime news of Oyston's arrest:

> Owen arrested today for sexual offence. Spoke to Sharon [Denby] and Brian [Hargreaves]. On news and papers. Melanie [Hardy] rang – will meet on Tuesday.

But on the day before she was due to meet Melanie Hardy, Monday, February 13, Lysa noted that:

> Police [Alan Fitzsimmons] and 6 officers came to search house and hotel – took this Filofax and papers.

The police retained Lysa Rubotham's Filofax diary for twelve weeks, not handing it back until May 4, yet still declining to take any statement from Lysa about the night-time car journey to Claughton Hall.

As Oyston's solicitor Sammy Lee was leaving the interview room late on February 9, he told the reporters outside the police station:

> Mr Oyston is angry and shocked at these ridiculous and untrue allegations relating to events said to have happened years ago – in some cases as long as seven years ago.

Alerted in London, Anthony Scrivener QC, a former chairman of the bar council, travelled overnight to start defending Oyston in Altrincham police station on February 10. His client was charged with four counts of rape:

In London, between April 1 and April 30, 1988

At Claughton Hall between October 1 and December 31, 1992

At Preston between April 1, 1988 and June 1, 1988

At Claughton Hall between January 1, 1989 and December 12, 1989

He was also charged with three counts of indecent assault and a count of conspiring with Charles Peter Martin to procure young women under the age of 21 with a third party in any part of the world.

Oyston appeared in the dock at Trafford Magistrates' Court with Peter Martin and Tracey Grainey. Oyston was being given bail on a £50,000 surety. Peter Martin was taken ill with chest pains and returned to Strangeways Prison, charged with 64 sexual offences, including 19 rapes. The magistrates remanded Tracey Grainey, 28, in custody, accused of 24 indecent assaults. Sammy Lee assured fans of Blackpool Football Club that Oyston would be at Saturday's match with Oxford United. The Blackpool team manager, 'Big Sam' Allardyce said

> I think the players know there is no point in over-dramatising what is already a dramatic situation.

And when Saturday came, the Blackpool fans were delighted to see Oyston out on bail, wearing his big hat and walking through a friendly crowd to sit in the director's box alongside his wife Vicki. The crowd cheered when he said he would fight to clear his name.

Michael Murrin kept up the conspiratorial pressure on the police, writing on February 25 to Det Chief Supt Hacking at Lancashire headquarters, alleging that Oyston was illegally employing an accountant who was facing charges after the collapse of the Maxwell publishing empire and telephoning, on February 13, to say he had been approached by Oyston to give evidence in civil proceedings against Lord Blaker, Bill Harrison and Robert Atkins and that the journalists Julian Allitt and Paul Halloran would soon be alleging that the charges against Oyston were a Conservative smear.

On February 14, Murrin wrote to the chief of Operation Chittering, Bill Roberts, making allegations against the British Airways media chief David Burnside and saying he had a report of Oyston 'providing children' and women for sex.

On February 16 he faxed Det Chief Supt Hacking to claim that a man from the *Sunday Mirror* had been talking to Oyston and his barrister in chambers in London. He telephoned Ann Foulger at Lancashire Constabulary HQ the next day to tell her that the reporter Andrew Rosthorn was planning to breach *sub judice* rules by writing stories to put Oyston in a good light before the forthcoming trial. He phoned later to report that a man in Fleetwood had been working for Oyston procuring prostitutes and paying them on Oyston's behalf.

In an unorthodox move on March 6, 1995, Oyston sent Murrin a last-minute invitation to a fine dinner and a bizarre legal conference in a private room at the Broughton Park Hotel, near Murrin's home in Preston. The arch-conspirator, suffering from a head cold that night, ordered a Drambuie with his double whisky and took a chair alongside Oyston at the head of the table. The diners included Sammy Lee, Gill Bridge, managing director of Blackpool Football Club, Andrew Rosthorn, the Manchester solicitor Tom Burke and Oyston's much-admired financial adviser, Michael Connolly.

Owen Oyston asked Connolly, 'Phone McGrath and get him down here' and the deputy Labour leader of Preston, who lived nearby, arrived within a few minutes. Frank McGrath walked into the private room, saw Murrin sitting alongside Oyston at the head of the table and asked, 'Is this some kind of joke?'

Everyone then listened to an analysis of the case against Oyston, conducted by a maverick lawyer Charles Buckley, fresh from victory in three recent 'political' cases, but restricted by the Law Society to acting as a consultant on an annual 'non-practising' certificate.

Operating from a series of alcoves in a disused wine bar under the Drury Lane Hotel, Buckley had recently bragged to a journalist that lawyers now viewed him with suspicion and that

> ... the Law is a profession of automatons. The idea of the fearless and free advocate is a joke.

Charles Buckley's client, Lord Spens, had been cleared in the Guinness share-trading fraud case. Another client. the former Manchester Conservative Association chairman Kevin Taylor had been acquitted in the John Stalker 'shoot-to-kill' case and a third Buckley client, John Morris, known at the time as 'Mrs Thatcher's favourite double glazing salesman' had been acquitted on a £20 million fraud charge. Buckley and his practising solicitor, Tom Burke, outlined a tactic which was not unlike the one that Murrin had described two weeks earlier in a telephone call to Lancashire police.

As this strange conference closed, Michael Connolly, known in the City of London for cool management in takeover battles, decided he had heard enough from Murrin. After calling Murrin 'nothing more than a blackmailer' he threw a gilded chair at the arch-conspirator who was still suffering with his heavy cold. In Connolly's mind, Murrin had already robbed Oyston of an estate agency and a media empire and was now threatening to rob Oyston of his liberty.

Next day Murrin wrote a 10-page report on the Broughton Park conference and sent it, complete with a sketch of the seating plan, to Det

Chief Supt Hacking. He complained that Connolly made his 'flesh creep' and declaring that his own life was in danger.

> Oyston asked if I was still in contact with Harrison, Blaker and Atkins and I replied no, because no-one would talk to me. When Oyston said he was going to destroy the three men I said, "I thought you might make it four – ME". Oyston said, "No. I want you on my side.

Oyston kept up the pressure on Atkins, Blaker, and Harrison. On March 13 Tom Pendry, the Labour MP for Stalybridge and Hyde, tabled a Commons motion calling Atkins and Blaker to apologise to MPs for having been 'privy to obtaining by clandestine means private papers and bank account details of Mr Oyston' and failing 'to reveal the extent of their financial and personal involvement in the squalid investigation. [82]

In June 1995, Oyston appealed against a decision by Mr Justice Ognall that was blocking his civil case against the conspirators. One month later, at the age of 50, Robert Atkins left John Major's government, revealing that he had written to the prime minister back in 1994, asking to leave his post as countryside minister at the next reshuffle and 'spend more time with his family'. The resignation letter of 1994 had come after the editor of the *Cambridge Evening News*, Robert Satchwell, had told John Major about Oyston's pending litigation against Atkins, over a Sunday lunch at Major's house in Huntingdon.[83] Robert Satchwell had been one of the *Lancashire Evening Post* reporters who revealed the Osmond Report and reported Robert Atkins's notorious remarks about the two mothers killed by Miss Harrison's car on the Kirkham Bypass. Robert Atkins was knighted in 1997 when he left the House of Commons and re-entered politics as a Conservative member of the European Parliament in 1999.

---

[82] Early Day Motion 747, 'Conduct of Honourable Members for Blackpool and South Ribble and the *World in Action* Television Programme of March 1992.'

[83] Author's interview with Robert Satchwell.

Murrin reminded Det Chief Insp Maloney at Lancashire Police that Melanie Hardy had told him about links between Peter Martin and Derek Zissman, brother of Sir Bernard Zissman, Lord Mayor of Birmingham. Murrin pointed out that Derek Zissman was a senior partner at the accountants KPMG and had acted for Oyston. Murrin asked for the return of tape recordings he had sent to the police.

Oyston's unorthodox legal consultant, Charles Buckley, soon to be replaced by corporate lawyers in London, had calculated that the authorities had delayed starting committal proceedings against Oyston in order to benefit from a change in the law concerning rape trials.

Section 32 (1) of the Criminal Justice and Public Order Act 1994 had abrogated in November 1994 the mandatory statutory warning that a judge was obliged to give to any jury considering a sexual offence. English judges had been required to give the 'corroboration warning' in their summing up, reminding the jury that it can be unsafe to convict a man of rape solely on a woman's uncorroborated evidence. Oyston had been charged with sex offences against six women and each case depended on uncorroborated evidence.

CHAPTER 16

Trawling

The young women who made allegations against Owen Oyston, Peter Martin and Tracey Grainey were all over the age of 16. They were children under English law but since the age of consent for sexual activity had been fixed at 16 in 1885, only a few experts noticed how closely the investigation of Operation Chittering was following tactics adopted by other police forces in the big English and Welsh child abuse investigations of the 1990s.

Police detectives were gathering evidence with techniques never previously seen in Europe. They were achieving hundreds of convictions using tactics permitted under English law but unlawful under Roman law, in police operations that would eventually be described in Parliament and in the appeal courts as 'modern-day witch hunts.'

The procedure was officially known as 'retrospective investigation' but after a string of human catastrophes the members of the House of Commons Select Home Affairs Committee described it in 2002 as 'trawling for witnesses'. Chief Superintendent Mike Langdon told the committee that he preferred to call it 'dip sampling' but the committee chairman, Chris Mullin, MP for Sunderland, decided on 'trawling'. David Rose, giving evidence as legal correspondent of the *Observer,* told the select committee:

> The problem with trawling as it is now carried out is that it is an absolutely unregulated process and it is a process which... is almost tailor-made to

generate false allegations.[84]

The procedure was pioneered in Leicestershire in the 1990 investigation of Frank Beck, a local councillor and a previously well-regarded childcare worker. The police tracked down and interviewed 400 people who had been previously in the care of this former Royal Marine. They gathered twenty complaints. Beck was acquitted of half the charges but died in prison awaiting a promising appeal against five life sentences. His defence team included a former policeman who had discovered that whenever documentary evidence had been uncovered by the investigators it had always confirmed Beck's innocence. The author Richard Webster, a witness at the Home Affairs select committee, said Beck was:

> the victim of an unprecedented trawling operation in which police officers, in their anxiety to gain a conviction, had inadvertently suggested allegations to the witness they were interviewing.

Edward Garnier QC, a Leicestershire MP who became Solicitor General in the 2010 coalition government, condemned another Leicestershire trawling investigation known as Operation Magnolia. In a Commons debate in 2002, he described the fate of two arrested care workers in his constituency:

> the massive growth in police trawling operations has become a danger in itself: it is different from the danger of child abuse but every bit as corrosive to our justice system as child abuse is to the public care system. Even on the limited information that I have concerning my two constituents, it is clear to me that the presumption of innocence that should have been made in their favour—both publicly as a matter of course until conviction and privately within the police and the social services department employing them—at least until evidence of probative value became available to warrant precise

[84] Select Committee on Home Affairs, Fourth Report, October 22, 2002.

charges that would stand the scrutiny of the Crown Prosecution Service and independent prosecuting counsel, never existed.[85]

In the decade after the Beck case, hundreds of millions were spent on similar retrospective investigations in Leicestershire, North Wales, Cheshire, South Wales, Northumbria and Merseyside. The investigations were launched in spite of a clear warning about 'recovered memory' from Professor Sydney Brandon, in a 1998 paper commissioned by the Royal College of Psychiatrists:

> There is no reliable means of distinguishing a true memory from an illusory one other than by external confirmation.
> Therapist and/or patient expectations, reinforced by guided reading, particular techniques and survivors' group participation, may distort any existing memory or implant a wholly new one.[86]

The House of Commons Home Affairs Committee, including future prime minister David Cameron MP, reported on expert estimates of the numbers of innocent people convicted in the police trawling operations:

> We sought views on the scale of the problem. David Rose guessed that 50 or more of the 120 or so former care workers convicted of sexual abuse had been wrongfully convicted. Chris Saltrese, a criminal defence solicitor specialising in these cases, estimated that over 100 had been wrongly convicted. Richard Webster, who singled out South Wales as the home to "one of the most dangerous trawling operations", said that in excess of 80 or 90 per cent of the 581 or so suspects trawled by South Wales Police were "completely innocent". Claire Curtis-Thomas MP, Chair of the All Party Group on Abuse Investigations, told us that she had 20 cases in which, she believed, there was "an overt indication that there have been significant abuses of the criminal justice system". Although she did not speculate about the statistics,

---

[85] https://publications.parliament.uk/pa/cm200102/cmhansrd/vo021016/halltext/21016h02.htm

[86] Reported recovered memories of child sexual abuse, Psychiatric Bulletin, October 1997

she said that she was convinced that miscarriages of justice had occurred in these investigations.

Richard Webster, a historian of mediaeval witch hunts, published a 716-page account of a notorious 9-year North Wales investigation.[87]

The paedophile ring turned out to be a figment of the investigators' imagination. Yet rumours of its existence led to the largest child abuse investigation in Britain. The police trawled allegations from 650 witnesses, who accused 365 people of abusing them at homes throughout North Wales. When only six prosecutions followed, with only two new convictions for sexual abuse, the police and the authorities were accused of mounting a cover-up. Police officers themselves were said to belong to the very paedophile ring they were supposed to be investigating. The story became a national scandal. A senior police officer, publicly accused of raping adolescent boys at Bryn Estyn, sued for libel and won.

The figures which are available indicate that by now between 5,000 and 10,000 former residential care workers and teachers have been accused of physical or sexual abuse as a direct consequence of police trawling operations. Some of these allegations are true. The evidence presented in the book, however, suggests that the overwhelming majority are false. Many other false allegations of sexual abuse have been made in other contexts – including the recovered memory movement and satanic abuse 'scares'.

In 1996 the government opened a tribunal of inquiry into the events in North Wales just as Det Supt Bill Roberts, the senior investigating officer in the Manchester model agency case, was describing Operation Chittering to the crime reporter John Burke-Davies:

> This is the largest case of child abuse Greater Manchester Police has ever investigated.[88]

---

[87] Richard Webster, *The Secret of Bryn Estyn: The Making of a Modern Witch Hunt* (Halesworth: Orwell Press, 2005)

[88] Interview notes of John Burke-Davies.

In April 1996, Merseyside Police launched Operation Care, an open-ended investigation of child abuse in 106 care homes run by five local authorities. Richard Webster interviewed Det Supt John Robbins who led a team of 12 detectives, supported by social workers based at the Operation Care headquarters in Upton police station on the Wirral. The SIO memorably described his method in 1996 as being 'the reverse of normal police procedure.'

> Normally, he explained, police officers start with an offence and are unsure who committed it. In trawling investigations, however, this process is reversed. He then went on to utter the words which have become famous. 'Corroboration,' he said, 'is generally done by volume.'
> His characterisation of trawling was entirely accurate. It remains accurate now. Of course, it is quite true that, in the course of investigating serious crimes such as murder, the police may go to great lengths in order to discover fresh witnesses who have not come forward of their own accord. But in this case the police are seeking evidence about a crime which has already been reported, and whose reality is not in doubt. In trawling operations, they are, of course, effectively seeking crimes which have not been reported – and which may not, in fact, have taken place at all. There is a difference between conducting a search for witnesses and conducting a search for complainants. As Detective Superintendent Robbins himself clearly recognised in 1996, the latter approach turns traditional police methods on their head. [89]

In 1997, Det Supt Robbins sent the following letter to five hundred former residents of a care home:

> I am the senior investigating officer of the above operation which is currently investigating allegations of child abuse reported to have taken place within a number of residential establishments in the Merseyside area. I am aware from records provided to me that in times past you have been a resident at

[89] *How the police trawl the innocent* by Richard Webster, New Statesman Special Report, July 19, 1999.

> [*a boys' home*], whilst in the care of a local authority. I am concerned that there is a possibility that such abuse may have taken place whilst you were in residence there. If you have any information or if we can help with any complaint you may have, please respond by completing and returning the attached slip using the enclosed pre-paid envelope or by contacting a member of my staff using the above telephone number. MAY I TAKE THIS OPPORTUNITY OF ASSURING YOU THAT ANY INFORMATION GIVEN OR COMPLAINT MADE WILL BE TREATED IN THE STRICTEST CONFIDENCE.

There were two notable arrests, Mike Lawson, 62, a social worker with 15 years previous service in the Merseyside police force, and Dave Jones, a former Everton footballer and the manager of Southampton Football Club. In June 2000 Lawson was convicted of 17 counts of indecent assault and jailed for 7 years.

Amidst huge publicity, the high-profile case against Dave Jones collapsed at Liverpool Crown Court in December 2000, 11 months after his arrest and four days after he had entered the dock. He had faced 14 charges of physical and sexual abuse of children. The Crown offered no evidence after the original complainant from the original trawl refused to come to court.

Mike Lawson was freed three years later at the Court of Appeal. A 'victim' had confessed to fabricating evidence to get compensation to pay for a gender reassignment operation. The former policeman said on the day of his release:

> Trawling is just touting for complaints when there is often no crime in the first place.[90]

On the following day, Merseyside police announced that Operation Care would be closed down, after 27 convictions and 4 acquittals.

---

[90] *Liverpool Daily Post*, March 18, 2003.

In 2002, at Newcastle Crown Court, Judge Maurice Carr freed Esme Allenby, 54, accused of nine indecent assaults dating back 27 years. She was the last of 32 care workers and teachers to face trial after Operation Rose, a £5 million, 5-year trawl gathered 558 claims of assault and rape from 277 residents or former residents of 61 care homes. When the judge lifted a two-year reporting ban it was revealed that five people had been found guilty, one had pleaded guilty, 12 had been found not guilty, nine cases had been withdrawn and four people had died before their cases could be heard.

Northumbria police had written to 1,800 former care home residents announcing the investigation and the setting up of a Manchester-style 24-hour telephone hotline. Assistant Chief Constable John Scott said, 'We would conduct the inquiry in the same way, were we to do it again. However, recommendations have been made to establish best practice.'

In a 2018 research paper on *The Origins of the Jimmy Savile Scandal* Mark Smith and Ros Burnett referred to international studies of false and distorted memories.[91]

> The realist position adopted by the police and activists on the status of people's stories extends to their understanding of memory, which is assumed to correspond to actual events (or which, reprising the memory wars of the 1990s... might be thought to be repressed and subsequently recovered). This is essentially a videotape understanding of how memory operates, which assumes that it can be accurately played back and that similar accounts might be thought to corroborate one another.
> Memory, however, does not work like this. Nash and Ost[92] capture the consensus in the field that memory is shaped by social, political and political forces and is thus amenable to manipulation, either active or passive, through therapeutic engagement or through the assimilation of cultural

[91] https://www.emerald.com/insight/content/doi/10.1108/IJSSP-03-2017-0029/full/html

[92] Robert A. Nash and James Ost (eds) *False and Distorted Memories*, Routledge. 2017

stories. In this sense, it links with the way that people use stories to make sense of their lives.
Haaken[93] suggests that when women struggle to speak openly about their experiences they may do so through storytelling, in ways that introduce layers of meaning but which blur the boundaries between 'true' and 'false'. Tavris and Aronson[94] describe how the lives of unhappy and vulnerable individuals become open to exploitation, by therapists, prosecutors, police officers and personal injury lawyers who profess to offer a solution, often labelled "closure" to vague feelings that something is not right in life. The authors go on to identify how lives can be destroyed by these intractable and sincerely-held, yet false, beliefs.

In 2016, the former high court judge Sir Richard Henriques reported on his independent review of *the Metropolitan Police Service's handling of non-recent sex offence investigations alleged against persons of public prominence*. The report appeared just as the police were closing down their £4.5 million Operation Midland without any convictions.

On the uncorroborated evidence of Carl Beech, code-named 'Nick', the police had raided the home of Field Marshal Lord Bramall. Bramall was a 91 years old D-Day veteran and former head of the British armed forces. Acting on information from the same tainted source, the police searched the home of Lady Diana Brittan, widow of a former home secretary, and the Barn House in the grounds of Belvoir Castle, where the former MP Harvey Proctor, 71, had been living and working as private secretary to the Duke of Rutland. Three years later, Carl Beech, 51, a complainant described as a victim in Operation Midland was jailed for 18 years at Newcastle Crown Court on 12 counts of perverting the course of justice. Sir Richard found

---

[93] Janice Haaken, *Pillar of Salt: Gender, Memory, and the Perils of Looking Back,* Rutgers University Press, 1998.

[94] Carol Tavris and Elliot Aronson, *Mistakes Were Made (But Not By Me): Why We Justify Foolish Beliefs, Bad Decisions and Hurtful Acts*, Harcourt, 2007.

> The principal cause of the many failures in this investigation was poor judgement and a failure to accurately evaluate known facts and to react to them.
> A major contributing factor was the culture that 'victims' must be believed. Whilst the responsible officers assert that they kept an open mind, several failures can only be explained by an unwarranted and disproportionate belief in 'Nick's' credibility.

Twenty-five years before the Henriques Report, after the raid on Peter Martin's model agency, no-one in Manchester would have seen setting up the 1994 Operation Chittering telephone hotline as a dangerous 'trawl for witnesses.' Yet in hindsight, asking the parents of the three thousand young women on the books of Model Team International to call a telephone hotline advertised on the front pages of the *Manchester Evening News* and the *News of the World* was as risky as Det Supt Robbins's Operation Care decision to send a 'fishing' letter to 500 former residents of a boys' home.

In 1994, Bill Roberts told the *Manchester Evening News*:

> We have an inquiry under way which is progressing. We want to hear from any parent who has taken their daughter to Central Models in Portland Street, Manchester. Parents can contact police from Monday on 061 856 7832.

Det Supt Flaherty described what happened:

> Two phones were manned from 8am to 10pm and the shortest time between putting a phone down and picking it up again was 13 seconds, but of course not all calls mentioned any allegations of impropriety. On the proforma we asked the question: 'Did anything untoward happen?' and we were able to prioritise the calls that way.

CHAPTER 17

Committed for Trial

Wearing a Marks & Spencer suit with the customary fedora, Owen Oyston arrived at Crown Square, Manchester, on May 12, 1995, to face committal proceedings before a stipendiary magistrate, Mr Alan Berg. The lawyers called it 'an old-style committal' to be conducted for five days under a procedure that was about to be changed by Home Secretary Michael Howard's recent Criminal Justice and Public Order Act of 1994.

Flanked by photographers, Oyston walked across the broad square with Mrs Vicki Oyston and his barrister Anthony Scrivener QC. According to the old law, Mr Scrivener would be allowed to cross-examine witnesses at the committal proceedings.

Peter Martin was now facing 60 charges, including rapes, indecent assaults, taking indecent photographs of girls under 16, and under 13, and accused jointly with Oyston of the rarely prosecuted Victorian offence of conspiring to procure women under the age of 21 to have sexual intercourse in any part of the world with a third party. Anthony Scrivener cited precedent to suggest that the conspiracy charge, the only charge directly linking the cases of Oyston and Martin, should be abandoned. He was unsuccessful, but the case was never pursued by the Crown and 'lay on the file' long after Oyston had been convicted.

Four women gave evidence against Oyston in a small modern court room rigged up with television screens to allow the magistrate to watch spy videos from the model agency changing room. The women were giving evidence about events said to have occurred up to seven years earlier, when they had been teenagers. They could not be named and even their evidence could not yet be reported in the media.

Mrs L, a tall red-haired woman in a brown trouser suit, was now married with two children. She said she had been 20 when Owen Oyston raped her in the Hilton Hotel in Park Lane, London:

> I was taken to London by Martin. We stayed at the Hilton Hotel. I was taken to Stringfellows by Owen Oyston. He behaved perfectly. Martin and Oyston arranged for me to go to London again. It was a business meeting. Again, Peter said he had to leave and go back to Manchester. I was to leave my things in Owen's room and then put them in my own room. It was probably about mid-day.
>
> He said he had a business meeting. He gave me £150 to go and buy a new outfit for that evening. He said we were going to meet some businessmen. I returned about four o'clock. I met Oyston again. He said something about there not being enough rooms, so we would have to share for the night. I was worried. I didn't know what to think. I didn't have enough money of my own for a room.
>
> I got dressed. We went for something to eat in the hotel. We had a drink, one or two glasses of wine. Owen needed to make a telephone call so I just went up to the bedroom and got ready for bed. It was about 10.30 p.m. I was wearing cotton bikini knickers and a night shirt. I then felt a heavy weight on me. I could not get the weight off. Owen had his penis inside me. He had made no attempt to awaken me. I tried to push him off. After a while I succeeded. I asked him, "Stop, please." I half managed to push him off then he got off. I needed a lot of strength to get him off. I was upset. I was crying. I managed to get out of the bed. I started to grab my clothes as quick as I could and got my bags.

She said Oyston had done nothing to prevent her leaving the Hilton after she had telephoned her boyfriend and asked him to meet her at Manchester Piccadilly railway station.

When the train rolled into Piccadilly, she was surprised to see Peter Martin waiting.

As her boyfriend went back to his car, she said that Martin 'told me not to say anything to anyone.'

> I did not complain to anyone else because I had been told not to and I was frightened of Peter and Owen. I mentioned to the police I had been raped by Mr Oyston. I never mentioned it to the girls at the agency because I did not know them.

She did not tell her boyfriend about the incident for four weeks but:

> He knew something was wrong because I was not having sex with him.

Oyston gave her no explanation,

> If he had, it's possible that would have been the end of the matter.
> In June 1988 Peter rang me at home out of the blue. Owen wanted to see me. I had to go to Preston to meet them. I wanted an explanation from Owen. I wanted to know why.

She met Oyston at a function on the *Manxman*, a former Isle of Man ferry moored in Preston Dock.

> I sat next to Oyston. He just said to sit there and be quiet. In a quiet moment he asked me to go to the hall for a weekend. I refused. I went for a taxi. I knew what he had in mind. I got no explanation from him. On Christmas Eve 1991, Peter and Owen together telephoned me, wished me Merry Christmas and asked me how I was. Again in 1992 they did the same.

Sitting behind the defendant, Vicki Oyston leaned forward from time to time to put peppermints behind the silk handkerchief in the top pocket of her husband's suit.

A second model, Miss W, said Oyston had raped her between April 1, 1988, and June 1, 1988. She had been introduced to Model Team at the age of 15, when her mother attended an introductory meeting with Peter Martin.

She said Martin had teased her by saying, 'You know what is going to happen when you are 16, don't you?'

She was 16 when she heard that Oyston had taken over the model agency and she went with Peter Martin to see Oyston at the Tickled Trout Hotel, near Preston. She said Martin needed to get petrol for his car and left her with Oyston.

> Owen went into the bedroom. The next thing Owen shouted to me from the bedroom. I went there. He said, "Can you sit next to me?" I did so.
> Prior to this, I had looked up to him as a father figure. I trusted him. He then said how sweet I looked and how much he liked me. Then he started undoing my blouse and I said I didn't want to. He said, "You know what you're here for, don't you?" Then he started to fondle my breasts and asked me to take my clothes off. I knew what Peter was like and did not know if Owen was the same.
>
> We had sexual intercourse. I just lay there. I did not respond in any way. I did not return his kisses."
>
> I was upset by what had happened. I was quiet. If anything, I felt he had betrayed my trust.

Miss W did not tell anyone what had happened. She had sex with Oyston on about eight occasions afterward. Once after they had been talking about her poor family background, she said he had given her an envelope containing £250:

> I felt cheap and disgusted and basically that I was just a prostitute.

When Miss W said she had sex with Martin regularly for a year and described him as a family friend, Peter Martin's barrister Daniel Janner asked her, 'The fact is that you did not go to the police, did you?' Miss W said, 'No.'

Anthony Scrivener QC asked Miss W:

You knew Mr Oyston was influential?

Yes.

You knew he had a media interest?

Yes.

You thought he could further your career?

Yes.

You knew him to be wealthy?

Yes.

During interview, did you make any complaints about Mr Oyston?

No.

Miss W admitted meeting a man from the *Daily Mirror* called Damian who had not left a visiting card but had offered money for her story, Scrivener asked her:

You know you are on oath. What do you have to say about the newspapers?

I am saying on oath it is not my intention to sell my story to a newspaper.

A clinical psychologist Dr Valerie Mellor appeared to support an application for the other complainants to be allowed to give their evidence unseen by the court, hidden behind screens. This was rejected after Scrivener and Janner elicited an admission from Dr Mellor that she had never met the young women and was basing her opinion on thirty years of experience and on the statements that she had read after talks with police and lawyers. Scrivener said:

> I do not wish to cause you offence but I am putting it to you that you have no right to make an opinion of those actions when you have not examined the girls.

Dr Mellor replied:

> I do not take offence. My opinion is based on previous experience when young children have described similar problems. There is a strong risk problems may occur.

Two young women then came into court and agreed to give their evidence without screens and in the presence of the accused.

Miss J said she had joined the agency in 1989 when she was 17 and was living in Grimsby. Martin had suggested that she move into his house in Sale with four or five other 16 to 18 years old girls. Receiving telephone calls and answering the front door were forbidden.

> On the first occasion I slept at the house I was told to sleep on the top floor with Peter Martin. I locked the door. The following day he said jokingly in front of the other girls that I had locked the door and he could not get in.
> We had to have a shower every night before we went to bed and sometimes, they gave us pills, either water tablets or sleeping tablets.
> During the evenings, Martin would sit in jeans and a sweater shirt. But later he would take them off and just wear underpants. He would ask Tracey Grainey to massage his feet while the other girls were in the room. I thought it was unusual.

She had noticed a double bed and a single bed joined together in his bedroom,

> I know for definite three girls slept with him because they had nowhere else to sleep at night. He was a strict man and could be frightening.

Chocolate and cakes were banned at the house, but Martin regularly took the girls out for Chinese meals. Miss J said Martin introduced her to Owen Oyston in a Chinese restaurant in Manchester in 1989, at the age of 17, but she was immediately corrected by her father, speaking from the back of the court. She had been 19 when she met Oyston.

> I did not like him and was not drawn to him in any way. He came across as sleazy.

When Miss J told the court that Martin had taken her by car at night to Claughton Hall, she began to sob:

> He took me out on a country lane, leading to a house that looked like a castle. It was about midnight and dark. Mr Oyston would be waiting. I was scared because I was in the middle of nowhere and didn't know Mr Oyston and why I was there.
>
> Peter Martin told me to go into the house. We went into a big hall. He said Mr Oyston would show me around the house. Peter Martin said, "Do as you are told and you will be all right. I will wait in the car."

Claughton Hall MINISTRY OF INFORMATION

On her way upstairs in the castle she had noticed a suit of armour. In the bedroom there was a four-poster bed:

> He told me to come and sit down on the bed. I said, "No. Can I go into the bathroom?" He said, "Yes." I went into the bathroom for about ten minutes,

> thinking, "What am I going to do?" because I did not know what was going to happen.
>
> I came out and Mr Oyston was sat there. He just had a shirt on. The lower half of his body was naked. He told me to lie down next to him so I did because I was scared. He told me to remove my underwear, just my knickers, but my dress and jacket remained on. Mr Oyston climbed on top of me. I tried to push him away. He said, "You will be alright. Don't be silly." I said, "No, I don't want to do this because it is wrong." He then put his hand on his penis and forced it into my vagina. He was just moaning heavily. I was crying. I did nothing because he had me pinned down. He had one hand across my shoulder, one on his penis and his weight on top. It was painful because I was a virgin. I forced him off. It was before ejaculation. He said, "You are silly. You should have done as you were told." I quickly got my knickers back on. He tried to kiss my face but I had turned my head away and he kissed me on the neck.

She said Martin was waiting for her in the car. She thought she had been in the house between twenty and thirty minutes.

> He said nothing to me about what had happened in the house. He had absolutely no sympathy. I did not say anything because they are both very powerful men.

On the journey back she said Martin had given her two hundred pounds from his wallet.

> Afterwards, I felt absolutely disgusted. I could not really tell anyone, not even after I got back to the house. I had a shower and then Peter Martin gave me a sleeping tablet.

She alleged that on another occasion Oyston had come into the house at Sale and put his hands on her vagina. Questioned about her police interview by Anthony Scrivener, Miss J admitted:

> I did not tell them I had been raped by Mr Oyston.

She denied her picture had appeared on the front page of one of Oyston's magazines and insisted she had not asked Oyston for two thousand pounds to buy a car or invited him to a party in Grimsby, or invited him to dine with her parents, or help her set up a boutique. She denied telling Oyston's associates that she loved him, but did admit that she had never told police about telephoning Oyston's personal assistant several years later, just a few days before his arrest:

> Why did you make a call to her in January of this year?
>
> I wanted to, because she is a close friend of mine.

Miss Y told the court she had been indecently assaulted by Oyston between September 30, 1989, and September 30, 1990:

> Prior to my sixteenth birthday, it was mentioned that the legal age for sex was 16.

On her birthday she met Oyston with other girls in a Manchester hotel. He had given her a twenty-pound note. A few months after her birthday he met her on the stairs in Martin's house, grabbed her arm and told her to go to the bedroom.

> He sat beside me. He put his hand on my shoulder and told me to lie back. He put his hand on my thigh in the middle of my thigh and knee.

She admitted to Scrivener:

> After the incident, it did not occur to me to go to the police. Had the police not come around five years later, I would not have done anything about it at all.

The next witness, Miss H[95], was the woman from Accrington whose account of her experience in Oyston's bedroom at Claughton Hall would eventually send him to prison for rape. Miss H said she had joined the agency at 14 when she was still at school. She had stayed weekends at the model house, been ordered not to wear knickers in bed and was introduced to Oyston at a restaurant in Manchester. On the night she met Oyston, she said she had been invited to travel with him on a journey to Claughton Hall on the back seat of Peter Martin's white Toyota Supra car. Martin was driving and Lysa Rubotham was in the front seat. Miss H was now nineteen.

> It was late at night. Owen got hold of my hand and put it on his pants. He moved my hand up and down on his penis. Then he unzipped his pants. He got hard and then got my head on his penis and moved my head up and down on it. His penis was in my mouth. Owen never said anything.
> He thingied in my mouth.

Soon afterwards, arriving at Claughton Hall, she said she and Lysa had entered Oyston's bedroom, where she watched Oyston and Lysa have sex in the bed while sitting in a chair a few feet away.

> Owen told me to take my clothes off and get into bed. Lisa was still in the bed.

Miss H appeared to be in extreme distress and obviously under the influence of drugs as she told the court that Oyston had raped her in the bed with Lysa. She admitted in court that she had abused various drugs, cannabis, ecstasy and amphetamines since she was 13. She was not asked about LSD. Her use of LSD from the age of 14 would not be reported medically until after Oyston was sent to prison, when Miss H was claiming civil damages from him in 1998. During a 210-minute interview in Harley

[95] Known as Miss B in contemporary court reporting.

Street, Dr Fiona Mason, a consultant forensic psychiatrist at Broadmoor Hospital reported that Miss H

> told me that she experimented with illicit substances during her teenage years along with the rest of her peer group. She experimented with marijuana at approximately the age of 13 and tried other oral illicit substances such as ecstasy, amphetamines and LSD at the age of approximately 14. Miss H stated that she would use these drugs when out at clubs and then only if she was given them or could afford them (which was relatively rarely). Miss H said that she never used intravenous drugs and had never experienced physical withdrawal from the illicit substances that she had used. She said that eventually her drug usage (apart from marijuana) stopped as she wished to do well for herself at the model agency.

Cross-examined by Daniel Janner about why she had stayed at the model agency for three years after the incident, Miss H said she had nowhere else to go:

> I could not go home because for the first time in my life my parents were proud of me. I couldn't let mum and dad down again.

The fourth complainant, Miss R, said she had joined the agency at 16 and stayed at the house in Sale to save travelling costs from her home in Wigan:

> Peter Martin took me into a little room. He said I should not have a boyfriend because they hold you back in modelling. He pushed me against the wall. He was very annoyed. He scared me."
>
> Martin used to grab hold of me and drag me. He used to try and kiss me and he would slap me and pull my hair. I think he must have got some sort of kick out of it.

She said that Martin took her with a girl called Dawn on a 'modelling trip' by train to the Grosvenor Hotel in London but after they had checked in to their rooms, he told them that Oyston wanted to see them at the Hilton Hotel. She recognised Oyston, 'He always wears a cowboy hat and a long coat.' After dinner and a trip to a night club they went back to Oyston's apartment in 'Park Lane or Mayfair'.

> Owen sat on the bed with Dawn and me. When Dawn went to the toilet, Owen tried to put his hands on my breasts. I pushed him away. I was fully clothed. He tried to kiss me and then Dawn came back and that was it. I had told him, 'I don't want to do that.'

On a later occasion Miss R said she went downstairs at the Sale house for a glass of water and met Oyston. She said Martin told her to go to Tracey Grainey's room and get into bed with Grainey.

> After a couple of hours, it may not have been one, I heard two people at the side of me. It sounded as if they were having sex. At first I thought it was Peter and Tracey but - with the door open - I could see it was Owen Oyston on top of Grainey. Martin then rushed into the bedroom and pulled Owen off Grainey. He said to Oyston: "What are you doing? How have you got into the bedroom?"

The cross-examination entered uncharted waters when Miss R appeared to claim that she had sex with a number of men against their will:

> They did not rape me but forced me into sex. At the time, I was 16 and I was scared to leave. I was also scared of my dad.
>
> Some of the sex you had with Mr Martin lasted for hours?
>
> Yes.
>
> And you had sex in different positions, including you being on top of him, didn't you?
>
> I was never on top of him.

Despite Mr Janner reminding her of a video of 'certain individuals' having sex, she refused to reconsider her reply and declared:

> I never said I liked rough sex.

She told Anthony Scrivener she was now a housewife, married to an unemployed man and living on social benefits. Her last job had been in a fish and chip shop.

Has it ever occurred to you to report what happened to the police?

No.

Can you supply dates, months or times?

No. I think it was in the summer of 1990.

Miss R told the court that a man named Julian Allitt had sex with her without consent:

Peter gave me a key to his room in a hotel in Preston. I thought if I didn't do it Peter would go mad with me.

Did a man called Giorgio rape you?

I didn't know it was him because I was blindfolded at the time.

She told Mr Scrivener that she had sex against her will with a man she knew as Derek Zissman, a man called Warren, and a man named Nino.

Did you consent then?

Not really.

Did you tell the police you were consenting?

Yes.

Were you ever involved with other women?

Yes - but only once.

Were you ever involved in a threesome?

Yes.

Was that rape?

No - but I felt I had to do that as well.

Mr Berg, the magistrate, had to contend with unexpected problems during the committal. At one moment, a well-known face appeared in the window of the courtroom door. The politically sensitive Oyston hearing was briefly interrupted by the appearance of a face from Manchester's last big political trial. It was the face of Kevin Taylor, the businessman whose friendship with John Stalker, deputy chief constable of Greater Manchester Police, had been used to engineer the removal of Stalker from the sensitive 'shoot-to-kill' inquiry in Northern Ireland in 1986.

The Poisoned Tree, by Keith Mumby, Sidgwick & Jackson, London, 1990.

Political dirty tricks had finished Stalker's brilliant police career in 1987, although the fraud case mounted against the blameless Kevin Taylor eventually collapsed in 1990, when Judge Michael Sachs memorably described evidence gathered dishonestly by Greater Manchester Police as 'the fruits of this poisoned tree.' It had been the maverick lawyer Charles Buckley, now dropped from Oyston's defence team, who discovered hidden links between the arrest of Kevin Taylor for allegedly defrauding the Co-operative Bank and the politically motivated attacks on the reputation of Deputy Chief Constable John Stalker.

Buckley had been talking about similarly linking the recent arrest of Oyston with the well-documented conspiracy against him, run by Michael Murrin and Chris More and funded through Robert Atkins, Lord Blaker and Bill Harrison. Regional politics in North West England in the days of Margaret Thatcher began to look dangerous. Kevin Taylor had been chairman of the Manchester Conservative Association. Oyston had entertained Neil Kinnock as the Labour Party's biggest private donor.

Kevin Taylor's compensation claim, one of four Stalker Affair malicious prosecution cases, had been looming over Greater Manchester Police when they were launching Operation Chittering. Their insurers would eventually settle out of court with Taylor for over a million pounds but Chief Constable David Wilmot revealed to the House of Commons Home Affairs Committee in 1998 that 'the total sum for damages and costs of all the parties involved in the four cases was £10,593,574.'

In another unnerving moment, Peter Martin's barrister Daniel Janner asked for a clip from a seized video to be transmitted to the magistrate's television screen, intending to demonstrate that Peter Martin had been videoed having sex with a consenting woman. The wrong section of videotape was transmitted to Mr Berg's screen. The reporters and the members of the public could not see the pictures, but they could hear the cries of a woman in sexual ecstasy. As Tracey Grainey, the third defendant, rose and ran from the courtroom, Det Sgt Harrison solemnly identified the woman on the video to Mr Berg: 'That was Tracey Grainey.'

Mr Berg eventually decided to commit Owen Oyston for trial at Manchester Crown Court on only three charges of rape; Miss L in the London Hilton, Miss J at Claughton Hall and Miss H at Claughton Hall. He would also stand trial on two charges of indecently assaulting Miss J and Miss H. Mr Berg found no case to answer on the charge of the rape of Miss W or on the indecent assault charges involving Miss Y and Miss R. Anthony Scrivener QC reserved Oyston's defence and successfully applied for the return of his client's passport and the continuation of his £50,000 bail.

The many charges against Peter Martin and Tracey Grainey would be heard at a trial that would not begin for another year and Martin would remain in prison.

CHAPTER 18

Disclosure

By the autumn of 1995, Oyston had travelled to so many legal meetings in the Chancery Lane offices of his corporate solicitors Denton Hall, that on at least one occasion a railway guard held the London train for four minutes at Preston station after hearing that his notorious first-class passenger was running late.

People in all OJO's regular haunts were being asked for details about his previous movements, at the Hilton Hotel in Park Lane, at the Portland Hotel in Manchester, at the Don Antonio Restaurant in Sale, at Blackpool Football Club, at the Preston offices of *Lancashire Life* and especially up at Claughton Hall, known to Oyston's staff as 'Hassle Castle.' A team of private detectives and solicitors from London set up temporary offices in Oyston Mill, a former First World War searchlight factory near Preston Dock.

Oyston was still regularly seen in the City of London and the West End. Friendly journalists in London offered to give evidence about his many appearances during the four years in which the complainants said they had been raped or assaulted. The crimes were alleged to have been committed on various unspecified dates between April 1, 1988, and December 31, 1991.

One complainant refused to state in what month, season, or even what year, the alleged offence had taken place. Miss H, still a teenager, claimed she was indecently assaulted and later raped during and immediately after a car journey from Manchester to Claughton Hall but refused to commit to a date. The Crown later decided that this must have happened on a certain night between October 4, 1991, and December 31, 1991.

In the detailed 'action books' kept by Oyston's staff, in his appointments diary and in thousands of hotel bills and travel tickets lay evidence that would eventually cover almost every day and evening in the 21-month allegation period. But it was to all to no avail. Seven days into his third trial, when serious inconsistencies appeared in the timing of Miss H's evidence, the trial judge agreed to a request from the Crown to extend the indictment period by a further twelve months, running on from October 4, 1991, to December 31, 1992, thereby devaluing all the expensive research performed by the defence, who had, of course, never bothered to account for any of Oyston's movements in the year of 1992.

For nearly a year the defence solicitors had been combing tons of evidence gathered by the police but 'unused' in the case against Oyston. English law, since weakened by statute, gave them in 1995 free access to this 'unused material' under powers granted after the Court of Appeal had noted that non-disclosure lay behind some of the most shocking injustices of the previous decade.

There had been the tragic case of Stefan Kiszko, who served 16 years for the murder of a young girl because the prosecution failed to disclose available evidence that the semen stains on the dead girl's clothing could not have come from him because he was infertile.

Judith Ward had served 17 years for murder after forensic scientists failed to disclose test results and after the Crown had failed to disclose that Ward had a record of compulsively confessing to crimes she had not committed. The key to the unused evidence was a huge paper printout from the HOLMES computer known as the HOLMES Log.

For 11 months solicitors, private detectives and Owen Oyston's daughter Heidi had checked the HOLMES entries for thousands of documents and statements logged by the police officers. Yet on the morning of February 9, 1996, only two weeks before the opening of Oyston's first trial, two hundred documents on the HOLMES Log had still not been disclosed to the defence. The Crown Prosecution Service had talked about applying for some documents to be denied under the Public Interest Immunity legislation which protects sensitive investigation techniques, although no such application was ever made. The notebooks of the senior investigating officer had been suggested as a subject for PII.

On February 9, Det Sgt Harry Harrison logged a number of documents on to the HOLMES computer system with the following declaration:

> During the course of this enquiry I have prepared the unused material schedules. These schedules have exceeded 2000 separate items.
> One of the documents that I have previously supplied to the Crown Prosecution Service is a police report dated 17th July, 1992. This report was compiled by Detective Inspector Robishaw and accompanied some notes I had made in 1992.
> On Thursday 8th February, 1996 I was on duty and in the process of checking that all the documents in the HOLMES system were filed in the correct order, when I saw that the above mentioned document had a further report attached to it. I had not seen the additional report previously.
> This document related to a Greater Manchester Police Fraud Squad Intelligence Document and associated documents.
> I immediately made the additional document available to the Crown Prosecution Service.

Harry Harrison was the detective who had investigated Michael Murrin's allegations about the Model Team agency back in 1992. He was also the detective who had accompanied Det Con Julie Sharpe in October 1994 to interview Miss H at Accrington police station, when the interview notes went missing. The documents logged by Det Sgt Harrison were not seen by Owen Oyston or his lawyers. Most of them referred to the 1992

Model Team investigation which was unknown to the defence team, until a journalist told them about it in September 1995, six months after Oyston's arrest.

The late-appended documents had one other thing in common. They either mentioned the name of Michael Murrin or they referred to media coverage of the Longridge chip shop owner's campaign against Oyston and his involvement with Robert Atkins, Lord Blaker and Bill Harrison. There was Murrin's angry letter to Det Insp Robishaw of GMP Fraud Squad, dated July 15, 1992. It had been handled by an assistant chief constable on July 28, 1992 but not appended to the HOLMES Log until February 9, 1996. On August 3, 1992, Det Chief Insp Anson of GMP had reported:

> MURRIN is a prolific writer of letters to the police, MPs, ministers, government departments etc. and has made a series of complaints to Lancashire Constabulary alleging corruption and malpractice by Preston Borough councillors in respect of land deals: however, no hard evidence has ever been uncovered which would justify criminal proceedings in respect of his allegations.
>
> MURRIN is said by Det Chief Insp Maloney of the Lancashire Constabulary Commerce Branch to have developed a personal vendetta against Owen OYSTON who MURRIN believes has manipulated Preston councillors to his own advantage in respect of land deals in which OYSTON has concealed interests.
> In February / March 1992 MURRIN appeared in a Channel 4 television documentary which focused on the leader of Derbyshire County Council, David BOOKBINDER, and his alleged association with OYSTON. There was an inference, at least, of malpractice.

Det Sgt Harrison's note about the unused material being misfiled was later contradicted by John Lord, a Crown Prosecution Service solicitor who said quite openly that the documents were held back because they were 'sensitive'. The sensitivity of the documents only became obvious during the third trial of Owen Oyston, after Oyston had asked his barristers to raise the existence of the political conspiracy in court. That move appeared to badly damage Oyston's case when the Senior Investigating Officer said that when he took the decision to arrest Oyston he had not known that Michael Murrin had been supplying information about the model agency in 1992.

In the various editions of the HOLMES Log disclosed to Oyston's defence by the Crown Prosecution Service there was a gap between entry 462 and entry 464. A document, dated October 5, 1994, said to be the text of A463, turned up after Oyston's trial in papers connected to the case against Peter Martin:

> A463
> Liaise with VO14 child abuse section re-any further information on N1 Martin
> and N2 Grainey or Central Models Agency.
> 051094 0944
> DS Harrison DC Sharpe.
> Sir. Checked with VO14 re Martin, Grainey, Central Models and Jennifer Cooper. Nothing known with the exception of 1992 report from Insp Robishaw, Fraud Squad.
> DS Harrison.

This early October date, just after the first raid on the model agency, shows that there was an immediate reference to the 1992 investigation an event entirely triggered by Murrin, the leading conspirator against Owen Oyston. The report section of the entry, addressed to "Sir" suggests that it was directly addressed to Bill Roberts, the SIO of Operation Chittering. Significantly, it presumes that Roberts knew about Murrin's connections with the Lancashire Constabulary which had led to the 1992 investigation.

A year and seven months later, in the witness box at the third Oyston trial, Det Supt Bill Roberts told the jury:

> I only found out afterwards that Murray [sic], to my knowledge now, had been giving information to the Lancashire police.

If the A463 text referred to Oyston, it would indicate that accidentally or on purpose the Crown Prosecution Service and the GMP had kept it from defence lawyers who might have used it in the third trial, or even in later appeal proceedings. They had, perhaps accidentally, concealed evidence of the conspiracy by Murrin and Melanie Hardy to incriminate Oyston in a police investigation at Model Team agency in 1992. Evidence of efforts to hide Murrin's 1992 activity shows that someone might have decided that it could weaken the prosecution case against Oyston.

The unusual charge of conspiring to procure women that was laid against in Oyston in 1995 but allowed to lie on the file, was very significantly exactly what Murrin had accused Oyston of doing in 1992. The allegation by Murrin and Melanie Hardy that Oyston actually owned the agency had been investigated and rejected as untrue in 1992 by Det Insp Robishaw. When it resurfaced as one of the 1995 charges it became further proof of the strong links between Murrin and the Manchester police, links that the CPS and Det Sgt Harrison kept away from the HOLMES Log until February 9, 1996.

CHAPTER 19

First Trial

On February 27, 1996, Oyston appeared before a jury for the first time. The clerk in court five at Manchester Crown Court asked at 10:43: 'Would Owen John Oyston surrender to bail?'[96] The tall man in a dark blue suit, with a Blackpool FC tangerine handkerchief in his top pocket, stepped into the glass-screened dock. Mrs Vicki Oyston and their five sons and daughters waited on seats in the long glassy corridor outside the courtroom, high above Crown Square.

Leading the defence was the Queen's Counsel who the year before had raced to Altrincham police station after Oyston's arrest. Anthony Scrivener was even taller than Oyston. Despite his origins, as the only son of a Canterbury ironmonger and despite his politics, as an outspoken republican and Labour Party activist, Tony Scrivener had been elected chairman of the Bar Council in 1991. He had been earning half a million pounds a year for commercial advocacy in Hong Kong, Singapore and Malaysia but was also famous for taking *pro bono* cases from the Caribbean, appealing before the Privy Council in London for men on death row in Jamaica.

In the true English 'cab rank' tradition, Scrivener at 60, had represented both the rich and the poor, from striking coal miners and Gerry Conlon of the 'Guildford Four' to the tycoon Richard Branson.His clients included the stock market wizard Asil Nadir and Dame Shirley Porter, the Tesco heir

---

[96] Court reporting from Harold Heys and from transcripts

surcharged by a district auditor for 'disgraceful and improper gerrymandering's

His adversary was Helen Grindrod QC, Manchester's leading feminist barrister and a very tough woman. She had battled for years to reach her important place on the Northern Circuit. As the daughter of a Liverpool warehouseman she had won an open scholarship to Liverpool's oldest grammar school for girls and then an exhibition to St Hilda's College Oxford.

She was fresh from her most important feminist victory, the 1995 appeal against the murder conviction of Emma Humphreys, only 17 years old when she killed a pimp who had repeatedly raped and beaten her. After seven years in prison Emma had contacted a feminist pressure group Justice for Women, co-founded by Julie Bindel, a campaigning journalist who once argued in *The Guardian*:

> We live in a culture in which rape is still an everyday reality, and yet women are blamed for it, as it is viewed as an inevitable feature of heterosexual sex. Domestic violence is still a chronic problem for countless women in relationships with men. Women are told we must love our oppressors, while, as feminists, we fight to end the power afforded them as a birthright.[97]

Julie Bindel wrote in 2002:

> I first met Helen Grindrod when Justice for Women set Emma Humphreys' appeal in train, and saw, at first hand, her amazingly creative thinking and tenacity when dealing with miscarriages of justice, particularly when sexual violence played a part.[98]

Mrs Grindrod persuaded the Court of Appeal that extreme provocation after long-term abuse was a sufficient defence to a murder charge. The conviction was reduced to manslaughter. Emma was released after serving ten years of a life sentence, establishing a precedent that provocation can be cumulative and that it does not have to occur immediately before a murder to form a legitimate defence.

Mrs Grindrod threw dark and furrowed glances at two rows of reporters crowded on the press benches for the Oyston trial. The reporters had been solemnly warned by Mr Justice McCullough that all reporting of the case was now forbidden under Section 4 [2] of the Contempt of Court Act 1981, to avoid prejudicing other juries in two later trials. News and television deadlines would therefore be stretched until the end of Oyston's third trial, expected later in the year. The ruling thinned personnel on the press benches. Only the lubricious *Daily Sport* could justify the continued full-time

---

[97] *My sexual revolution* by Julie Bindel, The Guardian, January 30, 2009.

[98] The Guardian, July 17, 2002.

presence of a reporter.[99]

The scarlet robed high court judge, thirty years on the bench, understood that Mr Oyston was a little hard of hearing in one ear. If the defendant was having difficulty in following any of the evidence, all he had to do was raise his hand. Oyston nodded and thanked him. Seven women and five men were sworn as jurors to try two charges, the rape and the indecent assault of Miss J between January 1989 and June 1990.

Miss J, a 6-foot tall silver blonde former model from Lincolnshire, now 25, was dressed in a brilliant white Dolce & Gabbana designer jacket, buttoned over a navy-blue top with tight polka dot trousers. She took her place in the witness box only 3 metres away from Owen Oyston.

Mrs Grindrod asked Miss J to describe the rape in Owen Oyston's Jacobean bed at Claughton Hall that she had described in earlier committal proceedings. Miss J told the Manchester jury that after she had been raped and indecently assaulted by Oyston she had been invited by his personal assistant, Mrs Gill Bridge, to join Oyston and Mrs Bridge at dinner in the restaurant of the Grosvenor Hotel in London, where Oyston was dining with the press tycoon Robert Maxwell. She told the court that on this, and on other occasions, Gill Bridge had helped her to get Oyston drunk so that she would not have to have sex with him. Scrivener asked her:

> If you were raped, as you suggest, you might think you might remember the year, the month, the season?

Miss J replied:

> I can't recall what date or what month, but I'm clear I was 17 years old.

She admitted telephoning Oyston's personal assistant in January 1995,

[99] John Burke-Davies

just before Oyston's arrest but denied telling Mrs Bridge that she would like to see Mrs Bridge and Mr Oyston again:

> I rang her just to say hello. She was a friend of mine. She is not now, because she is being paid by Owen Oyston.

She denied that Oyston had attended her 21st birthday party or that she had told magazine editor Brian Hargreaves that she was hoping to marry Owen Oyston:

> I should hope not.

She admitted going with Oyston and Gill Bridge to see the musical *Miss Saigon*, but said it was only to keep Mrs Bridge company. Mr Scrivener suggested:

> You shared a suite with Mr Oyston on numerous occasions.
> You first had sex at the Hilton Hotel in London. Mr Oyston was already there. You went shopping in the West End. You bought high-heeled shoes. You went to the suite, slept with him and later went for a meal at an adjoining restaurant.

On the morning of the third day of the trial, the judge told the jury that the indictment against Oyston would have to be changed, since Miss J was now saying that she had been raped in 1988, rather than in 1989 as she had originally told the police. Miss J, now wearing a short quilted black bomber jacket with a red skirt, denied staying with Oyston at the Royal Trafalgar Thistle Hotel in London in February 1992. When she was shown a signed hotel bill, she denied that it carried her signature. Mr Scrivener asked:

> It would be unbelievable if you would stay in a hotel with such a man in February 1992 if he had raped you?

As she left the witness box she said, 'I just want to get on with my life now.'

Det Supt Roberts, the senior investigating officer, then gave evidence that

Oyston had not been arrested as part of any political conspiracy:

> The decision to arrest Owen Oyston was mine and mine alone. There was no outside influence of any sort whatsoever.

Mr Scrivener then opened the case for the defence by noting Miss J's refusal to offer details:

> We do not know the date, the month, the year, or even the season of the year when the alleged rape took place.
>
> In addition to that, she never reported it to the police and never complained to anyone about it not even her friends, not even her family.
>
> These allegations are denied by Owen Oyston. Whether he was wise to have a girlfriend of that age at that time is not a matter of direct concern. We are concerned about whether he is a rapist.
>
> Is Miss J behaving like someone who has been raped by Mr Oyston? She was behaving like someone who was having an affair with him for quite a long period of time.

Scrivener outlined Oyston's life story of business success followed by the dirty tricks campaign that culminated in libellous *Sunday Times* articles and asked Oyston:

> Did you come across a gentleman called Mr Murrin?
>
> Yes. He passed me 48 hours of tapes which were recordings of conversations with Lord Blaker, Robert Atkins and William Harrison, the drugs squad, the Inland Revenue and others which proved Mr Murrin had conspired against me.
>
> Mr Murrin was paid by these gentlemen, it transpires, and this was made public in the *Sunday Times* case. He was paid by them to carry out dirty tricks against me and other members of the Labour Party in Lancashire.

Oyston told the court he had first met Miss J towards the end of 1989 and that they had a sexual relationship lasting four years.

> I know it was towards that date because it was around the time of the *Sunday Times* onslaught against me. It was quite a traumatic time.

The jury inspected pictures of Claughton Hall, the late mediaeval building which Oyston had bought 22 years earlier. There was laughter when Oyston described his rickety 'full tester' bed.

> It is very old and it can be quite unnerving if you are not used to it.
> What is unnerving?
> Well, Your Honour, if you were having sexual intercourse on it, the bed and canopy would move quite vigorously.

The laughter grew louder when Scrivener suggested that the jury could visit Claughton Hall and test the movement of the bed themselves, a facility which was later arranged by the judge. Oyston claimed he had never had sexual intercourse with Miss J on the full tester bed at Claughton Hall. He could certainly remember meeting her 'in the beginning of 1990. I never met her during the course of 1988 when she was seventeen.' He remembered exchanging telephone numbers with her early in 1990 when they began a sexual relationship

> Mostly at the Hilton Hotel. Sometimes the Royal Trafalgar Hotel. Sometimes in Manchester. Once at least at the Tickled Trout. The Portland Hotel in Manchester also.
>
> We agreed we would meet when she had an appointment in London and I was also there on business. Eventually she came to meet me whether she had business or not. She must have stayed at the Hilton Hotel at least 20 or 30 times with me in the same suite in the same name.

Oyston told the court he had given Miss J two thousand pounds to buy a second hand car and had arranged for two hundred and fifty pounds to be paid to her when she had difficulty paying her rent.

> The first time we stayed at the Hilton Hotel we went shopping. We went to the West End, to Miss Selfridge and bought some clothes there and to a shoe shop and bought further items, a pair of high-heeled shoes and an evening dress.

Miss J had been photographed for the front cover of one his magazine supplements. He had arranged a twenty-first birthday party for her at the

Windows on the World restaurant on the top floor of the Park Lane Hilton. He recalled going to see *Miss Saigon* with both Miss J and Gill Bridge.

> She proposed to me on at least one occasion. Of course, I was already married. I did not take it seriously.
>
> She would ring me and tell me she was getting engaged. On at least one occasion she rang me to tell me she was getting married.
>
> If I wasn't there, she would leave a message with Gill Bridge. I had the distinct impression she was trying to drive me into a permanent relationship.
>
> I expressed my concern that she should be careful with the Press if they made contact with her. I was concerned by investigations not just by the *Sunday Times* but also by the Inland Revenue, the Takeover Panel, the Stock Exchange, IMRO, the regulatory body in the City, the drugs squad and also Lancashire Police, one private detective and most tabloid newspapers at that time.
>
> That was inspired by Mr Michael Murrin who was employed by Lord Blaker, then a member of parliament, by Robert Atkins, a member of the government, and by William Harrison, who was a personal friend of Robert Atkins. Michael Murrin hounded me for 12 to 14 years and the ensuing inquiries were a direct result of his activities.

Mrs Grindrod began to press on the question of the political conspiracy and Oyston appeared to withdraw:

> I have no comment to make about any conspiracy. I shall pursue the conspiracy matter in the appropriate court. When the police came to see me three weeks before my court case, I naturally thought something was going on. I assumed there was a connection.

On the morning of the fifth day of the trial, Kevin Maxwell, the son of the dead media mogul Robert Maxwell, gave evidence to say that he had known Oyston in a business capacity for a long time. Oyston had written to him and his brother Ian to offer condolences after his father died at sea and Oyston had offered them support. Kevin Maxwell was shown a magazine picture of Miss J:

> I believe I may have met her on at least one occasion, possibly two. I met Mr Oyston at least five days after my father's death, between January and June 1992. I believe I met this lady with Gill Bridge and Mr Oyston. It was June 17. I am more certain of that date but I may have also have met her earlier that year.
>
> I had dinner with Mr Oyston that evening in the company of Gill Bridge and, I believe, this lady as well. I recall it with precision, because on June 19, about five or six hours after I left Mr Oyston, I was arrested in a dawn raid on my home by the Serious Fraud Office. I have just been acquitted of those charges.
>
> We met in the Hilton Park Lane Hotel, London. I recall going to one of the bars and watching part of a football match between England and Sweden. It was a game we lost. I then went upstairs and we had a drink there in the company of Gill Bridge and, I believe, this lady. We then went on to dinner in an Italian restaurant close to my home. I picked it. Because at that time I was an object of a lot of press harassment and there was a lot of journalists camped outside my home. I wanted to go to the local pizzeria instead of anywhere more public. We sat at different tables from the ladies. Dinner finished to the best of my recollection just after midnight.

Earlier that evening they had all been together in Oyston's room for a few minutes, probably not longer than a quarter of an hour.

> The atmosphere was perfectly amicable and to my eyes she appeared to be Owen's girlfriend. She appeared to have friendly relations with him.

Oyston's witnesses on the sixth day of the first trial included one of his former lovers, two journalists and the head waiter at the Hilton Hotel. All reported seeing him conducting an affair with Miss J. Angelo Sorelli, the head waiter at the Park Lane Hilton, said he organised a twenty-first birthday party for Miss J.

> He introduced her as his girlfriend. I remember she had short hair and long legs.

Paul Halloran, now a former *Private Eye* reporter and co-author of the biography of Mark Thatcher, told the court he remembered first meeting Oyston on the day after a *Private Eye* Christmas party, when he had a hangover. He had first met Miss J with Oyston's assistant Gill Bridge at a restaurant in May or June 1992. He said Miss J tried to fool him into thinking she was foreign.

> At that time, I thought her name was Laetitia. We had a few drinks and went to restaurant in Greek Street.
>
> She did not talk a great deal. I had some difficulty understanding her because Gill spoke to her in French and with this name Laetitia, I thought she could possibly be French. Later on, she was forced to order her food and had an accent which was decidedly Grimsby-ish. I thought they were having a little bit of fun at my expense.

The next time he saw Miss J was in the Windows on the World restaurant on the roof of the Hilton Hotel, 'They were on friendly terms. She seemed to be having a good time.'

Paul Halloran told the court he had volunteered to give evidence for the defence because,

> I thought, in this respect call me old-fashioned, if you like, but if someone comes along and accuses someone of rape it is highly unlikely they would be entertained by the alleged rapist some years later. I was horrified.

Sharon Denby, a former model and consultant at Model Team, said Miss J was a new model at the agency in 1988. She remembered that Miss J and Oyston had dined together at a Manchester restaurant in the summer of 1989 and seeming

> on friendly terms and to be relaxed in each other's company. I assumed them to be having a personal relationship with one another.

Now Mrs Sharon Denby-Sedgewick and reading law at the University of

Central Lancashire, she remembered lending a new dress to Miss J in August 1989 so that she could go out to dinner with Oyston. Mrs Denby said she left the agency in 1989 when she had become pregnant but had returned in February 1992. She told the court that Miss J, who had claimed to have left the agency in 1990, had still been on the agency books in 1992. When questioned by Mrs Grindrod, she admitted that in 1988 she had been having an affair with Owen Oyston, 'It finished a few months later in 1988.'

Brian Hargreaves, a retired magistrate and former editor of the *West Lancashire Evening Gazette* described volunteering to be a witness:

> The day after Mr Oyston had been charged - I read it in the papers - I came out to see him and suggested he should call witnesses among the women of his acquaintance who could testify how alien this was to him. I suggested Miss J. And to my horror he told me she was the plaintiff.

Mr Hargreaves, formerly an editor of glossy county magazines for Oyston, told the court that Miss J had said that she hoped to marry Oyston.

> Mr Oyston suggested to me that it would be a good idea to use Miss J's picture in the magazines. I agreed with this. We were publishing this supplement. I thought she would be most suitable to appear on the cover. Mr Oyston gave me her number. I rang her and arranged to meet her. I had seen them together on several occasions - informal dinners with a few other people. They seemed to be on most affectionate terms. They seemed to have a very happy relationship.

Hargreaves lunched with Miss J after the photo-shoot.

> She talked very affectionately about Mr Oyston. On some occasions she talked about her intention to marry Mr Oyston.

Brian Hargreaves told the jury he had given Miss J a cheque for a hundred pounds when she was a finalist in the Miss UK contest and Oyston had repaid him. The last time he had seen the couple together was in late 1990 or early 1991 at the Royal Trafalgar Hotel in London where they again appeared 'happy and affectionate.'

Mrs Grindrod suggested to Mr Hargreaves that Miss J had actually been booked for the magazine photo-shoot through the model agency and had been a friend of Gill Bridge, rather than Oyston. Mr Hargreaves replied:

> I must disagree with that. She was clearly Mr Oyston's friend. Mrs Bridge's association with her was quite secondary.

John Thompson, a retired director of the Independent Broadcasting Authority, said that Oyston had turned up unexpectedly in a distressed state at his Chelsea home in August 1988. Mr Thompson said:

> Having remarried, Mr Oyston clearly hoped the relationship with his wife would be harmonious and upbeat. But immediately after his marriage there was a problem with another man involved. Mr Oyston was pretty put out and low. In the course of the conversation he asked to be put in touch with a marriage counsellor We recommended a psychotherapist.

Mrs Vicki Oyston told the jury that she did indeed have an affair after she had remarried Oyston. She had continued visiting Claughton Hall after her 1982 divorce. Although she had bought herself a home in Lancaster, Claughton Hall 'was still treated very much as the family home.' In the seven months before their August 1988 remarriage, her visits to the hall had become more frequent and she had stayed the night in Oyston's bed a couple of nights a week. They went on combined business and holiday trips together, including a long excursion through the Soviet Union, China and Hong Kong. The scene at Claughton Hall was usually hectic with constant business meetings, even at weekends. Meetings started as early as 8.30am and would often continue until the early hours.

> In my opinion it was a nightmare. The business was being run almost totally from there. This was one of the reasons I had initially left. My father in law was living there and maybe four or five live-in staff, apart from people who came on a daily basis, secretarial and domestic staff.

Gill Bridge, managing director of Blackpool Football Club, said she had worked for Oyston as his travelling personal assistant in July 1990, before taking up her post at the football club in March 1994. All calls from 'young ladies' wanting to speak to Oyston had been put through to Mrs Bridge.

> Miss J always rang to speak to Mr Oyston. The only time she rang to speak to me was if Mr Oyston had asked her to ring me.

Oyston had asked her to arrange for money to be put in Miss J's bank account, when Miss J had trouble paying her landlord in London.

> I would have preferred the accounts department did not know that Mr Oyston wanted to raise a cheque for a girl on his personal account. I didn't want all and sundry to know he was giving money to a girl - and I did not think he did either.

She denied lending the money on her own account. She could not have afforded to give Miss J two hundred and fifty pounds, at a time when her weekly pay was only two hundred and forty. She was then asked about an invoice to Miss J from the Royal Trafalgar Thistle Hotel, on which was written: 'Friend of Gill Bridge - GB to repay.' Mrs Bridge explained that Miss J had arrived early at the hotel and booked her own room, before later moving into Oyston's suite. Oyston's firm had then paid the bill for the extra room. Asked if Miss J had really been her companion at the hotel, Gill Bridge said:

> No. She was having an affair with Mr Oyston. I may have been friendly towards her but she was not my friend.

Mrs Bridge told the court that Miss J had telephoned her on January 26, 1995, a few days after Miss J had made allegations against Oyston to the police.

> I found it strange because I had not spoken to her for two years. She said it would be nice to see us both again.

Mrs Grindrod asked:

Mrs Bridge. You worked for Mr Oyston for a long time, have a great loyalty to him, you owe him your promotion?

No. I worked hard for my promotion.

On every occasion you saw Miss J with Mr Oyston it was because YOU were with him. You are simply twisting the facts to make it appear that Miss J was conducting an affair with Mr Oyston.

Gill Bridge denied protecting Miss J from Oyston's sexual advances by getting him drunk:

That's untrue. If she was so frightened of Mr Oyston and his advances, why was she in London? I would not sit at the same table as a rapist.

The widow of the Lancashire comedian Les Dawson, Mrs Tracy Dawson, gave evidence that Oyston had sponsored a charity show for her late husband and raised £85,000:

I think he is an enormous ambassador for Blackpool. He has always been terribly helpful and supportive of all charities.

On the ninth day of the trial Mrs Grindrod summed up the case for an hour:

The issue is not, 'Did he have sexual intercourse at Claughton Hall and she consented?' The issue is, 'Did that incident happen at all?'

Miss [J] is unable to remember the date and it is true she is hopeless with dates. She is firm on the incident, but was it 1988 or 1989? She insists she was 17, but does it matter? According to the defence there was no occasion when it could have taken place. The place would have been lit up and it was teeming with people like Euston station, all the hours of the day and night. He has agreed she must have been to the house. Put yourself in the place of a young girl taken there in the middle of the night and left there.

Mrs Oyston said she stayed there at least two times a week. But Mr Oyston did not include her in his list of people who were there, even though he included people who were there from time to time. Miss J went back to the model agency. She stayed on at the Model House. Why, oh why, did she not leave? She speaks of two powerful men and the pressure from her parents to do well. The defence say this is all fantasy. The only suggestion, you may think, as to why she made up this fantastic story was that she had been paid by a newspaper. But she said she had given no information and done no deals with the papers: 'I wouldn't sell my story for the world.'

If she had done a deal you can be sure Mr Oyston would have found it out. Mr Oyston told the police he had had an affair with Miss J for one year or more. In evidence the affair has stretched to four years from the beginning of 1990 to the end of 1993. He also had other girlfriends during that period. It was a period, he told you, when he was being pursued by the Inland Revenue, the Stock Exchange, private detectives and most of the tabloid papers.

Mr Halloran's strange tale of Laetitia and her broken French. How did he know it was a Grimsby accent? How much can we rely on that as evidence of Miss J carrying on an affair with Mr Oyston?

If it happened, and you are sure it happened, it was rape. There are no two ways about it.

Anthony Scrivener said:

The date of the offence is relevant to whether or not you can believe Miss J beyond reasonable doubt. Miss X can't tell you the month, the date, the season of the year and changes her mind about the year.

If you had been raped you would have told someone about it. It would be unbelievable that you would not tell someone, a friend, a parent. Miss J told nobody. Would you wait six and a half years before you told anyone about it - she did.

If you had been raped, would you have remained on affectionate terms with your rapist thereafter? It is inconceivable you would sit at the same table. Is she lying in the witness box? Miss J gave the wrong date of her birth to the police. There is absolutely no evidence that she was working at the agency in 1988. Sharon Denby-Sedgewick says after she arrived at the agency it moved to Portland Street. It moved on June 26, 1989. She says Miss J was a new model - I knew that from the state of her portfolio which was undeveloped.

Miss J was still at the agency in 1992. She stayed at the Grosvenor Hotel, several months after the indecent assault. She was contacted by Gill Bridge. We know Gill Bridge did not join the Oyston Group until July 1990. She couldn't have talked to Gill Bridge shortly after the indecent assault. A short time is not two years. The police have not been able to produce one girl from the agency who was able to support what she says. Would you bottle yourself up for seven years? It's an enormously long period, longer than the Second World War. Is that the reaction of someone who has been raped?

After the alleged rape, did she see the doctor? No. She was asked did she see her GP in July 1991 because of stress, because she had received a large tax bill. She replied, 'I can't recall that'. In November 1992 she apparently took a drugs overdose.

This is a most unusual rape. There was no complaint at the time and no witnesses to support it. She says there was no other way out of the bathroom except back into the bedroom. But there were two doors. She is wrong about that. Her conduct was totally inconsistent with her being raped and what is more, she was lying about it. She would not have been friendly with her rapist. There are 30 recorded messages from Miss J in the message and action books. Miss J says she met Mrs Bridge because Gill was accompanying Mr Oyston.

Mr Oyston is not an establishment figure. He is not someone the establishment would understand or like. He has not been to public school, not inherited wealth. He came up the hard way. His first reaction was, 'This has something to do with a conspiracy'. That's what he first thought.

You should take into account the passage of time, first for Miss J and more importantly for Mr Oyston. He says he did not meet her until late 1989 or early 1990 and she was 18 or 19.

This is not a court of morals. It is of the utmost importance that you look at her evidence with great care. There may be all sorts of reasons why false allegations of a sexual nature are made.

The jury took two days to consider the two charges. After staying at an hotel overnight, they returned to court on March 13 to say that by a 10 - 2 majority they had found Oyston not guilty of indecent assault. In the rape case they had completely failed to reach any verdict. The judge then discharged them and announced that the rape case would have to be retried by another jury. Since he would be sitting in Liverpool in April, the retrial would take place before him at Liverpool Crown Court on April 22.

CHAPTER 20

Second Trial: A Kim Novak Look-alike

On March 20, 1996, Oyston appeared before Mr Justice McCullough and a second Manchester jury to face the charge that he raped Miss L before she fled by taxi from the Hilton Hotel in Park Lane to catch a train to Manchester. When Miss L was asked why she did not ask the taxi driver to take her to a police station to report that she had been raped, she said, 'I wasn't in a fit state.' She then took an aggressive line:

> Can I just say I've been looking at Mr Oyston while I've been making my statement and he can't look me in the eye? If he was an innocent man, he would look me in the eye.

Anthony Scrivener raised an immediate objection to point out that he had specifically asked Owen Oyston not to stare at witnesses, to avoid being accused of intimidation. Miss L's boyfriend then told the court that he went to Manchester Piccadilly station after Miss L had telephoned him around midnight:

> She was obviously upset. Her character had totally changed. The sparkle in her eyes had gone. She was a completely changed person.

Det Con Martyn Hughes said Oyston had originally told him he could not remember whether he had ever had sex with Miss L. He quoted Oyston:

> There was a time when I owned Miss World and I was also divorced at the time. If you like it was my last chance to enjoy myself.
> To be blunt I had a lot of girlfriends over those years, sometimes Miss World contestants I was going out with.

Oyston had sent two of his own daughters to train at Model Team and at one time had considered buying Peter Martin's agency but had been advised that the records were not in good order. About his first meeting with Miss L, he had said,

> I think it was sometime before the end of 1987.
> When I first met her, she had very short white blonde hair. She looked like a young version of Kim Novak - a film star from the fifties and sixties.

He had seen her at the Model Team agency in December 1987 and invited her down to London around January, when they had sex for the first time in his suite at the Hilton Hotel.

> She was staying with me in my suite. We went to the Windows of the World restaurant and then on to Stringfellows. We spent the night at my suite.

In March 1988 he said Miss L telephoned to say she was coming down to London to have some pictures taken. She asked for her own hotel room:

> because she didn't want Peter Martin to know she was having a relationship with me.

He said he paid for the photographs, paid a £150 deposit on her room and gave her cash to go shopping. They went to Stringfellows nightclub and had sex in his suite after dinner She went back to her own room later.

He had met Miss L again in April. On the 18th he had travelled to London with two business colleagues, Terry Bate and Michael Connolly. Miss L had arrived at the hotel with a change of clothes but told him she had to go back that night because it was her father's birthday on the following day. They went for a meal at a Polynesian restaurant in the basement of the Hilton and in the cocktail bar they met Frank McGrath and an Irish woman called Nuala Douglas. He said Miss L then left to take a taxi to Euston Station and he and Frank McGrath had seen her off. He said he stayed in contact with Miss L after April meeting and in June had invited her to meet him in Preston. He said they went to the *Manxman* disco and then on to the Tickled Trout Hotel, where he told her he was going to re-marry his ex-wife. He had given her a thousand pounds 'to help her with her portfolio.'

> I thought she liked me, I thought she was a friend. I've never raped her or anyone else.

When Mrs Grindrod asked Oyston how many other women he had been having affairs with at the time he was seeing Miss L, he said, 'Quite a lot.' When she asked what connection existed between the 'alleged conspiracy' he had mentioned in his police interview and the rape case, Oyston said that he had insufficient evidence to prove a connection between the two. The jury would have to make up their own minds. Mrs Grindrod accused Oyston: 'You gained her trust on the first occasion you took her to Stringfellows and on the second occasion you betrayed that trust. You were someone she looked upon as a grandfather.' Oyston replied, 'Not true. She was quite happy to climb into bed with me.'

Nigel Askew, a photographer and music video director from Belsize Park told the court he had sex with Miss L twice in Japan when she was modelling there in 1985. He said he had taken her on a tour of Tokyo night clubs and taken photographs for her portfolio free of charge. He admitted he had not known her surname but recognised the photograph shown in court as one that he had taken. Mrs Grindrod said:

> The suggestion appears to be that she was willing to have sex with you in order to have her photographs taken?
>
> I'm not saying that. She liked me. I never charge a model I've slept with.

James Kimber, a director of hairdressing firms sponsoring the Miss World contest, told the jury that when the Red Rose firm was merging with Eric Morley's Miss World, he had met Oyston and 'a young lady he referred to as Kim Novak' at the Hilton Hotel Roof Top restaurant around 1988. 'I clearly remember her face and her hair being blonde.'

Kathleen McGlynn, a secretary at Claughton Hall in 1988, told the court she had taken messages from a woman that Oyston called 'Kim Novak' and the jury listened to a statement from the former model agency manager Gloria Askew, 55, who now worked as English language teacher in Japan and was undergoing an operation for a hernia in Tokyo hospital. Askew said Miss L had been one of the models from Peter Martin's agency who had travelled to Japan in January 1985. She had been a very pretty girl who became good friends with her own daughter Nicola and had sometimes stayed at her home. Her nephew Nigel Askew had prepared a portfolio of photographs. She said that Miss L met the pop star George Michael in a Tokyo nightclub:

> [She] was excited to be picked out by George Michael one evening and he went back to the models' apartment with her. I had the impression that George Michael's bodyguard was also there.

The next time she had met Miss L had been at Peter Martin's agency in December 1987. Oyston had talked to her about starting his own chain of model agencies and after the meeting Miss L had stayed behind.

> Mr Oyston then offered her a lift home in his Rolls-Royce. I remember this clearly as the chauffeur had to get a map out to find the way to her home.

Miss Askew did not at first recognise Miss L. Her appearance had changed dramatically. She had very short, bleached blonde hair and wore a lot of makeup, 'I can recall Mr Oyston referred to her as Kim Novak and with her new appearance I could see looked more like her. '

The next witness was a journalist who had met the real Kim Novak. Brian Hargreaves had been in charge of the *Red Rose Advertiser* in 1988 when Oyston invited him for a drink in a nightclub aboard the former ferry *Manxman* at Preston Dock, where he had met Michael Connolly, Frank McGrath, Julian Allitt, and 'a lady Mr Oyston referred to as Kim Novak.'

> The young lady was pleasant, happy, cheerful and relaxed.
> She was affectionate. At one time while I was going to the bar, I noticed Mr Oyston had his hand on her hand under the table. It wasn't very obvious.

On the fifth day of the trial Mr Scrivener introduced a number of witnesses who all claimed to remember the appearance of a Kim Novak lookalike with Oyston in the late 1980s. These 'alibi' witnesses included the accountant Michael Connolly, the Preston politician Frank McGrath and Nuala Douglas, an Irish dancer who gave her address as the Gulf Hotel in Abu Dhabi and arrived at Manchester Crown Court carrying a huge teddy bear. Oyston had invested £20,000 in a lingerie shop that Nuala Douglas started with her sister in Oxford Street. He had mentioned a couple of times that he had a friend who was the spitting image of Kim Novak and in 1988 Nuala and Miss L met in Trader Vic's cocktail bar at the Hilton in Park Lane.

> I met a chap called Frank McGrath. And Owen was there with a woman who was the Kim Novak look-alike. She was sitting next to him. She did not say much. She did not talk to me and had a strange look on her face. She wasn't happy that I was in Owen's company. That was the impression I had.
> We had a few cocktails and the girl I now know to be Miss L left. She had to go and catch a train and got a cab outside. Owen escorted her to the taxi.

Nuala Douglas, when questioned by Mrs Grindrod, said she slept that night in Oyston's hotel bedroom but denied having sex with Oyston.

> On many occasions I went to the hotel and sometimes slept in the extra bed and sometimes I just lay on the bed. I was always fully clothed. He made a joke that I could take my shoes off.

On the morning of the sixth day of the trial, the foreman of the jury passed a note to the judge, asking why Peter Martin had not been called as a witness. Mr Justice McCullough then had to explain the quirks of the English adversarial system to the jury:

> If either side had felt that Peter Martin could give reliable evidence, then that side would have called him. You have taken an oath to try the case according to the evidence, which is of course the evidence you have heard.

Mrs Grindrod summed up by saying, 'This is a story of naivety exploited and trust betrayed.' The Kim Novak look-alike evidence had been a diversionary tactic and the documentary evidence of the Hilton Hotel bill for March 1988 supported Miss L's claim to have stayed in her own room, booked by the model agency.

Anthony Scrivener told the jury that there had been no independent evidence to support Miss L. She had not complained to the police until seven years after the alleged rape: 'The Second World War was over in a shorter period than seven years. It is an enormous period of time.'

There had been no reason for Miss L to stay overnight with Oyston after her photo shoot in March 1988, unless she had been on intimate terms with him. The evidence that Miss L was a Kim Novak look-alike had not really been challenged. The evidence of the photographer showed that Miss L was willing to give sexual favours to help her career. If Miss L was right, every one of the defence witnesses had to be wrong. As for the complaint about the conspiracy:

> Mr Oyston is not popular with the Establishment. His initial feeling was that this was part of a conspiracy waged against him by politicians. We cannot prove that. And we cannot speculate.

The judge summed up on the seventh day of the trial before sending the jury out at noon to consider their verdict. After six hours of deliberations, on the eighth day of the trial they sent a note to the judge asking for a definition of rape. Late in the afternoon, after eight hours 42 minutes, he told them he would accept a majority verdict of at least 10-2.

Oyston stared straight ahead when they returned 37 minutes later with a not guilty verdict. Gill Bridge burst into tears. Miss L was wringing her hands. The reporters were still barred from publishing the news but Oyston told them:

> It's been like a form of mediaeval torture. It's with you when you go to bed and every morning when you wake up, but you just have to fight it. I'll never know why she did this to me. She was a girlfriend. I treated her with great kindness, and she repaid this kindness with the kind of attack we have seen in this court.

CHAPTER 21

Third Trial: Prosecution Case

On April 23, 1996, Mr Justice McCullough let slip the attack dogs of Fleet Street. Owen and Vicki Oyston came with their daughters Heidi and Karen for the third trial, held this time in a vast concrete Brutalist building in Liverpool known as the Queen Elizabeth II Law Courts.

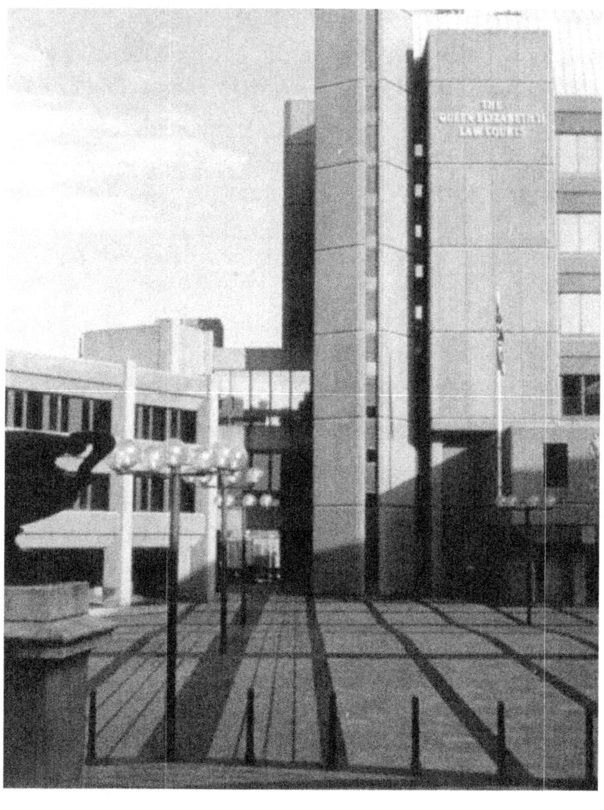

The judge lifted his restrictions on contemporary reporting during the hearing of the three remaining charges. Since the judge had been due to sit at Liverpool Crown Court, he announced that he would bring the cases with him from Manchester to be tried in Liverpool by a jury of eight women and four men. This Liverpool jury would re-examine the allegation that Oyston had raped Miss J at Claughton Hall. They would also try charges that Oyston had indecently assaulted Miss H on a midnight car ride to Claughton Hall and raped her a little later in his bedroom at Claughton Hall in the presence of Lysa Rubotham.

In Blackpool, the *Evening Gazette Late Final* reported:

Blackpool Football Club chairman Owen Oyston stood in the dock before a judge and jury on charges of rape and indecency. The 62 year old multi-millionaire faces two charges of rape and one of indecency against young girls... He is accused of raping one girl between January 1, 1988 and December 31, 1989 and a second girl between October 4, 1991 and December 31, 1992. The indecent assault is an alleged offence against a girl between October 4, 1991 and December 31, 1991.

Helen Grindrod's outline provided the headlines for April 24:

Terror of virgin

LANCASHIRE EVENING POST

Wife listens as Owen Oyston is accused of raping two models

DAILY EXPRESS

Three-in-a-bed on 4-poster

DAILY STAR

I wouldn't marry Oyston says model who accuses him of rape

MANCHESTER EVENING NEWS

She thought him quite sleazy but was told he could help her

INDEPENDENT

Blonde told how a millionaire soccer boss raped her on his four-poster bed

SUN

Young model tells of ordeal on Owen Oyston's bed after midnight drive to his mansion

DAILY MAIL

Mrs Grindrod summarised the allegations of Miss H, the girl from East Lancashire.

She sat on a chair. Lysa seemed to know more about why she was there, went into the bathroom, undressed, got into bed with Mr Oyston and had sexual intercourse. Oyston then ordered her to ... get into bed with them. She did what she was told. Oyston had sexual intercourse with her with Lysa still in the bed. She lay still and unresponsive making it clear that she was not consenting, Ms Grindrod said.

INDEPENDENT

There is no suggestion that he asked whether she was willing to have sexual intercourse, but he had it all the same. When he had finished with both girls, he redelivered them to Mr Martin, waiting in the car, and he drove them back to Sale. Mrs Grindrod said Oyston saw Mr Martin, the two girls and another girl again a couple of weeks later and again they returned. This time Oyston had intercourse with the other two girls while [Miss J] sat on a chair in the bedroom, but on this occasion, she was spared the order to get in bed and have sex with him because the other girls told him she was on her period.

EVENING GAZETTE

The petite Miss H would be giving evidence for the first time since her harrowing drugged appearance at the committal proceedings. The tall Miss J would be giving her evidence for a third time. Prominent friends of Oyston were in the public gallery; Louise Ellman, the leader of Lancashire County Council and future Labour MP for Liverpool Riverside and Billy Bingham, director of football at Blackpool FC, a former manager of the Northern Ireland international team and winger when Northern Ireland reached the quarter final of the 1958 FIFA World Cup.

Miss J told again how she had first met Oyston in a Chinese restaurant in Manchester when she was 17:

> I detested him from looking at him. He did not look right and I felt uncomfortable with him being there.
> He came across as being slimy and creepy. He smelled of aftershave. It was Calvin Klein's *Obsession*. Now that smell makes me feel sick.

Once again, Anthony Scrivener set out to challenge her claim that she had been a 17 year old virgin in 1988:

I will make it perfectly plain from the beginning that Mr Oyston's case is that you were never raped and you had an affair with him that was quite well-known for a long period of time.

Miss J: That is incorrect. I was raped. This incident did happen in 1988 when I was 17 years old. Talk about who is on trial…

Mr Scrivener: My client is. You are in the happy position of not being on trial.

Anthony Scrivener had come armed to this re-trial with fresh documentary evidence, a recently discovered sales record book found in a dress shop in Lincolnshire. When the 1988 book was passed to Miss J, she looked at her name, waved the book in the air and said:

> What a waste of time. You are trying to prove I was not available for work at the agency and be raped because I was at [the dress shop]. How can I be in two places at once? Is this all you can come up with? How pathetic.

Mr Justice McCullough intervened:

> You have insisted that the man in the dock raped you when you were 17. Counsel is exploring where you were and what work you were doing.

Miss J: I now realise what happened to me was in 1989 when I was 18 and not 17.

Mr Scrivener: You've been caught because we produced evidence that shows conclusively that you were working at the shop in 1988 and not at the agency.

Miss J: I have not been caught out. I was confused about dates.

Mr Scrivener: You swore it was 1988 and that you were 17.

Miss J: I was confused at the dates you were chucking at me.

Mr Scrivener: If my client had been convicted at the last trial it would have been on the basis that it happened in 1988 to a 17 year old.

Miss J: I swore on oath to tell the truth and I apologise to the court, the jury and the judge. I now realise it was 1989 and not 1988 and I am putting it right now. I can understand now why girls do not come to court.

Scrivener thereupon named a young man. He suggested to Miss J that this young man had sex with her before she had ever worked in Manchester. He asked Miss J if she knew the young man.

Miss J: I know him. He's a local lad in my hometown, which is close-knit… Everybody knows everybody. He liked me and asked me to go out and I said no.

Mr Scrivener: I put it to you that you had sexual intercourse with him on two occasions in 1988.

Miss J: I was a virgin when I was raped in 1989.

Mr Scrivener: Here was a man you detested. You did not even like his aftershave. You claim he raped you. That must have generated a good deal of hatred. So you would certainly not want to meet him. But on certain occasions you did meet him.

Miss J: I was sent down to London as I was ordered.

Mr Scrivener: You were never raped but you had an affair with him.

Miss J: That is incorrect. I was raped.

Mr Scrivener: It must have been very traumatic to have been raped in the way you described.

Miss J: Yes.

Mr Scrivener: Do you remember the date you were raped?

Miss J: No.

Mr Scrivener: The day of the week?

Miss J: No.

Mr Scrivener: The month of the year?

Miss J: No.

Mr Scrivener: The season of the year?

Miss J: No.

Mr Scrivener: Did you say you intended to marry him?

Miss J: What – after he raped me?

Two suits of antique armour were then brought into the courtroom and propped up against the witness box so that Mr Scrivener could invite Miss J to examine them and identify the 'silver knight' she had seen in Claughton Hall on the night she was raped.

Mr Scrivener: Is it either one of these?

Miss J: No. The one I saw was the same shape as the bigger of the two, but it was a silver armoured knight. You could have got these from anywhere. It doesn't prove anything. I am not an expert in describing silver knights. I don't remember the size. I will never forget the silver armoured figure. It is etched in my mind.

Miss J sobbed and asked:

"Have you brought the four-poster bloody bed? Would they like to see that?"

Scrivener then informed Miss J that the jury would be visiting the hall to look around.

"Well I hope you remember me in that bed. Bring in the drapes, everything, the décor."

Trembling, she asked:

"Do you like bullying people? Do you know what it's like? You are a bloke for God's sake. You don't know. "

Mr Justice McCullough ordered a break for Miss J to recover from this exchange.

On the fourth day of the third trial, **Anthony Scrivener QC** returned to the cross-examination of Miss J.

Mr Scrivener:	In July 1991 did you see your doctor about stress?
Miss J:	I had a tax bill of forty thousand pounds.
Mr Scrivener:	You didn't see him about rape but you were sufficiently distressed to see him over a tax bill?
Miss J:	Wouldn't you be? But then you could afford it.

After being questioned for nearly an hour about her age, Miss H finally declared:

I have always lied about my age. If you asked a hundred people, ninety of them would say women always lie about their age.

After a weekend break, judge, jury and barristers boarded a coach for a 70-mile journey from Liverpool to examine Claughton Hall, with its foyer, its great hall, the Oyston bedroom in the tower, its four-poster bed and its adjacent bathroom. Owen Oyston was present but his son Karl, who farmed the 1,500 acre estate, was standing guard at one of the gates to turn away reporters.

After five days in the witness box at Liverpool, Miss J admitted that she had received £1300 in six months from Oyston but she denied ever telling him that she had been pregnant:

> I would never mention to Mr Oyston anything to do with that. That's private. I know exactly what you are all thinking, when you look at me and think why did she accept all that money. It was owed money. I know what you are thinking. When I look back to the age I was then, I was younger and brainwashed and torn apart by big people. It all looks different now.

On the seventh day of the trial, Det Con Denise Lloyd described how she had travelled to Lincolnshire in January 1995 to interview Miss J about the Model Team agency:

> As I was about to leave, she stood up and began to cry. She said, "I have got to tell you I have been raped by Mr Oyston". She was extremely upset.

The deputy manager of the Royal Trafalgar Thistle Hotel gave fresh evidence that Miss H had stayed at the hotel on February 3, 1992, and that her bill had been paid by the Oyston Group. He said that Oyston and his travelling personal assistant, Gill Bridge, had booked into two rooms at the hotel earlier in the day and that an extra third room had been taken by Miss H around midnight.

It was now clear to many observers that the prosecution looked unlikely to prove that Miss J had been raped. Only one remaining prosecution witness, Miss H, stood between Oyston and freedom. The slight 20 year old Lancashire girl entered the witness box wearing a stark black shift dress and appeared to be under great stress. The *Daily Mail* reporter described how Miss H:

> shook as she as she began to give evidence, clasping her thin arms around her body and kneading a paper tissue in her hand.

Miss H told Mrs Grindrod about modelling lessons at the Manchester agency when she was 14 and still a schoolgirl. She had stayed with other girls, aged between 13 and 20, at Peter Martin's house in Sale on Friday and Saturday nights.

Q. Were there any rules you had to keep?

A. Yes. We had to be told to go to bed. We had to be told to have a shower and have a wash. We couldn't go to shop or anything. We weren't allowed to wear knickers for bed.

Q. What about where you slept?

A. Well. Peter told us which bedroom and which bed in the bedrooms to sleep in. We were told what to eat, told everything.

Q. Told everything?

A. Yes.

Q. Can we move to when you left school? Do you remember when it was that you left school?

A. Yes, it was Easter 1992

Q. Up to that stage you had been going to weekend classes and staying at the house at weekends?

A. Yes

About eight weeks after she began staying almost full time at the model house, Miss H said she saw Oyston at an Italian restaurant called Don Antonio. She said that Peter Martin told her Oyston was a very important man and 'dead rich.' A few weeks later, after a dinner at Don Antonio, 'Peter said that we were… he were going to take Oyston home and he were going to drive him home.'

Helen Grindrod QC was putting the questions to Miss H.

Q. Who was to go with him?
A. There were Peter and Lysa and me and him
Q. Whose car did you go in?
A. Peter's.
Q. What sort of car was that?
A. It were a white Toyota Supra.

Mr Justice McCullough intervened and asked Miss H

Were you and Lysa the only girls there or were there other girls at the meal too?

A. I think Tracey might have been. She might have been there, but she will have gone home. I can't remember.
Q. How did it come about that it was you two who went in the car when Mr Oyston was to be taken home?
A. Because Peter said.

Mrs Grindrod continued

Peter said to you and Lysa. Where was Mr Oyston at that time?

A. He were with us.
Q. How many doors did the Toyota Supra have?

A. Two.

Q. Where do you sit in the car?

A. In the back seat, not behind the driver, behind the other side.

Q. Where did Lysa sit?

A. She sat in the front with Peter.

Q. Where did Mr Oyston sit?

A. Next to me.

Q. Whose suggestion was that?

A. It will have been Peter's suggestion.

Q. Were you given any reason why you should sit in the back with Mr Oyston?

A. No, we were just going to take him home Peter said.

Mr Justice McCullough. Sorry?

A. Peter said we were just going to take him home.

Mrs Grindrod:

What time of night was it when you set off from the restaurant?

A. It were late. I'm not sure of an exact time but I think when we were driving home it were after midnight.

Q. Did something happen while you were driving?

Mr Justice McCullough:

No, no, no, Tell us about the journey. Nothing leading please.

Mrs Grindrod:

Did you know where you were going?

A. No.

Q. Tell us about the journey?

A. Well, we were like in the car and he unzipped his trousers and he got his penis out. He put my hand on his thingy and be moved it up and down until it were hard.

Q. And then?

A. Then he pushed my head down on to it. I didn't want to do it so I pulled my head up and he just pushed my head down on to it again.

Q. And then?

A. He were moving my hand up and down

Q. Where was his penis?

A. In my mouth.

Miss J was now in tears and shaking violently. A woman juror began to cry. There were even tears in the press box.

Some years later, Anthony Scrivener QC had to described the scene to the Court of Appeal:

> [Mr Shaw] is saying I must emphasise the impression this girl gave to the jury. There were actually six members of the jury in tears, including two men, during her evidence in chief.

Mr Justice McCullough to Miss H:

Would you like to sit down?

Mrs Grindrod:

How long did that go on for?

A. For about five minutes.
Q. How did it end?
A. He thingied in my mouth.
Q. I do not know whether the jury heard the word.

Mr Justice McCullough:

Did you hear the word? That will do.

A. He ejaculated in my mouth.

Mrs Grindrod:

Had anything been said?

A. No.
Q. Did the car eventually stop?
A. Yes.
Q. Did you know where you were?
A. At his house.
Q. Describe the house as you arrived at it?
A. Like a big castle. It were massive. It had a driveway. From the outside, it just looked like a big castle.
Q. What happened when you got there?
A. Peter said that we had to get out of the car because he wanted to show us around his home.
Q. We, being you and Lysa?

Mr Justice McCullough:

Did you say Peter said that?

A. Yes

Mrs Grindrod:

Where was Mr Oyston when he said that?

A. I think he was still in the back of the car.

Mr Justice McCullough:

He was?

A. Still in the back of the car.

Mrs Grindrod:

What did you think?

A. I had to get out because Peter said…

Mr Justice McCullough:

Pardon?

A. I had to do what Peter said. You had to do it.

Mrs Grindrod:

Why?

A. Because you had to do what Peter said. You had to do it.
Q. So did you get out?
A. Yes.
Q. Were there any lights on that you could see?
A. I think there were like, some lights. It were lit up where the car were parked.

Mr Justice McCullough:

Was that far from the front door or the door that you eventually…

A. Car were parked near the side door.

Mrs Grindrod:

What happened then?

A. I followed.
Q. Who went in first?
A. Oyston.
Q. Who opened the door?
A. It must have been Oyston.
Q. Where was Peter Martin when the door opened?
A. Sat in the car.
Q. Had he got out of the car at all… himself?

A. I don't think so, no.

Q. You went into the house?

A. Yes.

Q. Can you describe anything about the house inside?

A. Yes, it were like a museum.

Q. What do you mean by that?

A. It weren't like a normal home. It's a castle isn't it? It's not like a normal house, is it?

Q. Where did you go?

A. I followed him and Lysa and ended up at his bedroom.

Mr Justice McCullough:

Sorry, where did you go first?

A. I just followed him and Lysa and we got to his bedroom.

Q. Can you remember if you saw any of the house downstairs first?

A. No, I seen a silver... a silver knight thing.

Q. Then. You just held your hand up as you said that. Can you just do that again? (Witness held out her hand)

Mrs Grindrod:

Can you describe the bedroom at all?

A. It had a big four-poster bed. There were a bathroom next to the bedroom. There was a chair in the corner.

Mr Justice McCullough

Of the bathroom or the bedroom?

A. Bedroom.

Mrs Grindrod:

The bedroom. When you got into the bedroom… that was you, Lysa and Mr Oyston. What happened then?

A. Lysa and Oyston, they got undressed and I were sat in that chair.
Mr Justice McCullough
Sorry, I did not hear that.

Mrs Grindrod:

I think she said, "I was sat in the chair."

A. I was sat in the chair. Lysa with Owen Oyston. They got in the bed.

Mr Justice McCullough:

Let me know if you want to sit down.

Mrs Grindrod:

What did you see?

A. I seen Owen Oyston and Lysa have sex.
Q. Then what happened?
A. He told me to take my clothes off and get in bed,
Q. Did you?
A. Yes, I had to.
Q. Why?
A. Because I was scared, because he forced me. He forced me in the car. He forced my head on to him in the car. There were Peter outside

waiting and you had to do what Peter said. You didn't have a choice. You had to do everything what Peter said. Can you imagine if you had upset one of his mates what he would have done? He put me in a car boot did, Peter, he put me in a car boot and that's because he didn't want to afford a taxi. Can you imagine if I had upset one of his mates what he would have done? Can you imagine what he would have done?

Q. When had that happened?

A. Pardon?

Q. When had that happened?

A. Peter put me in the car boot?

Q. Yes.

A. After a meal. He knew I were... I'm claustrophobic. He knew I were claustrophobic and he shoved me in the Toyota Supra boot with another girl and be knew I were claustrophobic.

Q. Had that happened before?

A. Before?

Q. … you were at Oyston's home?

A. Yes. And then because I lost it in the car boot because I panicked. He dragged me out of there and he shouted at me and he said he would never take me out again because I had spoilt his night for crying.

Q. You were explaining---

Mr Justice McCullough:

Just slow down, please.

Mrs Grindrod:

You did as you were told?

A. Yes.

Q. What happened?

A. He had sex with me. I didn't even know him.

Q. Where was Lysa?

A. In the bed and she didn't give a damn.

Q. Did Owen Oyston say anything to you?

A. No.

Q. After he had told you to take your clothes off?

A. No.

Q. Can you describe how you were feeling?

A. Pardon?

Q. Can you describe how you were feeling?

A. I was frightened, I was in a house, in a bed with a guy I didn't even know, an old man, I didn't know old men did things like that. He is an old man, I didn't even know they did things like that, I was sixteen year old and he didn't give a damn. He's a selfish git.

Q. Did you say anything?

A. No, I were too scared. What could I have done?

Q. Tell us what happened. You said he had sex with you?

A. Yes.

Q. How long did that go on?

A. Five minutes, I don't know. I weren't counting,

Mr Justice McCullough:

What did she say after five?

Mrs Grindrod:

"I don't know, I weren't counting." How did it come to an end?

A. He thingied, he ejaculated in me.
Q. After that what happened?
A. We went back to Peter's car,
Q. Who is we?
A. Me and Lysa. I didn't even know him, I had never spoke to him, he didn't know me. He treated me like were an object and I'm not... I'm not.
Q. While he was having sexual intercourse with you what were you doing?
A. Nothing, just laid there.
Q. Was anything said after he had finished?
A. No.
Q. When you got back to the car where was Peter Martin?
A. Still sat in the car.
Q. Where did you go then?
A. Back to Sale,
Q. Did you continue to stay at Sale?
A. Yes. Peter used to say things to me every day, say how I were nothing without him, I were a nobody in Accrington, I'd really let my mum and dad down if I went back. I were nothing without him.

Mr Justice McCullough:

Is that how you felt or is that what he said?

A. That's what he said to me.

Q. Can you say the bit again about your mum and dad?

A. That I would let my mum and dad down.

Q. If?

A. Because they were proud of me.

Mrs Grindrod:

How would you let your mum and dad down?

A. Because he would put everything into it, they were proud of me for actually doing something with my life.

Q. Why did you stay on at the agency?

A. Because I didn't have a choice. I thought I would let my mum and dad down by going back, I thought... they were proud of me for the first time in my life, they were proud of me and if you have got someone saying to you every day that you are nothing, that you are a nobody without him (inaudible) I'd be nothing, you begin to believe it if it's said to you all the time. And I am not a nothing, I am not, I am a person. I've got feelings, I'm not an object, I'm not.

Mr Justice McCullough:

Who had said this to you about being a nobody?

A. Peter.

Q. Not your parents?

A. Peter.

Mrs Grindrod:

Did you see Mr Oyston again after this incident?

A. Yes.

Q. Where?

A. It were... It were at Sale.

Q. Had you been out for a meal?

A. Yes, I think so, although I am not sure, I think so.

Q. About how long after the incident at Mr Oyston's house are you going to tell us about now?

A. About, not long, about the week after.

Q. Who do you remember being at Sale? Was it at evening we are talking about? Who was there?

A. Peter, Lysa, and Sharon... her name...

Q. Do you know Sharon's surname?

A. Sharon Denby.

Mr Justice McCullough:

Sharon who?

Mrs Grindrod:

Sharon Denby. Where was Mr Oyston?

A. He went… He went on to the first floor and he went up with Sharon and Lysa and I stopped downstairs in the front room.

Q. Where was Peter?

A. He had gone to bed and he didn't tell me where to go. He told me which bedroom we were sleeping in. And he didn't tell me that night. He just went to bed.

Q. What happened?

A. Lysa came down, she came down first and she said, "He wants you upstairs."

Mr Justice McCullough:

Sorry, we have certain rules and one rule is that we cannot have in general what somebody said to somebody else. So I have got to stop you from saying that, I am afraid. I am not quite sure about the relevance of this incident.

Mr Scrivener:

I was not sure. Maybe we could have a short break. I know there are other points of law to raise.

On May 3, 1996, after a day of procedural discussions in the absence of Miss H and the jury, Mr Scrivener began to cross examine Miss H about her early life and her time at the model agency:

Q. You said, "One reason I went to the agency was to please my mum and dad because I had been terrible to them in the way I behaved. Basically, I didn't give a damn. I had started taking drugs at 13 years old. And I thought doing something else would please my mum and dad." Is that right?

A. Yes.

Q. You had been... you had been taking drugs since the age of thirteen. Is that right?

A. I tried them. I tried drugs at 13, yes.

Q. Sorry?

A. I tried.

Q. You tried at 13. Is that right? I am going to ask you...

A. It doesn't make me a bad person because I have taken drugs.

Q. I am not suggesting that at all.

A. It don't make me bad.

Q. I am just trying to work out all the problems you have got. Do you understand that?

(reply inaudible)

Mr Justice McCullough:

You are speaking in the present tense. She is speaking about when she was 13.

Mr Scrivener:

I will take it on from 13. 1 just want to ask you about that problem, do you understand? I am not making any judgment of your character at all. I just want to find what the facts are. Do you understand?

A. Yes.

Q. Since the age of 13, from time to time, have you taken drugs?

A. Yes.

Q. Cannabis?

A. Yes.

Q. Ecstasy?

A. Yes.

Q. Wiz?

A. Yes.

Q. And something called "E" I think. I am not sure what that is. Something called "E".

Mr Justice McCullough:

I suppose I ought to warn you that you do not actually have to answer these particular questions because they might, in theory at least, expose you to the risk of criminal prosecution.

A. I can get done?

Q. Pardon?

A. I can get done?

Q. I do not imagine anybody would do you, but it is my duty to warn you or to remind you that possessing dangerous drugs is a criminal offence.

A. Yes, but I want to tell, I want to be honest.

Q. If you choose to answer that is entirely up to you. As I say, I cannot imagine for a moment anybody is going to prosecute you.

Mr Scrivener:

Have you recently been taking advice about drugs?

A. No.

Q. Sorry?

A. No.

Q, Let me just see what it amounts to. Let us take more recently and work backwards. For instance, in 1995 were you taking drugs?

A. Last year?

Q. Yes.

A. I was smoking cannabis to forget.

Q. Did you go and see a doctor because of your tendency to lose your temper?

A. Yes.

Q. Was that in February 1995?

A. I can't remember...

Q. Were you finding it difficult to deal with ordinary people, like people in shops, without losing your temper? Is that right?

A. Yes.

Q. Because you hated everybody?

A. That were then.

Q. Then you started smoking dope heavily in about February?

A. Yes.

Q. You were smoking a lot of dope and felt paranoid. That is how you felt, how you have described it?

A. It just made me forget things. I didn't want to face up to things. It were the only thing that could calm me down.

Q. Were you having problems with your boyfriends?

A. Yes.

Q. Because you were quarrelsome. Did you accept that your use of cannabis was becoming a real problem?

A. Yes, because I have got to face up to things. I had to face up to things. I couldn't hide behind smoking, could I? I had to face up to things.

Q. Did you agree to go and see a doctor about drug abuse?

A. No.

Q. You didn't go and see a doctor about drug abuse?

A. No.

Q. Would it be right to say that you dabbled in drugs since a teenager?

A. Yes. It doesn't give him the right to do what he did though, does it?

Q. None at all. Not at all. Not at all.

Mr Justice McCullough:

Since a teenager. That covers, of course, 13 to 19. She is only 20.

Mr Scrivener:

I should say as a teenager.

Mr Justice McCullough:

Nineteen was last October.

Mr Scrivener:

I think the result of this is that you have been prescribed various medications by the doctors, have you?

A. No.

Q. Valium?

A. No. And it's not because of drugs why I'm taking it.

Q. I am not suggesting that. Have you received any medication in the last 24 hours?

A. Yes.

Q. What is it? Can you remember?

A. Dothiepin hydrochloride.

Mr Justice McCullough:

Pardon?

A. Dothiepin hydrochloride. That's an antidepressant. It helps me sleep.

Q. What is the effect of that particular drug?

A. It helps me sleep and it gives me… it helps me eat.

Mr Scrivener

Do you remember giving evidence in the magistrates' court? Do you want a break? Could we have another break, my Lord, perhaps fifteen to twenty minutes?

Mr Justice McCullough:

How much longer have you got?

Mr Scrivener:

Not too much my Lord.

Mr Justice McCullough:

You will finish today?

Mr Scrivener:

Most certainly.

Mr Justice McCullough:

You will finish this morning?

Mr Scrivener:

This morning I hope to, yes.
After the adjournment, Miss H returned to the witness box.

Mr Scrivener:

Are you all right?

A. Yes.
Q. Peter Martin has been charged with raping you, has he not?
A. Yes.
Q. His trial is coming on shortly?
A. Yes.
Q. The control of Martin over you was such that if you thought that Martin wanted you to have sexual intercourse with someone you would have had sexual intercourse with that person, is that right?
A. I couldn't say no.
Q. Pardon?
A. I couldn't say no.
Q. You could not say no?
A. I can't say no to Pete, I was scared of getting his coffee wrong, making

a cup of coffee, I were terrified of getting it wrong.

Q. When you were in the restaurant and you saw Mr Oyston, Martin said, "He is a rich guy". Is that right, something like that?

A. I think he said it before.

Q. On previous occasions, he said, "He is a rich guy."

A. Yes, before.

Q. He pointed him out as being a rich person?

A. Yes.

Q. Did you think that Mr Oyston was connected in some way with the agency?

A. No.

Q. Are you sure?

A. Yes.

Q. You do not think he was providing money for the Agency or anything of that sort?

A. No, I didn't know anything, I thought it were Peter.

Q. I am just going to go through the incident. The car was a sort of sports car with seats in the back. Is that what this car is?

A. Supra, a white Supra.

Q. It was quite small in the back?

A. Yes.

Q. There would be Martin driving?

A. Yes.

Q. Lysa in the front passenger seat?

A. Yes.

Q. You said that Mr Oyston had oral sex with you. Is that right? That is what you said, is it not.?

A. Yes.

Q. Did you protest?

A. What could I do?

Q. You could have said no?

A. You what? I put my head up and he put it back down.

Q. Did you protest at all?

A. How could I? He were Peter's friend.

Q. I am going to suggest to you that never happened at all?

A. You what?

Q. I am going to suggest that never happened at all?

A. You can suggest what you like, I know what happened.

Q. You could have shouted out perhaps for Lysa to help?

A. Lysa to help? Lysa? She were going out with him. As if she could have helped. I didn't know the guy. It happened. I am not lying.

Q. All right. Can I ask you what happened after you left the house later? You drove back with Martin and Lysa in the car?

A. Yes.

Q. Did you stop on the way back to get some petrol?

A. I can't remember.

Q. Did you complain to Lysa what had happened, that you had been forced to have sex?

A. No, but...

Q. Did you stop and have to get sandwiches at the petrol station?

A. I can't remember, I spent… When I came back from the house, I spent a year of my life trying to forget what happened.

Q. It was quite a long journey to the house, was it not?

A. Yes.

Q. When you got to the house did Lysa want to go to the toilet?

A. No.

Q. Do you remember?

A. No, I can't remember.

Q. Were you interested in looking round the house or not?

A. The house? Which one?

Q. The castle, you have described it as the castle?

A. Were I interested in looking at it? Were I heck. No.

Q. I am suggesting that you were, you went upstairs to the bedroom, Lisa went to the toilet, you sat on the bed?

A. I sat on the chair.

Q. I am suggesting you sat on the bed and Lysa came out of the toilet then you all left.'

A. What?

Q. That is what I am suggesting to you?

A. You can suggest what you like. I am not lying. I know what happened.

Q. Did you see a doctor at all during 1992 after this incident?

A. I can't remember. I probably went to see the doctor, yes.

Q. Did you ever complain to anyone that you had been raped?

A. No. I were ashamed I weren't...

Q. Just going now to the question of when you came to report this to the police. You saw something in the *News of the World*, did you?

A. Yes.

Q. You recall it was around the time of your birthday, your birthday was on 4th October?

A. Yes, it were the Sunday, either before my birthday or after, I'm not sure.

Q. Somewhere round about then, we will not be precise. It is a long time ago?

A. It were on a Sunday I find out, it all came out because I got back from the Lake District and it were on *Teletext*.

Q. I think what you are saying is for your birthday you had gone to the Lake District, had you?

A. Yes.

Q. Were you in the Lake District when you saw the newspaper which said; ring a number if you had been at this Agency?

A. No.

Q. You had come back from the Lake District, had you?

A. Yes.

Mr Justice McCullough:

I think you said, did you, when in the Lakes you had seen something on *Teletext*?

A. No, I went to the Lakes for the day and I come back in my house, my mum's and dad's house, it were on *Teletext*.

Q. What was on the *Teletext*, something about Mr Martin or the Agency?

A. Yes, that he'd been arrested with some video tapes.

Mr Scrivener:

Can I just ask, if you cannot recall tell me, but how long before 4th October 1994 had you left the agency?
A. Nearly two year.

Mr Justice McCullough:

Pardon?

A. Nearly two year.

Mr Scrivener:

During that period had you been working?

A. Yes.

Q. You had got in touch with the police following this advert that said contact this number?

A. Yes.

Q. Did you say that something like this: "I worked at the Agency, I want to tell you about the things he used to do and ask the girls to do. He used to make me love him so it was natural"?

A. What?

Mr Justice McCullough:

I have not got the ability to take a quick note of this?

Mr Scrivener:

I am sorry. Shall I dictate it, my Lord?

Mr Justice McCullough:

Yes. Can I just know when you are suggesting this was?

Mr Scrivener:

I do not think I can. It was her first contact, I am suggesting, with the police, when she left a message. The prosecution may be able to help me with that but it was shortly before 12 October 1994.

Mr Justice McCullough:

Are you suggesting she said this on the telephone?

Mr Scrivener:

I am looking at a computer log kept by the police which would record what she was saying.

Mr Justice McCullough:

Do you remember ringing them up and saying something or leaving a message?

A. To the police?

Q. The police?

A. I rang the police up.

Q. Sorry?

A. I rang the police up.

Q. I think what is being put to you is the sort of general substance of what you said to the police in that call.

Mr Scrivener:

Let us just find out exactly what happened. You rang the police up first. Did they ring back and you had a short conversation as to the way you could you help about this problem?

A. Yes.

Q. Am I right? I am not putting words in your mouth. That is right, is it not? I rang the police and I said I wanted to see them. They rang back and you explained what it was you wanted to see them about?

A. I… just over the phone… I just wanted to see them.

Q. I am just suggesting something like this is what you said. You said: "In 1990 I worked at the agency and I want to tell you about the things he used to do and ask the girls to do. He used to make them love him so it was natural." Then you say: "I work at..." you gave the address where you work, a telephone number where you worked. Was it something like that you said?

A. I can't remember.

Q. Then having left that message the police came round and then you went to the police station to make a statement. Is that right?

A. Yes.

Q. That was on 12th October as we have seen?

Mr Justice McCullough:

12th October?

Mr Scrivener:

I will just check the date of it, my Lord. Yes, 12th October 1994.

Mr Justice McCullough:

1994?

Mr Scrivener:

Yes. That took a long time to take, I expect, did it not? The statement?

A. Yes.

Q. Were they taking notes first? Can you remember how it was done?

A. Yes.

Q. They took notes, and having taken notes they then started to write a statement for you to sign?

A. Yes.

Q. Two officers present?

A. Yes.

Q. Were they both making notes? Or just one? If you cannot remember just say no?

A. I can't remember.

Q. Ultimately, after quite a long time, I expect several hours, you were asked to sign the statement?

A. Yes.

Q. You had been working up until that date. Is it right to say you have not worked since October 1994?

A. No.

Q. That is correct, is it not?

A. Yes.

Q. Thank you very much.

Mrs Grindrod:

My Lord…

Mr Justice McCullough:

Can you just clarify what she said the interval was between leaving the agency and October 1994?

Mrs Grindrod:

Before October 1994 she said she had left the Agency for about two years.

Mr Justice McCullough:

Two years.

Mrs Grindrod:

I think that is what she said.

Mr Shaw [defence]:

Nearly two years, my Lord.

Mrs Grindrod:

My Lord, there is a matter I need to raise with your Lordship before I re-examine.

Mr Justice McCullough:

Let me just ask you this. Do you happen to remember how long you were agency, altogether from start to finish?

A. Pardon?

Q. Do you remember how long you were Agency altogether? Can you put it in months or years or is that too difficult?

A. I used to stop at weekends but when I lived there…

Q. No, I mean from the very start, let us say from Easter 1992. Were you there months or years?

A. In Easter 1992?

Q. From Easter 1992 onwards, we know that date because you say that is when I left school?

Mrs Grindrod:

No. That was when she went to Sale.

Mr Justice McCullough:

Sorry, went to Sale. You started there earlier and you did your GCSE in the summer of 1992, I think you told us. We know you went to the police in October 1994, do you follow? Two years and a bit later. Can you tell me how much of the time you spent at the Agency?

A. When I were…

Q. Altogether. Was it months or a year? Or eighteenth months or two years or what?

A. A couple of year, I went when I were fifteen and I left when I were seventeen.

Q. You left when you were 17?

A. Yes. 14/15.

Q. Yes. Started at 15 and then stayed at the agency full-time from Easter 1992. GCSE in the summer of 1992, you left at 17 and you became 17 in October 1992, it was some time after that?

Leaving the jurors in tears, Miss H rushed out of the courtroom. Two particularly experienced observers were watching. One was John Burke-Davies, court reporter for the *Daily Sport*:

> She appeared to be extremely emotional, distressed and verging on what I would describe as neurotic. I noticed on several occasions that a number of the female members of the jury were in tears. Indeed, I was moved myself by the behaviour of Miss H, whilst she gave evidence. There were several adjournments, whilst time was given for Miss H to compose herself. [100]

As Burke-Davies went out to telephone his story:

> I actually followed Miss H out of the courtroom into the corridor, where I saw her throw her arms around a woman who appeared to be waiting for her. I kept walking down the corridor, but stopped to look back out of curiosity, and with a degree of sympathy for Miss H in view of what I had seen in the

[100] Court report to author.

> courtroom. I was surprised to see Miss H appearing to do a twirl, as she held her arms around the woman. This was a complete change in her composure, particularly as she was smiling, in complete contrast to the distraught person I had seen moments earlier. This was the first time in all my years as a court reporter seen such contrasting behaviour.

Miss H was closely observed by Mrs Frances Mason, a friend of the Oyston familyand a magistrate for fourteen years. Mrs Mason noticed that Miss H:

> Did a twirl, twisting her body to make her flared dress swish around at the bottom. When she did this twirl, I thought she was demonstrating that she looked nice. I think she was smiling when she did it. The officers acknowledged this action and then the young lady left through the doors. I think she was smiling when she did it. The officers acknowledged this action and then the young lady left through the doors. [101]

---

[101] Statement in appeal proceedings.

CHAPTER 22

'A very troubled lady, but I never laid a finger on her.'

On the eighth day of his third trial, Owen Oyston insisted on having his day in court. For weeks he had been pressing his barrister Anthony Scrivener QC to raise the question of political conspiracy. His legal team did not possess hard evidence of links between Greater Manchester Police and the two conspiring government ministers, Robert Atkins and Peter Blaker. Nevertheless, Oyston's wish was granted on May 8, 1996, when readers of the London papers heard for the first time about

Ministers' conspiracy against me

DAILY MAIL

Oyston names 'conspirators'

GUARDIAN

Oyston 'victim of ministers'

INDEPENDENT

I was set up says rape case tycoon

DAILY MIRROR

I'm too famous to rape anybody, said Oyston

DAILY EXPRESS

The *Daily Mail* used the whole of page 6 for Andrew Loudon's report:

OWEN OYSTON told police his arrest on rape charges was linked to the fact that he was suing two prominent Tories, a court heard yesterday.

The 62-year old media tycoon said Lord Blaker and ex-sports minister Robert Atkins had mounted a conspiracy against him and members of the North West Labour Party.

Following his dawn arrest at home in February last year, Oyston told detectives: 'I am amazed and shocked by this.'

Then at Altrincham police station in Cheshire, where he was taken for questioning, he said: 'Can I just give you some information first of all? It is curious I have been arrested at this time. It is three weeks before a High Court case in London.

'I am suing two members of the Government, one of whom has just retired and gone to the House of Lords. It has been ongoing for ten to 12 years. I have been subjected to some very nasty and vicious campaigns over that period. It may seem that I am looking for an excuse but the fact is I have tapes of the allegations I am making to you now.'

Mr Atkins has held a series of Government posts, including stints as a Minister in the Department of the Environment and the Northern Ireland Office.

Lord Blaker - formerly Blackpool South MP Peter Blaker - was a Minister at the Foreign Office and Ministry of Defence during his 28year Commons career.

Oyston told the officers that when the court case came up he planned to bring the allegations into the public arena, adding: 'I am sufficiently cynical in life after these vicious attacks over the years by newspapers and individuals to think there is a connection between what happened this morning when you arrested me and the court case in three weeks' time.'

A life-long Labour supporter, Oyston told Liverpool Crown Court he had 48 hours of tape recordings of conversations between Lord Blaker, Mr Atkins, Blackpool businessman William Harrison, a man named Michael Murrin 'and a whole range of other senior people in the Conservative party'.

'The tapes showed that Lord Blaker, William Harrison and Robert Atkins were in fact running a conspiracy against me and members of the North West Labour Party,' said the millionaire chairman of Blackpool Football Club.

Oyston failed to have his civil action heard in the UK because of a 'lawyer's mistake' but was now pursuing his case in the European Court of Human Rights. He told the jury at one time he was being investigated by the Fraud Squad, the Inland Revenue, the drugs squad, the City's regulatory takeover body, IMRO, international private investigators, the Insight team from the Sunday Times, and other newspapers.

'They tried to bring the world down upon me and others associated with me,' he said.

He told his defence counsel Anthony Scrivener QC that he had been cleared of wrong-doing by all those bodies.
In 1989, a series of three libellous articles by the *Sunday Times* had resulted in Oyston winning substantial damages, costs and an apology.
Oyston said he had mounted an action for defamation against Michael Murrin. In return for him not making Mr Murrin bankrupt he had received the tapes. Trial judge Mr Justice McCullough asked the detective in charge of the case whether he had known of the tycoon's forthcoming legal action when the decision was made to arrest him. 'I did not,' said Detective Superintendent Bill Roberts. 'No one tried to make my mind up. There was no interference from outside, or inside.'
Oyston denies raping two teenage models at Claughton Hall, his 15th Century mansion near Lancaster.
One of the girls has told Liverpool Crown Court she was an 18-year-old virgin at the time of the alleged attack four years ago.
Oyston also denies indecently assaulting the other girl, a 16year-old, by forcing her to perform a sex act in the back of a sports car.
Detective Constable Martyn Hughes said the tycoon had described the allegations of the first girl, who claims she was driven to his home in the middle of the night and forced to have sex on his four-poster bed, as 'fantasy world'.
Oyston claimed during an interview that he had a long-standing sexual relationship with her. 'I have known her for a long time,' he said. 'Until this moment I thought she was a good friend. I am amazed by this, that she should make these allegations about me. She actually proposed marriage to me, if you want to know.'
Oyston said the sexual relationship had lasted for at least a year.
When told that the girl had felt forced to comply with his wishes when she was allegedly told to lie on his bed and remove her underwear, Oyston said: 'No, I wouldn't do that. It is all a load of rubbish. Everyone knows who I am. I am a high-profile character. I can't go around doing things like that.'
He insisted he had no need to resort to rape to get sex.
Oyston claimed that between divorcing and remarrying his wife Vicki, a former Miss Blackpool, he had 'a lot of girlfriends in London and all over the country'.
The trial continues.

The *Daily Mail* reporter noticed how firmly the judge had shut down the question of political conspiracy by intervening in Anthony Scrivener's examination of Det Supt Bill Roberts.

Mrs Grindrod:

One or two matters, Mr Roberts. You referred to two or maybe three sets of notes have been lost.

A. Yes.

Q. In what size investigation is that? We are not just talking about this case?

A. Scores and scores of sets of notes have been taken in respect of this investigation and two or three have been lost.

Q. Thank you. Thank you, Superintendent.

Mr Justice McCullough:

Just a moment. Of which one? Is it the set of notes of the initial interview of Miss H?

A. That's correct, my Lord, yes.

Q. Mr Oyston, when he was arrested, said that he believed there was a connection between his arrest and the fact that a civil action, which he had initiated, was due to be heard in the High Court some three weeks after his arrest. Did you know of the existence of those proceedings when you took your decision to arrest him?

A. I did not, my Lord, no.

Q. Did you receive any instruction from higher up that you should form the decision to arrest him or was it a matter of your own mind being made up?

A. My own mind, my Lord. I was the officer in charge of the case and nobody tried to make my mind up for me. There was no interference from either outside or inside. It was my decision wholly.

Mr Justice McCullough:

Thank you.

Mrs Grindrod:

Thank you, Superintendent.

Mr Scrivener:

May I ask a question about that?

Mr Justice McCullough:

Yes.

Mr Scrivener:

I am sorry to keep you. You have said that you were not aware of the civil proceedings that Mr Oyston was involved in?

A. That's correct.

Q. Which he mentions in his interview?

A. That's correct.

Q. Had a man called Murrin been supplying information to the police?

A. Right. This will be complicated and take me a while my Lord...

Mr Justice McCullough:

What mattered, surely, is first of all whether he knew at the time he made his decision to arrest Mr Oyston, whether Mr Murrin had...

Mr Scrivener:

That is what I was going to ask next, my Lord.

A. Murrin, to my knowledge now, had been giving information to the Lancashire police.

Q. Did you know that at the time?

A. No, I only found out afterwards.

This denial, made under some pressure from the judge, closed off discussion of Michael Murrin's activities and marked the end of attempts to question Det Supt Roberts about the political conspirators. Yet there is evidence that Det Supt Roberts would have heard of Murrin and his activities earlier than December 12, 1994.

In September 1994, in the early stages of the investigation, two events involving Murrin would have been in the knowledge of the Operation Chittering team and their SIO, Det Supt Roberts. These concerned Melanie Hardy, the Boss model agency booker, introduced to Manchester police by Michael Murrin in 1992 and in touch with Murrin again in September 1994.

On September 23, 1994, on the day of the police raid on Peter Martin's home, Det Con Ashley had interviewed Melanie Hardy at the rival Boss model agency in Manchester. He reported that Miss Hardy had mentioned Oyston:

> Hardy suspects that girls from the agency were made available to a number of Martin's friends [including OJO].

Det Con Ashley already knew at this early stage that Oyston's nickname was "OJO", a business acronym revealed to police in documents carried forward from the investigation provoked by Murrin in 1992.

On December 12, 1994, Det Sgt Pinder of GMP had placed instruction A442 on the HOLMES computer for the attention of all officers working under Det Supt Roberts on Operation Chittering. All officers were ordered not to contact "*N937 Michael Murrin*" without liaising with their "*SIO*", the senior investigating officer, who was Det Supt Roberts. An entry before this, A440, referred to Det Insp Robishaw's 1992 report on the model agency, triggered by Michael Murrin.

Ten days later, on December 22, 1994, Det Con Alan Fitzsimmons was working on Operation Chittering in the area around Owen Oyston's home at Claughton Hall.

A police computer note on an entry in the diary of model agency owner Peter Martin had been logged as R13O3 and was shown to Owen Oyston soon after his arrest. He was asked questions about it. It was approximately dated to November 1994 in the last few weeks before Oyston's arrest. Once again, the entry referred to Michael Murrin, with another instruction to detectives not to contact Murrin without liaising with Mr Roberts.

Later that day the Blackpool *Evening Gazette* reported the tenth day of the trial:

MILLIONAIRE soccer boss Owen Oyston had a private meal at an Italian restaurant with Kevin Maxwell, the son of the late Robert Maxwell, the night before Kevin Maxwell was arrested for fraud.

The 62-year-old club chairman told of the meal that was also attended by a teenage model he is alleged to have raped on a four-poster bed at his, home Claughton Hall, near Lancaster.

Oyston said in evidence yesterday that the occasion was June 17, 1992.

He added: "He was arrested the following morning by police and charges were made against him on which he has recently been acquitted."

He met Kevin Maxwell at the Hilton Hotel in London and had drinks with Gill Bridge and the girl referred to as *Miss H* and then went on to the restaurant.

"Kevin must have had a premonition of what was happening and the Press were besieging his home and he came out to try and escape," said Oyston.

"He was frightened they would catch up with him. It was an awful experience. We sat at separate tables.

"Kevin and I sat at one table and the girls at another. We were only a few tables away."

Oyston told of another occasion when he was with Miss H and met a reporter from the satirical magazine *Private Eye* for a meal.

"He was the last person I would have introduced her to if I had raped her on some previous occasion," he said.

"It was decided to disguise Miss H's identity by pretending she was foreign, but she could not speak a foreign language so that was changed to her not speaking at all during the evening.

"That was maintained for the evening until she began to talk in a Northern accent and it was treated as a joke," he said.

Defence counsel Anthony Scrivener QC asked his client if Miss H had ever mentioned marriage.

Oyston replied: "Yes. She proposed to me on at least one occasion, possibly two.

"I was married at the time and didn't take her seriously. I think that was towards the end of 1992 or the beginning of 1993.

Mr Scrivener asked: "Did she mention pregnancy?"

Oyston: "Yes, she told me she was pregnant. She had previously told me on several occasions she could not have children so, to be blunt, I didn't believe her." He was then asked about the girl mentioning boyfriends. He said she had mentioned boyfriends in the first 18 months and added: "The boyfriend disappeared from the scene at the height of our relationship. Then in 1992 she began mentioning boyfriends again.

Oyston told the jury he had been invited to lunch at her home by the girl on several occasions but had never accepted. He had also been invited to lunch by the girl's father. Miss H had invited him to her home to celebrate her 21st birthday but he had been unable to go.

But Gill Bridge, his former personal assistant and now managing director of Blackpool Football Club, organized – on his instructions – a dinner party at the top floor restaurant at the Hilton Hotel.

"I arranged the dinner party by way of consolation and asked the head waiter to organise a birthday cake," he said.

Earlier in his evidence Oyston spoke of advising Miss H about a mortgage and property in London.

He had shown her the company flat in Mayfair and she said it would be nice if she could stay there but he said it was not possible because it was for the company executives.

After taking advice from various people he established Miss H would need a very substantial deposit to buy a property, even on the outskirts of London.

He said Miss H had also said she wanted to set up a boutique in her hometown and he had also advised her on that matter.

Oyston said he had been shopping in the West End with Miss H on one occasion and another time he had given Gill Bridge and the girl money to buy clothes.

Miss H had been photographed for a magazine, part of a group owned by Oyston.

He said he had introduced her to the then group editor Brian Hargreaves, who would have handled the matter.

Oyston agreed he had reimbursed Mr Hargreaves for money given to Miss H but could not remember the circumstances.

The first he knew of the rape allegation against him by Miss H was when the police came to see him in February 1995.

He said if people came to Claughton Hall and were interested he would show them round.

"I did it all the time," he said. "It is an unusual house and if people come and express an interest, I was very proud of it, and would show them round."

He said the most valuable piece of furniture in the house was the four-poster bed in his bedroom.

In August 1987, he gave a big dinner party for models from the agency and they had all used the bathroom in his bedroom and would have seen the four-poster bed.

Oyston admitted to Helen Grindrod QC that he had sex with four other girls connected with the Model Team agency but said he could not remember having sex with two other girls named by Mrs Grindrod:

> It may seem pompous but I didn't have tremendous difficulty in having friends or girlfriends. There was no need to take advantage or force sex upon any of them

After Mrs Grindrod had named Hazel Taylor, Sharon Denby and Lysa Rubotham, he said:

> I did not search them out. These were largely models looking for advancement. I was seen as someone who could advance them. I realise now I was pretty stupid. I realise now that I've been used.

Adrian Darbyshire reported in the *Evening Gazette*:

> PROSECUTING counsel Mrs Helen Grindrod put it to Owen Oyston that he was so used to having his own way with women that he didn't bother to ask if Miss H or Miss J had consented or not to sex.

Oyston replied: "I've always had a great respect for women and I've promoted women within my own organization. I've employed thousands of them. I've owned Miss World.'

"I've never had this kind of problem, - it's just not true. My character is totally without blemish. That's why I'm so distressed and I'm also angry – that's the only thing that's kept me going."

"You are angry, are you not, because you thought it was all safely in the past?" asked Mrs Grindrod.

"I'm angry because the police, the CPS and yourself are accusing me of things that are against my nature," he replied.

Mrs Grindrod pointed out that it was Miss J and Miss H and not the police, the Crown Prosecution Service or herself who had made the allegations.

Later Mrs Grindrod asked if Oyston's personal secretary, Rosemary Snell, knew her boss was having an affair with *Miss J*.

"She did not know I was having a relationship with anyone. She had her suspicions perhaps," replied Oyston.

Did Gill Bridge – Oyston's other personal assistant and now Blackpool FC's managing director know about his affairs, asked Mrs Grindrod. "She knew," he replied.

Asked if *Miss H* had made up her allegation, he said: "I think she's terribly confused – a very troubled lady but I never laid a finger on her."

Earlier, Oyston had claimed his trial was linked to a political conspiracy against him involving former Blackpool South MP Lord Blaker, South Ribble MP Robert Atkins, Fylde millionaire William Harrison and a private detective called Michael Murrin.

But under questioning from crown counsel, he said he was not putting the alleged conspiracy forward as his defence.

Oyston told the court it had "chilled his blood" to discover recently that Michael Murrin had made serious sexual allegations against him back in 1992.

"Are you suggesting in some way either Miss J or Miss H has been put up to make these allegations by someone who wants to do you down?" asked Mrs Grindrod.

"I believe that to be the case – I shall prove it in another place."

Under repeated questioning, he said: "I'm saying there is a connection but I'm not putting it forward as my defence."

Asked if the jury could forget about the alleged conspiracy, he replied: "No they can't. I can't forget about it. I've been through hell these last 14 months and I want the world to know what kind of people these are and what they've been doing.

"They want to lock me up and throw the keys away."

Sharon Denby, a university law student and future solicitor who had trained as a model at Model Team gave evidence that undermined Miss H's account of the evening in London. The *Evening Gazette* reported the eleventh day of the trial:

Ex-lover tells of night she saw alleged victim with accused

A FORMER lover of Owen Oyston told a court that she had seen alleged rape victim *Miss H* dining with the business tycoon in the summer of 1989 when they appeared on friendly terms.

Former model and university law student Sharon Denby, 31, of Blackburn, told the court that in 1988 she had run her own model agency and during that time had met Oyston.

Mrs Denby said she had started out as a model at Peter Martin's Model Team agency in Manchester and had much later set up her own business but it had not been a success so had gone to work for Martin's agency in early 1989.

At Model Team she worked both as a model on the books and also on the administrative side of the business. She returned there for a short time in 1992, she told the jury.

"Whilst there did you meet Mr Oyston?" asked Oyston's barrister Anthony Scrivener QC. "Yes," she replied.

"And did you have short affair with him?" he continued. "Yes for few months," she told the court.

While at the agency Mrs Denby said she had met a girl called *Miss H.* "She had a weight problem. She was quite a new model when I met her and she had to lose some weight."

"Did you ever lend her some clothes?" asked Mr Scrivener. "Yes, it was in August 1989. *Miss H* came to my house to borrow a suit," she replied.

"She was dressed casually in jeans and the such like and she said she had been invited to go out for dinner with Mr Oyston."

Mrs Denby said she let *Miss H* select a suit from her own wardrobe and she had chosen a new, expensive suit, which the witness said she had only worn once before.

She said *Miss H* was looking forward to dining with Oyston – "she was excited about going."

Mrs Denby said she had driven to the meal. Oyston and *Miss H* appeared "very close, very friendly "

Under cross-examination by Crown counsel Helen Grindrod QC, Mrs Denby

said she had been introduced to Oyston by Model Team boss Peter Martin.
"Mr Martin intimated that Mr Oyston supported him in plans to expand," she told the court.
"You assumed from that Mr Oyston considered putting money into Mr Martin's agency?" asked Mrs Grindrod. "I assumed so," she replied.
Asked when she had had an affair with Oyston, she said: "It was in 1988 – we were both unmarried at the time."
She said she had never been to Martin's house in Sale.
Asked about the dinner with Oyston, she said she thought it took place at a large hotel in Manchester and quite a few people were present including girls from the agency and business colleagues of Oyston.
"Was everybody being friendly?" asked Mrs Grindrod. "Not to the extent that *Miss H* and Mr Oyston were," she replied.
"Where was *Miss H* sitting?" asked Crown Counsel. "Next to Mr Oyston. I was sitting among other company. We were all sat at one big table dining together."
Mrs Denby said she had known *Miss H* for a few months when she had asked to borrow some clothes.
"Could it have been earlier than August 1989?" asked Mrs Grindrod. "No, it could not," she replied, adding that she fixed the date because she had just moved into a house with her husband and was embarrassed by the state it was in.
The witness said she had first been approached by Oyston's solicitors a fortnight before the first trial in February this year.
"And you are remembering back to 1989 – six years?" asked Mrs Grindrod. "Yes," she said.
"Did you have sex with Mr Oyston after 1988?" "No," she replied.
Judge Justice McCullough asked if Mrs Grindrod was going to ask the jury to reject Mrs Denby's evidence.
He said, "It seems to me that this lady and *Miss H* can't both be right."
Mrs Grindrod put it to the witness: "Mrs Denby, you came here to support Mr Oyston and your evidence is not true."
"My evidence is truthful and correct," she replied.
The jury then heard from TSB bank manager Richard Willoughby who confirmed that a cheque for £100 had been paid into the account of *Miss H's* husband in October 1992.
Oyston's defence claim that magazines Life series editor Brian Hargreaves had given *Miss H* £100 so she could enter the Miss UK competition but the alleged rape victim denied she or her husband had received such a payment.
Next was James Kimber, director of two hairdressing companies and a

publishing company.

Mr Kimber, of Chelsea Harbour, London, told the court that he had known Oyston from 1988 to the middle of 1990 and had sponsored the Miss UK competition and had even appeared as a guest judge one year. He said that Oyston had been in negotiation to take over his chain of hairdressing salons but nothing came of the deal.

"We became quite friendly when he was in London. He would normally be staying at the Hilton Hotel on Park Lane. I think he also had a company flat in Grosvenor Street, W1."

Asked if he remembered attending Oyston's birthday in 1990, he replied: "It was in early 1990 at a favourite restaurant of Mr Oyston's called Scotts in Mayfair."

"You had a lady with you?" asked Mr Scrivener. "Yes".

"And Mr Oyston had a lady with him?" "Yes", said Mr Kimber, adding that the girl was introduced to him as *Miss H.*

Shown a photograph, the witness said: "Yes. That's the young lady – very tall."

"Was this a pleasant evening?" asked Mr Scrivener. "Oh yes," he replied, "Mr Oyston, or Owen, asked if I would select a bottle of champagne as it was his birthday.

"I picked a bottle of Crux – I'm interested in wine so it stuck in my memory. It was £80 to £90, a vintage bottle – he shouldn't have asked me really."

Of *Miss H* that night, Mr Kimber said: "I assumed that was his young lady – they seemed very friendly." The witness said that after the meal Oyston invited everyone back to his Grosvenor Street flat for a nightcap but that Mr Kimber's then girlfriend decided she didn't want to go.

"We followed *Miss H* and Owen up the road for a while. We decided to get into a taxi and go home. They were linking arms and walking along as a normal couple would," he told the court.

Cross examining, Helen Grindrod QC asked: "When were you asked to throw your mind back six years?"

"A few months ago," replied Mr Kimber, adding that Oyston's solicitors had shown him a photograph of *Miss H.*

"Mr Kimber, you were asked after six years to look at a photograph and you say you remember this girl?" asked Mrs Grindrod.

"She's very striking," he replied.

Oyston was then recalled to the witness box to answer a question from the jury about other residential properties he had owned, used or let. He said that Claughton Hall was his only home but that his wife Vicki as part of a divorce settlement had got a property in Lancaster which had been let out to

students.
The eight women and four men on the Oyston rape trial jury are to examine a Toyota Supra sports car similar to one in which a teenage model claims she was indecently assaulted by Owen Oyston.
The girl has alleged during the trial that she was forced to perform a sex act with the multi-millionaire in the back seat of the car.
She said it took place as Manchester model agency boss Peter Martin was driving the car to Oyston's castle-like home at Claughton Hall near Lancaster. The girl referred to as *Miss H* also alleged, she was raped by Oyston on a four-poster bed in his bedroom after she watched him having sex with another woman.
The jury sent a note to the judge asking if they could see a Toyota Supra of the relevant year.

Kevin Maxwell, son of the late media baron Robert Maxwell, recounted the last hours before his arrest on fraud charges before the jury trying Owen Oyston. He told Liverpool Crown Court that after his father died in November 1991, Oyston had written to him and his brother Ian offering "condolences and moral support."
Shown a photograph of alleged rape victim *Miss H*, he said: "I believe I met this lady on at least one occasion and possibly two.
"I remember the date of one occasion with some precision – June 17,1992."
"Why do you remember?" asked Oyston's barrister Anthony Scrivener.
He replied: "On that occasion I went out to dinner in the evening with Owen Oyston, Gill Bridge and I believe this lady.
"I remember it well because a few hours after that I was arrested by the Serious Fraud Office."
"You were charged and recently acquitted?" asked Mr Scrivener. "Yes," he replied.
Mr Maxwell, who appeared in the witness box dressed in a dark blue suit and blue tie, said at the time he was being followed by a "substantial rat pack" of journalists.
Asked where they he had gone that night, Mr Maxwell said: "We arranged to meet at the Hilton Hotel, Park Lane, London.
"I went to the bar in the Hilton and I can recall after having had a drink making a telephone call first to Gill Bridge's room and then, getting no reply, to Mr Oyston's room and I was asked to go up to his room.
"I met Owen, Gill Bridge and I met this lady. "There was a few minutes spent having a drink in the room before going to the restaurant for dinner."
Mr Maxwell said he drove Oyston to an Italian trattoria near his home in his

wife's car while Mrs Bridge and the other lady went in a black cab.

At the restaurant the two women sat at a different table while the men discussed business, he told the court, adding that the seating arrangements were Oyston's idea.

"During the time you saw Mr Oyston with this lady on what terms did they appear?" asked Mr Scrivener.

"Perfectly amicable – there was no friction in the room. I remember assuming that she was his girlfriend," he replied.

Under cross-examination from junior prosecuting counsel Raymond Wigglesworth, Mr Maxwell said that he had become friends with Oyston in the six months after his father died.

He explained that Oyston had bought a series of magazines from one of his father's companies and had had dealings with another involving radio stations.

And he agreed that Robert Maxwell and Oyston could have met but added that his father "was not a great socialiser in the normal sense."

Mr Maxwell said he could not recall the name of the girl whose photograph he had been shown.

He told the court that during each of the five times he had met Oyston between January and June 1992, Gill Bridge had been present and had sat at a separate table so that the two men could talk about business.

When asked if the meal at the Italian restaurant had been purely business, he hesitated before replying: "At that stage I was under enormous personal pressure. I was very much a pariah.

"I had just resigned as chairman of Oxford United a couple of months previously and I recall talking about a radio station, in Albania of all places, that Owen was interested in.

"But I can recall receiving the absolute moral support he always offered along the lines of – 'keep your chin up' – in what was in June 1992 a pretty horrendous and ceaseless attack."

Asked why he could recall how the two women had behaved towards Oyston on that night, he replied: "I've only been arrested once in my life and you do not forget it. You don't forget what you were doing a few hours before. It's deeply engrained in my memory because of the shock I received a few hours later."

A FORMER magazine editor told a jury he had been "absolutely outraged" to discover that a girl he had seen enjoying herself in the company of business tycoon Owen Oyston had later alleged she was raped by the millionaire soccer boss.

Retired magistrate and one-time group editor of Oyston's Life magazine series Brian Hargreaves said the Seasiders' chairman had asked him to give the girl publicity to further her career as a model.

On the 11th day of the trial, Mr Hargreaves told the court that in the summer of 1990 he had met Oyston and *Miss H* at a business meeting in Staffordshire and Oyston had asked him if he could give the girl publicity in one of his magazines.

He said he had arranged a photo shoot at the Northcote Manor Hotel near Langho, Blackburn, and a photograph of her appeared on the front cover of a magazine supplement.

He said he had later given *Miss H* other photographs to include in her portfolio.

He told the jury at Liverpool Crown Court that he had seen Oyston in the company of *Miss H* on a number of other occasions in hotels in Preston, Manchester and in London.

Mr Hargreaves, of Rusholme, Manchester, said he had bumped into *Miss H*, Oyston and the tycoon's personal assistant Gill Bridge at the Royal Trafalgar Hotel in London in 1991 and they gone for a meal in a restaurant in Covent Garden. "They were on affectionate terms, relaxed, easy and happy," he said.

He claimed he had given *Miss H* £70 to pay off a speeding fine and was later refunded by Oyston.

And in September 1992, he told the court, he had given her £100 so she could meet the entry requirements of the Miss World competition, because she said she had to make a donation to charity.

Under cross-examination by junior prosecuting counsel Raymond Wigglesworth, Mr Hargreaves admitted that he had socialised with another model from the Model Team Agency but denied that he had ever had a sexual relationship with her.

He said he had met this girl about a dozen times and had seen her three times in 1994 but denied giving her a "beautiful diamond ring" at the Haydock Races or buying her an evening gown and leather trousers.

Mr Wigglesworth said: "You are simply here to help out an old friend."

He replied: "I'm simply here to help the cause of justice, I was absolutely outraged that someone who I had seen happy and enjoying herself in Mr Oyston's company should make these allegations."

Earlier the jury heard evidence from Mr Angelo Sorrelli, the head waiter at the Windows of the World restaurant at the London Park Lane Hilton Hotel.

He said that Mr Oyston had frequented his restaurant for many years and that the tycoon had once asked him to arrange a special 21st birthday cake for a girl whose photograph he recognised as *Miss H*.

He told the court that it was the first and only time that Oyston had asked him to arrange anything special for his guests and that he had organised: "a non-chocolate fraisier cake – strawberry and cream."

He said he remembered the event because it was one of the very rare occasions when Oyston had wanted to dance.

He said: "She was quite tall, had long legs and Mr Oyston wasn't a good dancer."

Junior prosecuting counsel Raymond Wigglesworth said: "I put it directly to you that the girl in the photograph was not the girl present at the 21st birthday party, that you have made a mistake."

Earlier, the jury were taken down to an underground car park beneath the law courts to view a Toyota Supra sports car, of identical model and age to the one in which Oyston is alleged to have forced a 16-year-old girl to perform an indecent act on him.

A female and a male juror squeezed into the back of the white sports car, watched at a discreet distance by the judge, barristers and a group of journalists.

The *Gazette* reported the evidence of Mrs Gill Bridge:

Mrs Gill Bridge said that a fashion model who alleges she was raped by Seasiders' chairman Owen Oyston had in fact said she was in love with him.

Mrs Bridge told the jury ay Liverpool Crown Court that the model had shared Oyston's luxury suite at the Hilton Hotel.

She said she had squirmed in her seat when two of the millionaire's girlfriends came face to face in a posh London restaurant.

Oyston, 62, who has already been acquitted of indecently assaulting the girl known as *Miss L*, denies raping *Miss H* and denies two further counts of rape and indecent assault against a second teenage model, now also in her twenties.

Giving evidence on the 13th day of the Oyston trial, Mrs Bridge took her stand in the witness box dressed in a dark blue suit.

The court heard that Mrs Bridge, of Blackpool Road, Ansdell, who speaks fluent French after studying at the Sorbonne, became Oyston's personal assistant in July 1990.

When the managing director of Blackpool FC resigned, she was assigned the post of temporary office and administration manager but soon took over full-time and was appointed MD of the club in February 1994.

Asked if she knew that her boss had girlfriends during her time as his personal assistant, she replied: "Yes. Obviously, we tried to keep it as discreet as possible.

"I probably knew more than the other two personal assistants because I was away on business with him more and I would be seeing him more in a social environment than perhaps the other girls did."

She told the court she had received telephone calls at the office from *Miss H* on "a regular basis – probably from 1990, 1991 and possibly into 1992 as well."

Oyston's defence counsel, Anthony Scrivener QC, asked: "Were these telephone calls to you personally?"

"No," she replied, "She was always trying to speak to Mr Oyston."

Mrs Bridge said she left notes in the Oyston's message book when *Miss H* rung for him.

If she had wanted to speak to you there would be no point in making a note?" asked Mr Scrivener. "No," she said.

The witness said that her boss had asked her to arrange £250 to be paid into *Miss H's* building society account in April 1992 when the model was having problems with a landlord.

"Did you lend her the £250," asked Mr Scrivener.

"No. It would have been over a week's salary," she said.

Mrs Bridge said that she first met *Miss H* at the Midland Hotel in Manchester in the summer of 1990 when she arrived there with Oyston just a couple of months after starting work for him.

"He had obviously met her before. She put her arms round him and kissed him on the cheek," she told the jury.

She said she had seen *Miss H* at the Hilton Hotel in London "perhaps half a dozen times and she "normally stayed in Mr Oyston's room."

"They were friendly and affectionate," she said. "She was quite flirty with him. He was perhaps a little more reserved. It was obvious she was attracted to him."

On one occasion, she said *Miss H* had given the tycoon a photograph of herself but Oyston had asked Mrs Bridge to get rid of it because he was "embarrassed about taking it home for obvious reasons."

Mrs Bridge said she had gone to see *Miss H* take part in a hair show in February 1992 because Oyston could not make it himself because he was appearing as a witness in a court case.

She said she thought *Miss H* had booked a room herself at the Royal Trafalgar Hotel that day and that the receptionist had not accepted her signature on the bill because it had not been booked by the Oyston Group of Companies.

Mrs Bridge said that Oyston had paid for the room himself but to prevent his accounts department from finding out about *Miss H*, his personal assistant had marked on the bill that she was a friend of hers.

"Did you ever meet her apart from when you were with Mr Oyston?"

"Never," she replied.

The witness told the court that she had gone to see Miss Saigon with her boss and *Miss H* and that Oyston had also arranged "a small get together" for the model's 21st birthday at the Hilton Hotel.

On another occasion she had seen the two together, Mrs Bridge told the court, *Miss H* had pretended to be her French cousin so that a *Private Eye* journalist would not discover Oyston's affair with the girl. And she said she had gone on a shopping spree with *Miss H* with £300 given to them by Oyston.

On one embarrassing occasion, she told the court, another girlfriend of Oyston, Hazel Taylor, turned up at the same restaurant in London where he was dining with *Miss H* and some people from Channel Four.

"I was squirming in my seat because the two girls were not getting on too well," Mrs Bridge said.

"She once said she loved him in my company," she told the court. "One of Mr Oyston's colleagues had asked what she was doing with a chap like him and she said she loved him".

In January last year -18 months after she had last spoken to her – *Miss H* rang Mrs Bridge at her Bloomfield Road office, the court was told.

"She asked how are you, how is Owen, what are you doing. She said she would like to see Owen and myself again.

"I didn't want to make any firm commitments because things had cooled between her and Owen."

Mr Scrivener said: "It's been suggested that you were a special friend of hers."

"No, never," Mrs Bridge replied.

"Never her friend at all?" asked Crown counsel Helen Grindrod QC.

"Being friendly with someone in not the same as being her friend. I've never been her friend, Mrs Grindrod," she replied.

Mrs Grindrod asked if the witness knew the names of Oyston's girlfriends.

"I knew *Miss H* and I knew Hazel Taylor," she replied.

"It appears, Mrs Bridge, that every time *Miss H* was down in London with Mr Oyston you were there too. You were always tagging along with them as it were."

"She would always stay at Mr Oyston's suite?" asked Mrs Grindrod.

"That's correct," said Mrs Bridge, but asked why *Miss H* had got a separate room at the Royal Trafalgar Hotel after the hair show, she replied: "I don't know".

"You are loyal to Mr Oyston are you not? You still work within his aegis, within his presence," said Mrs Grindrod, who added: "What you have done is seek to put a slant on the facts which can be shown to be true to suggest that *Miss H* was having an affair with Mr Oyston."
"She was having an affair with him," said Mrs Bridge. "She has put a slant on my involvement."
Re-examining, Mr Scrivener said: "You were asked about other girlfriends Mr Oyston may or may not have had. Have you seen any other girlfriends with Mr Oyston in his hotel room?"
"Yes, Hazel Taylor – a couple of times," she replied.
"Does she look similar?" he asked. "She's got auburn hair." "Any question of mistaking her?"
"No," replied Mrs Bridge.

The key witness for the defence of Oyston was Lysa Rubotham. She had been a key police informant against Peter Martin. But as soon she refused to support Miss H's rape allegation against Oyston, Greater Manchester Police dropped her, even declining to record her evidence.

Melanie Hardy, the *éminence grise* behind the police investigation and Michael Murrin's original informant put Lysa in touch with the *News of the World.* On February 14, 1995, Lysa gave Melanie Hardy a signed seven thousand pounds *News of the World* contract:

> The information I have to offer is of a personal nature concerning a two and a half year relationship between myself and Mr Oyston.

But no money changed hands and at the age of 22, expecting a baby by her boyfriend, the tall woman who had modelled around the world as Lisa French went into the witness box on May 15, 1996, to give evidence for Owen Oyston. The Crown said Lysa Rubotham was in the bed with Oyston when Miss H was raped. It would be Lysa's word against the word of Miss H.

The manner of her questioning by Mrs Grindrod and her treatment by the judge was eventually raised at the European Court of Human Rights on the grounds that the unequal treatment of the two witnesses breached

Article 6 [d] of the European Convention on Human Rights. In the later words of Ben Emmerson QC:

> The admission of evidence relevant to the credibility of the two young women therefore lay at the heart of the domestic criminal proceedings. Ms Rubotham was required, without the benefit of anonymity extended to J, to undergo unremitting and grossly intrusive questions about her sexual history which had no relevance to the case other than to besmirch her character in the eyes of the jury. She was asked about allegedly promiscuous sexual activity when she was 16. She was obliged to answer questions about sexual relations she had had, when aged 17 and 18, with four much older men who were named in court. She was obliged to concede that these encounters were "*almost dirty and sordid*". She was questioned about an abortion she had had at around the time of the alleged offences. And she was asked whether she had had "*three in a bed*" sex with another woman named Sharon Denby. There was no basis in domestic law for objecting to such questions since section 2 of the 1976 Act had (and has) no application to defence witnesses. The prosecution were therefore entitled to ask any question relevant to credibility, without restriction. Any defence objection to this course was bound to fail. Indeed, when defence counsel made a modest objection to one particularly irrelevant and intrusive question (about the alleged group sex with Sharon Denby), the judge rejected the objection and allowed the questioning to proceed. Indeed, far from restricting such cross-examination the judge himself asked questions about Ms Rubotham's sexual history, asking her to provide dates for her sexual encounters with other men. Even without the additional issues arising from the Court of Appeal proceedings, there was thus a stark inequality of arms at the trial itself. Questions of the sort which were put Ms. Rubotham could never have been put to *Miss H*, without the permission of the judge because section 2 of the 1976 Act prevents this. Section 2(2) provides that if an application is made to cross-examine on sexual history, the judge may only give permission if he is satisfied that it would be unfair to the defendant to refuse it. As the Court of Appeal held in the present case, questions designed purely to undermine a favourable impression which a witness is making in the witness box are prohibited by the section, and the judge is required under section 2[2] to refuse permission for such questions to be put. Had Ms Rubotham been an alleged victim the judge would inevitably have prevented the questioning which took place. In view of the importance of Ms Rubotham's credibility, the resulting unfairness strikes at the very root of the applicant's conviction.

> In a case in which the relative credibility of the two young women was likely to be decisive, the principal defence witness had been attacked as sexually immoral, with the acquiescence and support of the trial judge, in a manner which would never have been permitted to the defence.

In the *Manchester Evening News* Steve Panter reported her entry into the witness box:

> The courtroom was hushed as ex-model Lisa, 5ft 10in tall, with long copper hair, told of her romance with the multi-millionaire. She met him through the Model Team agency, which she joined as a child model at 11.
> When she was 15 she went out with other models and agency boss Peter Martin for meals and met Mr Oyston, who was then about 58.
> She became more friendly with Mr Oyston and met him at various hotels and restaurants before starting a relationship with him at 16.
> Under questioning from Mr Oyston's barrister Anthony Scrivener, QC, she said she developed a sexual relationship on a consensual basis. She replied: "I loved him. It was something to myself which appeared totally normal."

She gave a completely conflicting account of the encounter in Oyston's bedroom:

Mr Justice McCullough:

You made your way up to the bathroom?

A. Yes.

Q. That meant going upstairs?

A. Yes.

Q. At the moment where, as far as you were aware, was Mr Oyston and *Miss H*?

A. Behind me at the bottom of the stairs.

Q. As you go upstairs you lose sight of the downstairs and you made your way the bathroom?

A. Yes.

Q. So by the time you got to the bathroom door what was the last time that you had seen…

A. At the bottom of the stairs.

Q. You go into the bathroom. You are there for five minutes. You then come out and what do you see?

A. I see Mr Oyston and Miss H on the bed.

Q. How was Mr Oyston on the bed?

A. He was propped by the pillows on his side.

Mr Justice McCullough:

He was propped on his side?

A. By some pillows or something.

Mr Scrivener:

Dressed?

A. Yes, he was.

Q. Fully dressed, the same as when you left?

A. Just without his jacket and shoes.

Q. And *Miss H*?

A. Fully dressed,

Q. What was she wearing that night, can you remember?

A. Yes, she had a black velvet dress which had a bright

coloured panel up the front, black tights and Tracey Grainey's b"ac' heeled shoes.

Q. What were they doing when you arrived outside?

A. They were talking and giggling.

Q. I want to put this to you, did you have sexual intercourse with Mr Oyston…

Mr Justice McCullough:

Before we move on to that, you initially said, "When I came out of the bathroom door, I saw them", plural., "lying on the bed."

A. Yes.

Q. You explained Mr Oyston's position as being with jacket and shoes off propped on his side by some pillows?

A. Yes.

Q. Lying means with feet off the floor, does it?

A. Yes, it does.

Q. You have not told us about her position, you just told…

A. She was lying on the bed.

Q. She was also lying on the bed?

A. Yes. But as they were talking, she wasn't on her side but she was facing Mr Oyston.

Q. Not on her side. facing him. Shoes still on?

A. Yes, they were.

Mr Scrivener:

I can now put the question. Did you have sexual intercourse with Mr

Oyston in that bed in the presence of Miss H?

A. No, I didn't, no.

Q. What you saw when you came out, you saw the two of them lying as you described. Did it make you jealous or annoyed in any way?

A. No.

Mr Justice McCullough:

Pardon?

A. No.

Mr Scrivener:

When you came out of the bathroom what happened next?

A. We left straight away.

Q. Did Mr Oyston say goodbye to you?

A. Yes, he did.

Q. How?

A. He gave me a kiss and showed us the way out.

Q. How did he say goodbye to *Miss H*?

A. Just the words.

Q. No kiss?

A. No. No, I wouldn't have expected him to.

Mr Justice McCullough:

Pardon?

A. I wouldn't have expected him to.

Mr Scrivener:

Let us deal with the journey back. Did you travel back in the car with Mr Martin driving the three of you?

A. Yes.
Q. Were there any complaints from *Miss H* during that journey?
A. No.
Q. Was there a conversation?
A. Yes, there was.
Q. Do you remember where you stopped on the way back?
A. Yes, we did.
Q. Where did you stop?
A. At the service station.
Q. For what reason?
A. Peter to put petrol in the car and to get sandwiches.

A later report in the *Evening Gazette* described Lysa's torrid cross-examination by Mrs Grindrod

> Under cross-examination by Crown counsel Helen Grindrod QC she confessed that she had sex with a variety of other men while she was dating Oyston.
> These included former Pool director Julian Allitt – now boss of Bay Radio in

Morecambe - when she was 17, Peter Martin's osteopath Warren Hudson and an accountant who worked for the Oyston Group of Companies called Derek Zissman, the court heard.
After her affair with Oyston had petered out, she also had sex with a businessman named Michael Thompson when she was 18 or 19, she told the court.
And asked if the sex with these other men was the same as with Oyston she replied: "No, not at all. It was almost dirty or sordid."
Miss Rubotham told the court that she had first met Oyston when she was 13 or 14 at the Model Team agency in Manchester.
She said she had started seeing Mr Oyston for meals regularly with other guests from the age of 15 and then started a relationship when she was 16.
"Any complaints about the way he treated you?" asked Oyston's barrister Anthony Scrivener.
"No," she replied, "I loved him", adding that she had known he was married at the time.
She said the tycoon had given her gifts on her birthday and at Christmas and twice he had given her a new dress.
At one point she told him she had become pregnant and had an abortion and she said Oyston had been "very supportive".
The witness told the court that she had known Miss H "quite well" and described her as "quite unstable, very nervous and had strange behaviour".
Miss H openly admitted that she had taken drugs at parties in her home town, the court heard.
"Was she aware of your relationship with Mr Oyston?" asked Mr Scrivener.
"Not at first, but later," she replied.
Miss Rubotham told the jury that some time before January 1992 she, *Miss H*, Oyston, model agency boss Peter Martin and a couple of other models had dined at the Portland Hotel in Manchester.
After the meal Peter Martin drove Oyston back to Claughton Hall in his Toyota Supra sports car, she told the jury.
Miss Rubotham said she sat in the front and Miss B sat behind with Oyston.
She said that during the journey to Claughton Hall, everyone was singing and she had placed her hand on Oyston's shin and knee.
"I was very close to him and felt we had something which was quite special at the time," she said.
Asked if she would have known if any sex had taken place in the back of the car, Miss Rubotham said: "Yes I would, and I would have probably ordered the car to be stopped."
She said Miss H had never complained to her about anything that had

happened in the car.
Once they all arrived at Claughton Hall she had asked to use the bathroom, she told the court, and Miss H had been quite excited about seeing inside the tycoon's home.
She said that she and the other girl went inside with Mr Oyston and when she came out of the bathroom, she found the tycoon lying on his side of the bed propped up by pillows without his jacket and shoes.
She said Miss B was also on the bed facing him, fully clothed and wearing a black velvet dress.
Asked if she had sexual intercourse in the bedroom in the presence of Miss B she replied: "No, I did not."
She said that they had left straight away and Oyston had given her a kiss as he showed them the way out and said goodbye to Miss H.
Miss Rubotham said they returned at about midnight to Peter Martin's house in Sale where she was staying.
Miss H never made a complaint about Mr Oyston, the court was told.
And she said her relationship with Oyston had eventually petered out.
Under cross-examination by Helen Grindrod QC, she admitted that the *News of the World* had offered her £7,000 to sell her story but she decided against doing so and had been paid no money. She said that Oyston had often visited Peter Martin's house in Sale and had occasionally come inside.
Asked if she had had sex with the millionaire at Martin's home, she replied: "I can't recall but possibly yes."
"Have you ever had three-in-a-bed sex with Mr Oyston?" asked Mrs Grindrod. "No, I have not," she replied.
She told the court that she had stayed with Oyston at three London hotels including the Hilton and said she could only recall one occasion when his personal assistant Gill Bridge had been present at the hotel.
"Would it not be the case that when you went to London with Mr Oyston, Gill Bridge would be there?" asked Mrs Grindrod. "No, not at all," she replied.
She said she would ring Oyston's office to contact him but if he wasn't there, she would not leave a message.
Miss Rubotham denied Miss H's claims that she had only stayed at Martin's house regularly after Easter 1992.
"She had certainly been there when I was still living there prior to January 1992," she told the court.
Asked why she had travelled with Oyston when he was being driven home by Peter Martin after the meal at the Portland Hotel, she replied: "I wouldn't leave the dinner early, certainly not with my boyfriend present."

"Was Mr Oyston the one you called your boyfriend?" asked Mrs Grindrod.
"Yes, he was," she replied.
"Why didn't you get in the back of the car with your boyfriend?" pressed Mrs Grindrod.
"No particular reason. I very often sit in the front," said the witness.
She told the jury that she had visited Claughton Hall once before but on the second visit had been startled by a suit of armour in the hallway before going upstairs to the bathroom.
"You had sexual intercourse with Mr Oyston in that bed, didn't you, while Miss B was sitting on a chair?" said Mrs Grindrod.
"No," she replied: "We never had sex at his home.
Miss Rubotham told the court that she was expecting a baby in November and had a steady boyfriend.

DO YOU HAVE
ONDENSATION?
D OF SEASON SALE
IAL HIRE AVAILABLE
ESTON TV SERVICES

LANCASHIRE
Evening P

33,921 THURSDAY, MAY 23, 1996 26p COUNTY

250
JOBS TONIGHT
SEE CLASSIFIED

HALF PRICE
PIZZALAND
MEALS
OFFER PAGE 6

'st picture of woman 16-year-old claims watched he

SHE SA
OYSTO
RAPE M

THIS is the teenage model a court was told shared the same bed as millionaire Owen Oyston as he raped a terrified 16-year-old.

Lisa Rubotham was also the girl whose love for Oyston reduced his wife Vicki to tears.

Lisa, who used the catwalk name Lisa French, has admitted having an affair with the father-of-five. She was 18 – 42 years his junior.

ORDERED

Her former lover Oyston was today beginning a six year jail sentence for "horrendous" sex attacks.

A jury found the 62 year old guilty of the rape of a 16-year-old in his four poster bed at

By PAUL BALDWIN and JANE MACDONALD

...half hours to return their unanimous verdict that the millionaire Blackpool FC chairman was a rapist.

Before sentencing Oyston to six years yesterday afternoon, judge Mr Justice McCullough said the offences were horrendous and added: *"You have throughout placed your own feelings above hers. You have not shown a hint of remorse.*

"You were 58, she was 16. You were rich and powerful with a strong personality. She was young, dependent and vulnerable."

Oyston frowned heavily as the judge sentenced him to three years for the indecent assault and six years for the rape, to run concurrently.

During the 20 day trial Oyston also faced

TRA

In a later unsuccessful application to the European Court of Human Rights the advocate David Price expressed how the two witnesses, Miss H and Lysa Rubotham, were treated unequally at Liverpool Crown Court:

> Miss Rubotham, his defence witness, was subjected to extensive cross-examination about her sexual experience with other persons.
> Unlike "J", she was not given anonymity under Section 4 [1] of the Sexual Offences [Amendment] Act 1976. She was obliged to admit having a sexual relationship with the defendant and after having replied to one question by saying that she had "loved him", was asked to say whether she had sex with other men besides the defendant. She had then to admit to promiscuous sex at the age of 17 and 18 with four businessmen, who were all named in open court.
> Asked by the prosecuting barrister if the sex with these four men had been the same as sex with the defendant, she replied, "No, not at all. It was almost dirty or sordid."
> These questions were framed to demonstrate that although Miss Rubotham was a friend and colleague of the complainant, the admission that she had "loved" the defendant, suggested that she might be more loyal to the defendant than to her colleague and that she might even be prepared to lie on oath for him. Having admitted to "almost dirty or sordid" promiscuity, she was also obliged at the trial to reveal that she had undergone an abortion at the time of the alleged crimes.

Professor Anthony Bradley QC[102] described the difficulty faced by the Oyston defence:

> If a barrister facing a jury knows that the judge will not support his objection, intervention could damage his client further, in the eyes of the jury. This barrister was at a disadvantage here because both the prosecuting counsel and the judge were demonstrating by their questions to Lysa Rubotham that they regarded her as a different type of witness to *Miss H.* The judge's own

[102] Emeritus Professor of Constitutional Law, Edinburgh, Institute of European & Comparative Law, Oxford.

questions and insistence on establishing the time-scale of Lysa Rubotham's sex with the other men shows that he thought the questions being put by Mrs Grindrod were certainly not "*unnecessary*", under the common law, and that the questioning of Lysa Rubotham on her promiscuous sex life was relevant to the trial.

In this way, the judge demonstrated that he believed this witness [Lysa Rubotham] was in a completely different position to that of the complainant, Miss H, who was protected from such questions. Since the judge treated these witnesses differently, unfairness was inherent in those proceedings, especially when in his summing-up he put a stark choice to the jury, did they believe Lysa or Miss H?

The *Evening Gazette* reported Mrs Vicki Oyston's evidence for the defence[103]

The defence case in the Owen Oyston trial finished yesterday with the jury of eight women and four men hearing evidence about the Blackpool soccer boss's work for charity and other causes.

Since 1985, the court was told, Oyston had donated more than £1 million to various charities and also contributed funds to the Labour Party.

The jury then heard from Granada presenter Robert McLoughlin, who said Oyston had anonymously donated £10,000 to allow defendants in the Heysel Stadium disaster case to be released from custody in Belgium.

He explained that following the 1985 disaster 25 Britons were allowed bail by the Belgian authorities on a surety of £2,000 each.

Some families were able to raise the cash to get their sons home, but others could not until Oyston had stepped in with the anonymous donation.

Dr Ronald Heywood, of the Blackpool based Lancashire Free Legal Action Centre, then took the stand and told the court that Oyston had

103 Adrian Darbyshire, Evening Gazette, Blackpool.

given anonymous donations on a number of occasions to help people facing imprisonment over poll tax arrears.

Earlier Vicki Oyston, 56, the wife of the millionaire Seasiders' chairman, appeared in the witness box.

She began by guiding the jury around the Oyston's family home using plans and photographs.

Claughton Hall, she told the court, had been a very busy place in 1989. Living there was her elderly father-in-law Selsby and his two carers, together with a housekeeper.

The Oystons' son Karl also stayed there from time to time with his girlfriend and daughter Dawn and her friend were living in the tower.

The youngest child Adam stayed at Claughton Hall when he was home from school and the other two daughters Heidi and Dawn slept there occasionally.

"Apart from the domestic situation, the house was still being used an enormous amount for office work and social functions combined with business," Mrs Oyston told the court, adding that there was always someone in the house.

By 1992, there were fewer people living at the house. Oyston's father had died the year before, there was no housekeeper and the children were no longer living there full-time.

"For quite a bit of the year we did have Heidi who had just had a baby and immediately got pregnant and had another baby," Mrs Oyston told the jury.

"Karl used to come and stay if I was away and Heidi was away."

She told the court she had first married her husband in 1962.

But 20 years later, on her birthday, the two had divorced only to remarry six years later, in August 1988.

During that period of the divorce they continued to see each other, work together and go on holiday as a couple.

"It might sound strange but that was the way it was," she said, adding that Claughton Hall had always been treated "like a family home."

"After you married again was there a problem?" asked Oyston's barrister Anthony Scrivener.

"Yes," she admitted. "Whose fault was it?" he asked. "Oh, it was mine," she replied.

"Was someone else involved?" asked Mr Scrivener. "Yes, there was," she told the court.

Mrs Oyston said her husband had gone to London when he discovered her affair and she had joined him a week later.

They got back together, sought counselling but the marriage remained "very difficult" until comparatively recently.

In the years 1991 and 1992, she said she became very depressed.

"We were not communicating very well during that period," she told the court, adding that she was still living at Claughton Hall.

Mr Scrivener then asked the witness about Manchester model agency boss Peter Martin, a former business colleague of her husband.

"I didn't like him at all," she said.

"When Owen and I were having a problem, I discovered later that Peter Martin was following me and having me watched all the time," she added.

She said she would not invite him to the house.

Cross-examining, Crown counsel Helen Grindrod QC asked her if there was any occasion when her husband would be at Claughton Hall late at night when she wasn't there.

She said that in 1990, she would be there most of the time and in 1992 it was "unlikely but possible" that she would not be at home at night.

"I decided to seek help for myself and I had counselling.

"I started going out far more and I actually went away for a weekend with my daughters. It worked."

Mrs Oyston told the court she believed her husband had originally instructed Mr Martin to tail her.

"I think when he was very angry, he probably did discuss it," she said.

"He was very angry with you because he suspected you of having an affair?" asked Mrs Grindrod.
"He was upset," Mrs Oyston replied.
"How many of your husband's girlfriends between 1989 and 1992 did you know about?" asked prosecuting counsel.
"I rang two of them when I suspected," she replied.
"I did not know until the charges were put forward and I saw the names of the girlfriends. Nobody knows at the time - but I suspected."
Questioned about the evidence of one her husband's former lovers, Mrs Oyston broke down in tears. "I saw her arrive in court, yesterday," she said, sobbing.
"Did you know her?" asked Mrs Grindrod.
"No," she replied. "I've seen her photograph."
Sipping a glass of water, she said she would like an adjournment and the courtroom emptied for 10 minutes, allowing her time to recover her composure.

Under the headline **The Last To Know** the *Daily Mail* reported harshly on Vicki Oyston's evidence:

OWEN OYSTON'S long suffering wife tried hard to keep her composure while testifying for her errant husband yesterday.
She sailed through questions about his adultery, about how cheated wives were always the last to know and even about how he had her tailed by a private detective.
But when Lisa Rubotham's name was mentioned, the 56-year old mother of four could contain herself no longer.
Eye-dabbing turned to sniffles then a flood of tears, and proceedings had to be halted.

Elizabeth Gomm, women's editor at the *Evening Gazette,* sympathised:

IT looked as if Vicki Oyston was going to hold herself together.
For 70 minutes in the witness box she kept her emotions in check.
On the 15th day of the trial where her husband, tycoon Owen Oyston, is

accused of rape, she managed an uneasy composure.

In a soft, clear voice she answered questions about her personal and domestic life.

Sitting, she twisted the rings on the fingers of her right hand or toyed with the large handkerchief she had with her when she walked into court, wearing a blue silk suit.

The crunch came when prosecuting counsel Helen Grindrod asked her about one of her husband's former lovers.

Had she known her?

It was suddenly, too much. Biting her bottom lip, she failed to stem the tears.

And Vicki Oyston - wife, mother and grandmother - wept in the witness box.

It was with relief that she agreed she would like an adjournment to give her a chance to get a grip.

As the courtroom emptied, she refused to be ushered out. Instead, she asked to stay and walk around.

Her husband, who had looked uncomfortable throughout her testimony, asked if he could go to her.

Permission was refused. He would have to wait until she had completed her evidence.

After a short break Mrs Oyston, who is 56, regained her composure.

She appeared slightly embarrassed by her earlier lack of control.

Back straight and head high she went back to the witness box where, for the remaining five minutes she seemed to be at ease with herself.

As she left, she smiled at watching family and friends and gave them a thumbs up sign.

When the court broke for lunch Oyston could, at last, go to his wife.

He walked straight to where she was sitting, planted a kiss on her head and whispered "Well done".

CHAPTER 23

'There has been an attempt to deceive you'

Helen Grindrod QC, closing for the Crown, examined Miss H's account of the events in Oyston's bedroom:

> It may be suggested to you that because she "just lay there" and did not say, "No", you could not come to the conclusion that Owen Oyston, if it happened, which he denies, thought she was consenting. How could a man think that? A girl of 16, to whom he has behaved as he did in the car, forcing her to give him oral sex, who is lying there rigid, terrified. Does she really have to say no?
>
> You see there is no request, there is no foreplay, not unless you count what happened in the car as some crude kind of foreplay. He simply forced himself upon her.
>
> Owen Oyston seems to want it both ways with this. "It did not happen", he says, but if it did, then I must have thought she was consenting."
>
> He cannot have it both ways and if you decide it did happen you have no evidence from him to say she gave every appearance of wanting it. All the surrounding circumstances suggest that it must have been perfectly obvious to Owen Oyston that the girl was not consenting. But you see Owen Oyston was used to having young women, being surrounded by them, having sexual intercourse with them. He was not used to asking, and he did not ask, and she did not consent, and he must have known it.

Mrs Grindrod said it could not have been a coincidence that both the complainants had told similar stories about incidents nearly three years apart:

> The proposition put forward by the defence that there was never an occasion when either of these offences could have occurred late at night at Claughton Hall in the dark with nobody there is blatant nonsense. Of course, there

might have been somebody there, no-one would expect Mr Oyston's ninety odd year old father to get out of bed and say; 'What are you up to lad, would they?' Mr Oyston was master in his house, his own house. Of course, he would not bring women there when his wife was there. He was at least paying lip service to keeping her in the dark. But Lysa shows you that there were two occasions, and what happens, she goes into the bedroom, she comes out of the bathroom and here is the astonishing bit, not put to Miss H, when she comes out there is Mr Oyston lying on the bed, jacket off, shoes off. There is Miss H lying on the bed, fully clothed. That is it. They all leave. Lisa Rubotham has advanced the case, has she not, to this extent. There was an occasion when Miss H and Mr Oyston were in the back of that car, Lysa was in the front, they all went to Claughton Hall. There was something about showing Miss H the house, but it seems to have been her idea. They are all in the bedroom at some stage. The only bits missing, of course, are the indecent assault and the rape. That is hardly the picture that was being painted when *Miss H* was being cross-examined.

Members of the jury, you will have to consider many other bits of evidence. What you think important you will give importance to. I have tried simply to outline how the Crown put the case now. We say to you quite simply neither of these girls was shaken on the main issue. Both said similar things, so similar that you might well say to yourselves; how can these girls possibly be making It up? As far as Miss H is concerned, if you were going to make up an allegation of rape would you include Lysa in the story thereby openly inviting her to contradict it? Of course, you would not. It would happen alone, would it not? Not with witnesses.

It will be suggested to you, of course, that Miss H is so unreliable you can dismiss everything she says but keep your eye on the issues. If you come to the conclusion that defence witnesses have been called not to clarify the truth but to obscure it then you can only reach one conclusion, can you not? There has been an attempt to deceive you. Having carefully considered all that we say you are driven to the conclusion that Owen Oyston raped Miss H and indecently raped and assaulted Miss H three years later.

Anthony Scrivener began by giving the jury some guidance About the special difficulties of trying sexual allegations:

These are sexual cases and again there is a special principle which most judges would normally tell the juries about in sex cases. It is usually expressed in this way, that human experience in the courts has shown that complainants in sex cases for all sorts of reasons, and sometimes for no reason at all, tell a false story which is very easy to fabricate but extremely difficult to refute. That is a warning which is normally given to jurors. It is based on the experience of the courts, because the trial process is such that you may not ever penetrate the truth as to why a person is making an allegation. The system is not perfect enough. So that warning is given. Often it is put in another way. Another way it is put is that complainants in sex cases may well have purposes of their own to serve and may lie or fantasize for unascertainable reasons or no reason at all.

Scrivener tackled the question of Oyston's sexual conduct.

You have often heard this statement and I make no bones for reappearing, repeating it here, we are not a court of morals. You may disapprove of Mr Oyston's morals. I suppose nowadays we are much more cautious about criticising our fellow citizens in the area of morals than perhaps we were years ago. The date of hypocrisy has passed, good fortune though it may be. You are not here to try him as to whether he is a man of good morals or bad, if that were the case, we would have lost hands down. That is not the issue in this case. If girls are sixteen, they have passed the age of consent. We are concerned with probably the second most serious crime in the book. the most heinous crime of rape and the issue you have to decide is whether you are sure beyond reasonable doubt that the evidence in this case convinces you that Mr Oyston is guilty of those offences, it means eliminating the defence evidence.

ge 4 NEWS Evening Ga

THE OYSTON TRIAL

We'd lose on morals admits QC

Days of hypocrisy gone: Owen O

By ADRIAN DARBYSHIRE

THE jury in the Owen Oyston rape trial was told by his barrister today that if the tycoon was being tried for his morals "we would have lost hands down."

But Anthony Scrivener QC stressed to the eight women and four men that they were not in a court of morals.

Oyston, 62, the millionaire

The charges

- BETWEEN January 1 1988 and December 31 1989 he raped a teenage girl at Claughton Hall.
- BETWEEN October 4 1991 and December 31 1992 he raped another teenager at the Hall.
- BETWEEN the same dates he indecently assaulted the same girl.

have lost hands down."

Mr Scrivener was making his closing speech on the 16th day of

the first girl could not remember the date, the day of the week or the time of year when the alleged rape

rape, was "totally inconsistent" with what she had claimed happened.

"You do not become friends with your rapist. You do not go on meeting your rapist. You do not appear on affectionate terms with your rapist," he said.

He described the second girl, who claims Oyston forced her to commit a sex act in the back seat of a car, then made her watch him having sex with another girl before raping her, as "a very sad and mixed-up individual."

The prosecution has their similar fact lists and the defence have theirs.

1. Both of these girls came from the same agency.

2. Neither of them can remember the date of the alleged offence.

3. Neither of them made any complaint about these alleged rapes for years.

4. When they were first contacted by the police, they made no allegation against Mr Oyston and you will see in your admissions, number 8 and number 17, deal with that.
5. Both are alleged to have made their first complaint after the police started to interview them.

6. In both cases, the J and H cases, something unusual happened to the first record kept by the police of their interviews. In the case of J an interview note was taken, to which I will refer later, and in the writing of that note there is no references to rape. Not one word is written in that text. The police officer said it was mentioned at the end of the interview but she did not make a note of it. In the case of *Miss H,* the original interview note has mysteriously disappeared.

7. Both of these girls knew a woman named Melanie Hardy who worked at the agency for several years.

8. Neither of them, neither of these witnesses, is supported by any other evidence.

9. The police made no obvious follow up enquiries in this case because the police had decided to charge Mr Oyston even before he had been arrested.

There are nine strange features about this case. They are the similar facts the defence rely upon, both models, neither can remember the date, neither made any complaint for years to anyone. When they first contacted the police before they were interviewed, they were making no complaint about Mr Oyston. Both alleged to have made their first complaint during a police interview. In the case of *Miss H* no record of that has been kept in the note, in the case of *Miss H* the case note has mysteriously disappeared. Both knew Melanie Hardy, neither is supported by any supporting evidence and the police made no follow up enquiries in either of those cases.

Have you noticed other curious features? Let me mention Lysa Rubotham, and I suspect you noticed this. The police must have known from the moment Miss H made her written statement that Lysa was supposed to have been there all the time. It does not require a great brain to realise in the circumstances that Lysa Rubotham must be an important potential witness because she is someone who can corroborate what *Miss H* has said. She is obviously a material witness. Did the police contact Lysa Rubotham? They certainly did and she kept a note of the dates. They saw her on 27 separate occasions, 24 of those, if we look at the dates, would have been after *Miss H* made her written statement.

During that time until one instance, which I will tell you about in a moment, they never asked her about the incident with which you are concerned, a serious rape allegation involving *Miss H*. They never asked her. She was never asked to make a statement about what she knew about that incident. We know why. The material date is 30th January, 1995, because on that date, according to Lysa Rubotham, she received a phone call from Detective Constable Hughes, whose name you will see appears a little later on.

These are the questions I asked of Lysa Rubotham, and this is from the transcript not a summary. My question was: "How many written statements did you make for the police?" Answer: “Two”. Question: "In either of those statements were you ever asked by the police about this incident you have now been talking about in this case. Miss H?" Answer: “No.” Question: "Did any policeman ever ask you about Miss H? Answer: "Yes." "Who was it?" "Detective Constable Martyn Hughes." My Lord said: "Constable who?” and she replied, “Martyn Hughes." I said, "Can you look around and see him if he is in court?" She did and said: "Yes.' I said, “What happened?" Answer; "It was by telephone, a telephone conversation." Question: "What was the conversation?" Answer. "Along the lines of, do you recall going to Claughton

Hill, did anything improper take place?" My Lord said: "Pardon?" She said: "Did anything improper sexually take place?" My Lord said: "Yes?" She replied: "With yourself or Miss H? I said, no, and asked if he would come down and talk to me about it and he asked me again if I was saying that nothing... " My Lord interrupted: "Sorry, just a second, he asked if I could come and talk to him, he coming to talk to you or..." Answer: "Yes." "What else?" "He- asked me once more if I was saying that nothing improper took place and I said well, nothing like that happened but I would like to talk to you and I was told it wasn't necessary," I said: "Just a second, he said what? It will not be necessary?" "That's correct." "This was when?" "This was February, I have the exact date, but I believe it was either January 30th or February 1st or something 95. "1995?" Answer: "Yes."

So the answer was she was never asked to make a statement about it, obviously a material witness and when she was asked, she indicated to the police that she would not be corroborating the police's version of it and so it was not necessary to take a statement. That would either have been the 30th or 1st November.

D.C. Hughes was then present at the interview of the defendant on 9th February, nine days later. After lunch I am going to ask you to look with me at that police interview to see what was being said to Mr Oyston in the presence of D.C. Hughes nine days after he had said to Lysa Rubotham; it is not necessary for you to make a statement and he must have known that Lysa Rubotham was not going to support the prosecution case.

Scrivener claimed *Miss H's* behaviour was totally inconsistent with having been raped:

You do not become friends with your rapist. You do not appear on affectionate terms with your rapist. You do not go on meeting your rapist. She has misled you on oath.
She kept in contact with Mr Oyston, in fact was having an affair with him, seen by a number of people.
Her evidence is in direct conflict with independent witnesses, with no axe to grind, whose evidence you would have to say was perjured before you reject it.

Of Miss H, who had reduced members of the jury and members of the press to tears, Anthony Scrivener said she was a 'very sad and mixed up individual' who had exhibited 'strange behaviour' and 'not, in our submission, a reliable witness.'

CHAPTER 24

'You have been told lies.'

Mr Justice McCullough told the jury of eight women and four men that lies had undoubtedly been told in the witness box during the third trial. He said there was no red light to tell them when lies were being told and they would have to use their common sense and knowledge of human nature and their experience of life.

> In each case the evidence of the person making the allegations and the defendant differs starkly.
> Can it be explained by mistaken recollection or by imagination or is it that you have been told lies, indeed lie after lie, in the form of deliberate perjury designed to mislead you into delivering a false verdict?

The judge noted a number of similarities between the accounts of rape given by the two complainants and asked the jury to consider whether it was possible that they had put their heads together or that a third party had put them up to making false allegations against Oyston.

> Might the similarities simply be explained by coincidence, or is the only realistic explanation that the defendant did indeed behave in the circumstances and in the way they have described?

Mr Justice McCullough decided to give the jury the old statutory warning about convicting in rape cases on the uncorroborated evidence of a complainant, despite that requirement having been removed in 1995. He told the jury:

Remember you don't just take into account what witnesses say but the way he or she says it. Was he, she, trying to be frank and honest, or devious? Did witnesses appear to be trying to answer the questions? Did they appear to be trying to avoid answering the questions by side-tracking?"

David Ward of the *Guardian* reported:

As the jury left to consider its verdict, Owen Oyston's aides began distributing copies of an A4 booklet to reporters.
This was the *Oyston File*, a 72-page document printed on glossy paper and published by Oyston himself.
Having spent an estimated £1 million defending himself against sex charges in three consecutive trials, the northern tycoon had used still more of his considerable wealth to publish his own extraordinary allegations, detailed during the trial, of how former Conservative ministers Lord Blaker and Robert Atkins and Blackpool businessman William Harrison had conspired against him for years.
The document includes a four-page insert, which brings the story up to date by quoting extensively from the summary of the case for the defence presented by Oyston's counsel Anthony Scrivener QC.
A colour photograph of Oyston illustrates his "personal statement".
He writes: "I have taken the unusual step of releasing the enclosed documents after being prevented on a technicality in the High Court, the Appeal Court and the House of Lords from taking legal action. If, with my considerable financial resources, I am denied a hearing through no fault of my own, how can the ordinary man in the street ever hope to get his day in court?"
The central dossier charts the progress of the alleged conspiracy in great detail.
The supplementary insert concludes with a grim prediction: "The Oyston case will rumble on like a gathering storm with darkening clouds over many of those involved."

Two hours after entering the jury room, the jury were called back to be sent to their homes for the night of May 21. On the following day, after a further five hours deliberation, they returned with a verdict of not guilty of the rape of Miss H, but guilty of the indecent assault of Miss H in the car.

They said they were unable to reach a verdict on the charge of rape of Miss H in Oyston's bedroom. Consequently, after having already deliberated for seven hours and fifty minutes, Mr Justice McCullough told them to retire again and try to reach a verdict on which at least ten of them could agree. Fifteen minutes later, the foreman of the jury surprised the court by returning at 4:13 pm on May 22 with a unanimous verdict: guilty of the rape of Miss H.

Anthony Scrivener rose:

My Lord, it has been a long-contested case and your Lordship knows all the facts. If I can just draw your Lordship's attention to what I would call the salient facts for your consideration. The first is these offences occurred quite a long time ago. Secondly, there is the age of the defendant. Thirdly, the actual facts. When looked at from the point of view of rape cases as a whole, there was little force used in this case, and on any view *Miss H* on her own evidence was at most passive, although there was some force used in the car.

He is a man who reached the age of 62 years of age with a completely clean character. He is a man who became wealthy through hard work and industry. He has not just become more wealthy but has done a lot of good for the community. He has always had a social conscience and he has contributed a great deal to society, particularly for those who are most in need. Quite often it was done, as your Lordship heard, anonymously and that is much to his credit. My Lord, at a moment like this, all those factors a man is entitled to have taken into account and I ask your Lordship to do so.

The judge said:

Mr Oyston, the starting point for any Court considering a sentence for an offence of rape is five years' imprisonment. When one or more aggravating features are present this figure is increased. Where mitigating features are present, it is reduced. The most significant mitigating factor commonly found is a plea of guilty. This is because a plea of guilty is an acknowledgement of wrongdoing and, in particular, because it saves the victim from having to give evidence and face cross-examination designed to persuade a jury that their evidence is unreliable.

Miss H was subjected to that ordeal both here and in the magistrates' court last year. You said that you were very sorry for her; but had you cared for her you would have pleaded guilty. You have throughout placed your own interests above hers. You have shown not a hint of remorse. The defence that you advanced was false. It is to be regretted that another young woman was put forward to support it. This does not mean that your sentence will be increased on that account, it simply shows that the conduct of your defence provides no mitigation.

It is true that you did not threaten Miss H, nor did you use any weapon, nor did you use any violence in order to have your way with her. But you also have to be sentenced for what you did to her in the car. That incident substantially aggravates your conduct, and makes five years too low a starting point. I have no doubt that the other girl was being used to increase the chance that Miss H would comply with your wishes. You were 58, Miss H was 16. You were rich and powerful, with a strong personality. She was young, dependent and vulnerable. That too aggravates the offence.

I do not believe that Miss H led you on in any way. I am, however, prepared to assume that you hoped that your advantages of age, wealth and position would influence her to agree with what you wanted. But when it came to the bit she did not, and it must have been obvious that she did not. As she so accurately put it: "He treated me like an object and I'm not."

It is impossible to know to what extent Miss H has been traumatised by the experiences of that night having regard to the other matters of which she spoke concerning somebody else. But as you yourself said to the jury, these are horrendous offences. As you said in one of your previous trials: "Rape is an awful ordeal for a woman. Anyone who commits it deserves the worst kind of sentence." The worst kind of sentence is imprisonment and clearly this is a case where only a substantial term of imprisonment can meet the justice of the case.

You are now 62, considerably older than most who face their first sentence of imprisonment, and you have not previously been convicted- You have in many ways over many years been generous to the wider community, often anonymously. But in these cases, as the Court of Appeal has said, previous good character is of only minor relevance.

> These offences happened four years ago but this is not a case where a defendant has feared for years that he would eventually be brought to justice. Until early last year you thought you had got away with it. I accept, however, that for the last year the prospect of this trial and its outcome, should your attempt to defeat justice fail, will have caused you considerable anxiety. I have put all these features in the balance.
>
> It would have been justifiable to have passed consecutive sentences for the two offences, but if proper sentences for each alone were accumulated the total would be too long, particularly for somebody of your years. The sentences will therefore be concurrent. The length of each reflects the fact that it was committed in the context of the other. For count 2 you will go to prison for three years. For count 3, six years, both concurrent. Total six years.

Chris Blackhurst, the journalist who had revealed that the death crash conspirator Bill Harrison had funded Michael Murrin's campaign against Oyston reported the end of the trial for the *Independent* and described his departure for Walton Jail in Liverpool:

> As Oyston was being led from the dock, he mouthed "I love you to his daughter Heidi, who was in the public gallery. She responded by mouthing to her father, "I love you too."
> Detective Sergeant Harry Harrison of the Greater Manchester police investigation team said of the young model: "The last few years have been a very difficult time for the young lady and her family.
> "She has shown tremendous courage in coming to court and giving her evidence, which at times included details of an intimate and traumatic nature.
> "I hope that she can take some consolation from the fact that today's result can be seen as a victory for the average person by showing that no matter who an offender is, action can and will be taken when a person's privacy is violated."

CHAPTER 25

Flower Calendar

For fourteen months, between the arrest of Oyston in 1995 and his conviction for rape and indecent assault in 1996, Greater Manchester Police and the Crown Prosecution Service held two documents that could have been used to prove his innocence.

They had seized a 1992 calendar and a black notebook used as an attendance register in the raid on the Model Team dormitory, three months before the 1996 arrest of Oyston. When Miss H said in October 1995 that she had been raped in Oyston's bedroom after a car journey from Manchester to Claughton Hall, the Greater Manchester detectives correlated the calendar and the notebook to work out a single date, June 6, 1992, as the likeliest occasion on which Oyston committed the two offences of which he would eventually be convicted. Yet for reasons that remain unclear Crown prosecutors framed an indictment against Oyston specifying rape and indecent assault on a date in 1991.

The disastrous consequence was that solicitors wasted months researching Oyston's movements for 1991, for until the seventh day of his third trial, Oyston stood accused of committing two offences against Miss H on an unspecified evening between October 4 and December 31,1991. Yet the calendar and the notebook held by the authorities showed that the only possible date for those offences had been June 6, 1992, six months outside the indictment period.

The meaning of markings on the calendar and notes in the black 'Ostaline' notebook had been explained to Det Constable Julie Sharpe.

Greater Manchester Police knew from February 9, 1995, that the two documents indicated a 'likeliest' date for any offences against Miss H that lay six months outside the wide indictment period. This discrepancy was not brought to the attention of the defence, despite the law at that time requiring full disclosure of unused police material. The black 'Ostaline' model agency attendance book was never even seen by the defence.

At Oyston's May 1996 third trial, the police and prosecuting counsel did not put forward the June 6, 1992, date. Miss H, the rape complainant, was resolutely refusing to state in what month, season, or even year, the alleged offence had taken place, so the indictment in her case specified only that the two offences were committed during and just after a car journey from Manchester to the defendant's home at Claughton Hall on a night between October 4, 1991, and December 31, 1991.

Oyston's defence team conducted pre-trial research using 1991 business diaries and credit card records to track his movements for that year. There was no such car journey, nor any such visit to Claughton Hall on any evening in 1991. But on the seventh day of the third trial, after inconsistencies began to appear in the evidence of the rape complainant, Mr Ray Wigglesworth for the Crown applied in court before Mr Justice McCullough for the indictment period to be extended by a further fifteen months, to run from October 4, 1991, to December 31, 1992. The judge complied, so that the case proceeded with the prosecution not specifying any date for the journey and with the defence lacking any information to suggest one. The dates of the allegations against Oyston would ultimately be changed seven times in three years.

Greater Manchester Police had seized from Peter Martin, three months before the arrest of Owen Oyston, the 1992 calendar that became known as the 'flower calendar' and was listed as "MJH / 30D". The calendar had been kept at Peter Martin's home in Sale, Greater Manchester, and used to record his movements, meetings and sexual encounters. It dated the car journey exactly. Det Con Julie Sharpe listed notations on the calendar and Peter Martin's business partner and co-defendant Tracey Grainey explained the notation used on the calendar during a police interview on February 8, 1995.

Events and appointments marked on the 'flower calendar' were then compared with notes in the Ostaline notebook, indicating who had stayed overnight at the model agency dormitory in Sale. The police listed the calendar and notebook as R31O and R30O on the HOLMES computer. The entries were not dated but it is clear that by February 1995 Det Con Julie Sharpe was checking Martin's daily activities against the list of his overnight residents. This was fourteen months before Oyston's trial. Despite requests, the Ostaline notebook was not shown to the defence.

Det Con Sharpe's analysis of the notebook began:

With reference to exhibit (ASM/9) Black Ostaline notebook: - Log of girls staying at house in Sale.

Her correlation of the calendar and the notebook revealed that Martin, Oyston, Rubotham and Miss H had met at the Don Antonio restaurant in Sale on the night of Saturday, June 6, 1992. The calendar entry was '6.6.92 Saturday OJO LR [Miss H] Don Ant'. Det Con Sharpe had added information in brackets, 'DI : R31 reads: 2.6.92 Tuesday OJO 4.6.92 Thursday B'ham 6.6.92 Saturday OJO LR [Miss H] Don Ant (Don Antonio's Sale) 7.6.92 Sunday GEO.'

Photocopies of the calendar supplied to the defence were too indistinct for the Don Antonio restaurant to be identified but the eventual examination of the Ostaline register revealed that Miss H and Lysa Rubotham both stayed the night at the house in Sale on June 6, 1992.[104] There was no other

---

104 [Miss H]: author's brackets and identification.

occasion in 1991 or 1992 on which the calendar showed Peter Martin meeting Oyston, Miss H and Lysa Rubotham on any date when the register also showed Miss H and Rubotham staying the night at Martin's home. The documents were accurately analysed by the police. The calendar and the Ostaline notebook indicated that the journey to Claughton Hall could only have happened on the evening of June 6, 1992. Greater Manchester Police made that assumption long before Oyston's trial, when they were framing an abortive case against Martin and Oyston for procuring. But by setting the rape indictment period between two dates in 1991, the Crown prosecutors made it highly unlikely that the 1992 'flower calendar' would ever be closely examined by Oyston's legal team.

To make matters worse, the 'Don Ant' on the photocopy supplied to the defence was indistinct and the calendar's full meaning could in any case only have been gathered with the help of Peter Martin and Tracey Grainey, defendants not involved in the Oyston trial and both not available to Oyston's solicitors. The police work on the "floral calendar" was never handed over to the defence team, but in 2002 long after Oyston had served a prison sentence, Peter Martin explained to this author the notations that he had used on the calendar for the month of June 1992. A copy of his notes showed that he "had a meeting" on June 6 with Owen Oyston, Lysa Rubotham and Miss H.

The Crown Prosecution Service and Greater Manchester Police possessed, long before Oyston's trial, a document from which the only possible date for the alleged crimes could be fixed as June 6, 1992. Yet they allowed an indictment to be framed and served for a period running from October 4, 1991, to December 31, 1991.

The failure of the Crown Prosecution Service to let the defence know that the Crown could fix June 6, 1992, as the date of the car journey became suspicious as soon as Miss H took civil action for damages against Oyston.

In the civil case, long after his conviction, the Crown offered the date June 6, 1992, as a helpful suggestion for the likeliest date of the car journey which was then adopted as 'June 1992' at a late stage in the civil proceedings by Miss H's solicitors.

One of the prosecuting trial barristers, Mr Ray Wigglesworth, replying to an amended skeleton argument in Oyston's appeal against conviction, had also suggested the date of June 6, 1992. The agreed facts in Oyston's appeal [9604193Y4 Ind. No. T961028] eventually included a detailed chronology from April to October 1992 with June 6, 1992, as the only possible date for the car journey to Claughton Hall.

On February 14, 1999, solicitors acting in civil pleadings for the complainant Miss H amended the "likeliest date" for the rape and indecent assault of their client by Owen Oyston from "on or about September 1992" as stated in her claim to the Criminal Injuries Compensation Authority, to "on or about June 1992". The date was changed in civil proceedings after Oyston's appeal against conviction had failed. The complainant had of course at all times previously refused to say in what month, season or even in what year, the alleged offences. In four years of proceedings, indictment dates had been changed nine times.

Hiding the date of June 6, 1992, became particularly pernicious as fresh evidence of events in May and June 1992 were uncovered by Oyston's appeal solicitors. Fresh evidence, never heard by a jury, showed that Miss H had not been living at the Sale dormitory house, in terror of Peter Martin in May 1992, as she had suggested at the trial of Oyston. A letter, discovered after Oyston's conviction, showed that Miss H had been on holiday in Crete with her parents between May 7 and May 16, 1992. The letter revealed a sexual affair in Crete between Miss H and a young man named Jerome O'Malley. The letter was written after her holiday and posted from East Lancashire to O'Malley in Crete on May 21, 1992. The letter had been franked thirty miles away from Martin's home in Manchester. Miss H had not, as she had claimed at trial, been living in fear of Peter Martin at his model agency house in Sale before June 6, when she met Lysa Rubotham, Peter Martin and Owen Oyston at Don Antonio and travelled with them to Claughton Hall. On her return from her holiday in Crete she had taken school examinations on May 18, May 22 and June 2.

There was firm evidence that Miss H had taken a negative pregnancy test in East Lancashire on June 16. This had no particular relevance until the date of June 6 had been fixed and her holiday affair with Jerome in May had been discovered. She had always claimed that before the alleged rape by Oyston she had only ever had sexual relations with Peter Martin, who was infertile, and with a boy at school when she was aged 15.

In a note handed to Oyston's civil solicitors, the Crown later explained their view of the relevance of the pregnancy test:

> [H] did not take a pregnancy test after rape by Oyston because she started her period. After having sexual intercourse with O'Malley, she did not start her period when expected, thus she took a pregnancy test which was negative.

Yet the CPS and the police knew, in the phrase they used at the Court of Appeal, that the 'likeliest day' for the rape by Oyston was only nine days before the pregnancy test. That fact clashed with Miss H's assertion that she had not missed her menstrual period after rape by Oyston. If the journey to Claughton Hall was timed for June 6, Miss H's statement about the pregnancy test damned her. She had lied. The prosecution had gained a huge advantage by not allowing the jury to know that there had ever been a 'likeliest date' for the rape.

Once the date was fixed to June 6, another important piece of documentary fresh evidence, unseen by the jury at Oyston's trial, became relevant. This was a greetings card which Miss H admitted handing to Peter Martin and the staff at the model agency with a printed message:

> This very special 'thank you' is coming to express appreciation for all your thoughtfulness.

At the later trial of Peter Martin for the rape of Miss H, Martin's defending counsel produced the greetings card to try and shock Miss H at a time when she was angrily threatening to walk out of the witness box. The card was addressed to Lysa Rubotham, the woman said to have watched her being raped by Oyston, and also addressed to Peter Martin, a man said to have raped her four times before June 1992. Miss H's hand-written message on the card was:

> Thanks for everything, helping me and getting me sorted out. Love kisses and cuddles. XXXX J

In court again, during the trial of Peter Martin, Miss H admitted giving the card to Rubotham, Martin and another member of staff, but claimed that she must have given it to them no later than 'January or early 1992' well before the time she had been raped by Oyston or Martin:

> At the beginning, January, well the beginning of 1992. It was when I thought they were all right.

As soon as the card fell into the hands of Oyston's defence team it was discovered that the card had not been manufactured, distributed or even wholesaled, until late in June 1992. The card was not released to wholesalers until June 12, 1992, six days after the "likeliest date" for the alleged rape by Oyston. Miss H had therefore affectionately addressed the card and personally handed it to Lysa Rubotham and Peter Martin after the "likeliest date" of her alleged rape. Miss H had been given time to think about the consequences of her reply to questions about the greetings card. After a lunchtime adjournment she agreed that she could not possibly have given the greetings card to Peter Martin after he had raped and abused her. Yet she had been claiming that Martin had raped her four times in ten weeks, before forcing her to acquiesce to rape by Oyston, on the evening of June 6

– six days before the earliest date that she could have purchased the greetings card.

During Oyston's trial, Miss H told Anthony Scrivener on oath that she left the model agency house after her birthday, October 4, 1992, and re-started her education in East Lancashire.

Mr Scrivener: "I completely lost my temper, had a row with him and the whole thing exploded. The next day I left and went back home." That is what your statement says, is it not?

Miss H: Yes. It were my birthday and I had arranged to go home.

Mr Scrivener: Sorry. Your birthday?

Miss H: It were my birthday and I had arranged to go for a meal with my mum and dad on the Sunday and I told him about a week before and he knew about it and he said he were going to give me some money to go home. And then on the Sunday when I was going to go home, he said no I had to stop at the house and do his ironing. He said I should be on my knees to him.

Mr Scrivener: That is when you completely lost your temper and left?

Miss H: Yes.

Although there was much evidence that Miss H was in occasional and friendly contact with the model agency for another year, she no longer stayed at the model agency house. There was therefore no period between April 1992 and October 1992, in which she could have suffered ten weeks of abuse by Peter Martin at the model agency house as suggested at the trial of

Oyston. Ten weeks of abuse by Martin was the reason she gave for submitting without resistance to rape by Oyston. But for many good reasons it became clear that there was no occasion in 1991 or 1992, in all the various indictment periods suggested by the Crown Prosecution Service, on which Miss H could have surrendered to rape by Oyston, through fear of Peter Martin in the presence of Lysa Rubotham as suggested by Mrs Helen Grindrod QC at the trial of Oyston.

In June 1997, just a year after the jailing of Oyston, *Private Eye* reported that Anthony Scrivener QC would be presenting fresh evidence to Lord Bingham at the Appeal Court. The Eye noted that Helen Grindrod QC was simultaneously urging the 'curtailment of judges' discretionary powers' at a conference organised by the Centre for Research on Violence, Abuse and Gender Relations.

PRIVATE EYE

Legal News

LESS THAN two days after Owen Oyston heard on the little radio in his cell that three judges had given him leave to appeal against his rape conviction, his prosecutrix, Helen Grindrod, QC, was a 'keynote speaker' at a conference on rape and criminal justice.

Her most recent courtroom victory was the successful prosecution of millionaire rapist Owen Oyston," gushed the brochure for last week's conference organised by the Centre for Research on Violence, Abuse and Gender Relations of Leeds Metropolitan University. In her speech, Grindrod proposed the "curtailment of judges' discretionary powers to permit previous sexual history as evidence.

Over at the appeal court such evidence had just been admitted into Oyston's appeal case by the lord chief justice, Lord Bingham, sitting with Mr Justice Rougier and Mr Justice Kay. The evidence included a letter, apparently written in 1992 by Oyston's presumed victim, Miss B[105], to a boy she met on holiday in Crete.

Oyston's QC, Anthony Scrivener, reminded Lord Bingham that when the trial judge, Mr Justice McCullough, was jailing Oyston for six years, he declared that Miss B had been "young, dependent and vulnerable", and that when she was giving evidence about her rape in 1992 she said she had had sex only once before, with a boy at school. "I hate sex," she testified. She claimed that she never had an affair with Oyston, and had visited his Lancashire castle, Claughton Hall, only once – when she was taken there for the alleged rape.

"My Lord, it's a very frank and explicit letter about sexual matters." He said of the newly-discovered *billet doux*, before reading out some of Miss B's alleged phrases to the boy from Crete:

"Don't be fucking too many girls because you'll need some energy left for when I come back over… If you have, you won't have by the time I've finished with you because this time I'm going to be staying sober." Page 4, discussing holiday snaps reads: "I don't know whatever possessed me, but I've ordered one of us two to be blown up. I must be mental – ha ha. No, I like to know my men. I've got a few good one's though and one of them this guy's got his dick out!!"

Other new evidence includes a statement by a housekeeper, said to have worked out Miss B's true identity from the *News of the World* and to remember Miss B saying: "I've been to a castle and it was great. I've had a look round and I'm going there again."

---

105 'Miss B' was Private Eye's pseudonym for Miss H.

Two days after the appearance of the new evidence at the appeal court, and despite her conference billing as the successful prosecutor of the man in the big hat, Helen Grindrod QC took care to deliver her speech without once mentioning Oyston. Noting the presence of his solicitor Lindsay Moffatt, in the audience, Grindrod told a reporter: "Moffatt is here checking up on me and trying to catch me out. Does she really think I am so stupid as to talk about the case when it is sub judice?" Can this careful lawyer be the same Helen Grindrod described last November by *The Lawyer*, a trade journal? The magazine reported that, at a party in Manchester to celebrate the Oyston conviction, Grindrod "handed out gold-plated key rings in the shape of a man sporting a large fedora. But the hat wasn't the only large thing protruding from the extremely well-endowed gentleman…"

As well as being a QC, Helen Grindrod is a deputy circuit judge.[106]

[106] "*Private Eye*, Legal News, June 1997".

"Lord Campbell-Savours presented an unsuccessful application to the newly-established Criminal Cases Review Commission on May 21, 1998."

"Only the lubricious Daily Sport could justify the continued full-time presence of a reporter."

BEAUTIES OF THE BEAST

A WINK FOR THE CAMERA AS 9 MEN HAD HER

It was the size of a cucumber

THE SEX VIDEOS

MARTIN'S former lover, brunette Tracey Grainey, fled from the courtroom in tears as the jury watched nearly four hours of videos, secretly shot through a hole in the wall at Martin's offices.

The film showed in graphic detail the kinky sex she had with NINE men. Heavy sighs and groans, together with screams of "You f***ing bastard" and "No! No! No!" left the jury stunned.

TALK 0891 122 822

LINK 0891 445 666

THE FASTEST DATING SERVICE ON LINE

INDEX

A

B

C

D

H

I

J

M

N

O

P

Q

R

S

T

U

Printed in Great Britain
by Amazon

34482702R00258